THE MISSILE CRISIS IN CUBA

Keith Eubank

AN ANVIL ORIGINAL
under the general editorship of
Hans L. Trefousse

KRIEGER PUBLISHING COMPANY
MALABAR, FLORIDA
2000

Original Edition 2000

Printed and Published by
KRIEGER PUBLISHING COMPANY
KRIEGER DRIVE
MALABAR, FLORIDA 32950

FROM A DECLARATION OF PRINCIPLES JOINTLY ADOPTED BY A COMMITTEE OF THE AMERICAN BAR ASSOCIATION AND A COMMITTEE OF PUBLISHERS:
This publication is designed to provide accurate and authoritative information in regard to the subject matter covered. It is sold with the understanding that the publisher is not engaged in rendering legal, accounting, or other professional service. If legal advice or other expert assistance is required, the services of a competent professional person should be sought.

Library of Congress Cataloging-in-Publication Data

Eubank, Keith.
    The missile crisis in Cuba / Keith Eubank.
        p.   cm. — (Anvil series)
    Includes bibliographical references (p.   ) and index.
    ISBN 0-89464-890-X (pbk. : alk. paper)
    1. Cuban Missile Crisis, 1962.   I. Title.
E841.E75   2000
973.922—dc21   99-25624
                                                     CIP

10   9   8   7   6   5   4   3   2

To Marilyn

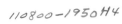

110800-1950 H4

CONTENTS

INTRODUCTION

As the American people watched their television screens on the evening of October 22, 1962, President John F. Kennedy announced that the Soviet government was in the process of setting up offensive missile sites on the island of Cuba. These ballistic missiles would have the capability of striking most major cities in the Western Hemisphere. Already American naval vessels were preparing to set up a quarantine to prevent Soviet offensive military equipment from being transported to Cuba. United States military forces had been ordered to prepare for an invasion of Cuba if necessary. President Kennedy warned that any nuclear missile launched from Cuba against any nation in the Western Hemisphere would be regarded as an attack by the Soviet Union on the United States, requiring a full response on the Soviet Union. For the first time in their history these two powers confronted each other in a crisis which could result in nuclear warfare.

The missile crisis involved the secret installation of nuclear ballistic missiles in Cuba which were aimed at the continental United States as well as the secret transportation of tactical nuclear weapons from the Soviet Union to Cuba. The crisis had been aggravated by the denials of Soviet government officials who claimed that only defensive military equipment had been shipped to Cuba. Because of the presence of nuclear weapons, the Cuban missile crisis became the most dangerous superpower confrontation in recent history. In this crisis two great powers went to the brink of war and both retreated, avoiding a confrontation that could have led to nuclear holocaust.

The documentation of the crisis is particularly abundant from American archives but only recently have some Soviet archival materials became available for study. So far Cuban archives are closed to researchers. Consequently researchers are far better informed concerning the American role in the Cuban missile crisis. The study of this crisis is unique because the sources include tapes of the meetings of the Executive Committee of the National Security Council, now more often referred to as "ExComm," established by President Kennedy to advise him during this crisis. These transcripts provide the reader with an opportunity to listen in on American officials as they debated the odds of war or peace. Selections from these transcripts have been excerpted for this volume. Included are selections from the correspondence between Nikita S. Khrushchev and John F. Kennedy.

For American officials at the center of the Cuban missile crisis, it became the classic example of what has been called "crisis management," which later was touted as the newest method to handle international crises. We now realize that the peaceful resolution of the crisis in 1962 was more often the result of luck rather than crisis management. As the Cuban missile crisis is studied it becomes more apparent that both sides misunderstood, misperceived, and misjudged the actions and motives of the other side.

The Cuban missile crisis was also a unique moment in the history of military intelligence. Thanks to reconnaissance photography using the U-2 spy plane, photo intelligence was provided which revealed that the Soviet Union was moving a nuclear strike force into Cuba.

Since 1962 explanations for the Cuban missile crisis have become more complex. No longer is it simply a tale of the Soviet Union attempting aggression in the style of Adolf Hitler as it may have appeared at the time. What influences led Nikita S. Khrushchev to devise Operation Anadyr? To what degree was John F. Kennedy responsible for initiating the crisis? How did American election year politics and personal ambitions influence the Cuban missile crisis? Why did Khrushchev imagine that nuclear missiles could be transported to Cuba and installed ninety miles from the Florida shores without the knowledge of the United States? What led him to embark on such a dangerous venture? What was the role of the United Nations? How did members of Congress react to the revelation of the crisis? How was this confrontation resolved? Why has there never been another Cuban missile crisis? These are some of the issues entangled in the history of this near disaster.

The study of the Cuban missile crisis is frightening because miscalculation, mistakes, or human error could easily have ignited a nuclear war. This was an event so terrifying in its potential for human destruction that we can only marvel that the two antagonists were shocked enough to avoid hostilities. For the American people these October days marked the moment when Cold War confrontation between the two super powers touched the shores of the United States.

 **THE ANVIL SERIES**

Anvil paperbacks give an original analysis of a major field of history or a problem area, drawing upon the most recent research. They present a concise treatment and can act as supplementary material for college history courses. Written by many of the outstanding historians in the United States, the format is one-half narrative text, one-half supporting documents, often from hard to find sources.

PART I

THE MISSILE CRISIS IN CUBA

CHAPTER 1

THE UNITED STATES AND CASTRO'S CUBA

High over Cuba on the morning of October 14, 1962, a U-2 photographic-reconnaissance airplane crossed the western end of the island from north to south. In a matter of minutes, the photographic mission was completed. When the plane landed at McCoy Air Force base near Orlando, Florida, two large rolls of film were removed and rushed by another airplane to the Naval Photographic Intelligence Center in Suitland, Maryland. It all seemed rather routine. However, the photographs from this flight would precipitate a nuclear confrontation, the Cuban missile crisis, when the Soviet Union and the United States seemed on the verge of nuclear conflict.

The roots of this crisis lay in the peculiar relationship between the Cuban government and the United States. Following the Spanish-American War in 1898, Cuba became independent, but the United States dominated much of the life of the island including mining, telephone, sugar, and oil. By 1959, the United States purchased seventy-four percent of Cuban exports and also furnished sixty-five percent of imports. Nothing, however, antagonized Cuban nationalists more than the American naval base at Guantanamo. It was a living symbol of American dominance.

Fidel Castro. By the 1950s many Cubans were tired of the series of corrupt governments which they had to endure. The current dictator, Fulgenzio Batista, supported by the United States government, so exploited Cuba that many Cuban businessmen and landowners were ready to throw their support to a replacement. It came in the person of a young lawyer, Fidel Castro Ruz, the son of a wealthy landowner. Young Fidel was a sometime baseball player who even dreamed of playing in the major leagues in the United States. A gun lover, he made a pistol hanging from his belt a part of his wardrobe. He was an inadequate law student at the University of Havana. By 1953 he began to assemble a group of followers who opposed the corrupt Batista regime. On July 26, 1953, Castro and a small group of poorly armed rebels attacked a Cuban army barracks in search of weapons. The rebels were easily defeated. Not only were there casualties but Castro was captured and imprisoned for two years, then released and exiled to Mexico The revolutionary movement which he headed took its name from the date of the unsuccessful assault on the barracks: the Twenty-Sixth of July Movement. In 1956 he returned from exile and began to launch raids from the Sierra Mountains. A confrontation with the United States became inevitable after Castro and his followers toppled the Batista regime in 1959. To Castro, the United States was an evil empire.

At that time Castro was not considered to be a Communist, but his two closest advisors, his brother Raúl and Che Guevara, were probably Communists, members of the Communist Party, *Partido Socialista Popular*. Fidel Castro was then considered a nationalist revolutionary with Socialist inclinations who intended to free Cuba from the influence and domination of the United States. To achieve this goal, however, he needed to find friends.

Castro soon found friends in Soviet Russia. By February 1960, the Soviet first deputy, Anastas Mikoyan, a wily, tough old Bolshevik who had escaped Josef Stalin's purges, had traveled to Cuba and negotiated trade and economic agreements, including $100 million in trade credits to lessen Cuban economic dependence upon the United States. Then after a ship loaded with arms from Belgium blew up in Havana harbor on March 6, frightening Castro, and convincing him that it was a prelude to an American intervention, he asked Moscow if Cuba could count on the Soviet Union to supply goods and weapons if the Americans invaded or blockaded Cuba. Within days the Soviet government agreed to supply Castro's needs. The cost would be borne by Czechoslovakia, Poland and the Soviet Union.

In June, the Castro government seized American oil refineries after their refusal to refine Soviet crude oil. In retaliation, on July 8, 1960, the United States suspended the Cuban sugar quota, but the next day the Soviet government began to buy sugar formerly shipped to the United States. Khrushchev promised the support of the Soviet government and its allies to their "brother" in Cuba. On September 2, Castro proclaimed the Declaration of Havana in which he condemned the "open and criminal intervention that U.S. imperialism has exercised in every country in Latin America." He repudiated the Monroe Doctrine and expressed his gratitude for the support of Soviet missiles if Cuban soil were to be invaded by United States military forces. Then on October 6, the Cuban government nationalized private American investments worth one billion dollars without any compensation. On October

19 the Eisenhower administration announced an embargo on all commodities sent to Cuba, except medical supplies and some foods. The Cuban government openly aligned itself with the Soviet Union on December 19. Even before this date, arms shipments from Soviet bloc members had begun to reach Cuba followed by Soviet and Czech technicians to aid in assembling and installing Soviet equipment. Military specialists came to instruct and advise the Cuban armed forces. Finally on January 3, 1961, after the Cuban government demanded that the United States reduce its embassy staff to eleven, the United States and Cuba broke diplomatic relations. Three days later, Nikita S. Khrushchev, the Soviet premier, welcomed Castro into the Soviet bloc. In April, Castro announced that Cuba was a socialist nation. Finally in a long rambling speech during the night of December 1/2, 1961, Castro at last proclaimed, "I am a Marxist-Leninist, and shall remain so till the last of my days."

John F. Kennedy. By the time that Castro made his announcement, a new president had taken the oath of office. John F. Kennedy was sworn in as president of the United States on January 20, 1961. Until then he was the youngest president in the history of the United States, a Harvard graduate, PT boat commander during World War II, and a former congressman and senator, whose political career had been bankrolled by his father, Joseph P. Kennedy.

The young senator had been influenced by the failure of appeasement in the 1930s to stop Hitler from dominating Europe. Consequently, Kennedy came to believe that dictators like Castro could not be tolerated. During the presidential campaign, Kennedy had used the issue of Cuba and Castro to prove that the Eisenhower administration had failed in the Cold War. Somehow the Eisenhower administration had "lost" Cuba to communism. "Today," Kennedy declared, "the Iron Curtain is ninety miles off the coast of the United States." Speaking in Johnstown, Pennsylvania, Kennedy said that Richard M. Nixon, the Republican presidential candidate, had never mentioned the need to confront the Cubans. "If you can't stand up to Castro," asked Kennedy, "how can you be expected to stand up to Khrushchev?" Kennedy tried to appear tougher on Castro than Nixon because Cuba had become a symbol of the Cold War. In Havana, the official radio described Kennedy as "an imbecile and a cowardly, despicable and miserable dog."

Once in office, Kennedy would have to fulfill his demands for action in regard to Cuba. Soon Democrats and Republicans alike, business-men, union leaders, and the Joint Chiefs of Staff demanded action against Castro because he had challenged the position of the United States in Latin America. If it became contagious, other Latin American nations might follow suit and seize American property.

The Bay of Pigs. From the Eisenhower administration, Kennedy had inherited a CIA-sponsored invasion plan for Cuba. The invasion force was composed of Cuban exiles who were undergoing training in Guatemala. Already the press had been reporting on the recruiting and the training of the Cubans. Once ashore in Cuba, the invaders would set up a government and seek to rally support from the Cuban people in a campaign to overthrow the Castro regime. The CIA had no evidence that Cubans in significant numbers would join the invaders in overthrowing the Castro regime. It had convinced itself that the invasion would magically create an organized resistance. Members of the Kennedy administration voiced criticism of the proposed operation. Kennedy, however, could not cancel the project because the Cuban exiles would spread the news that he was soft on communism. Consequently, Kennedy allowed the operation to continue, but he forbade American forces to participate in the invasion, known to history as the Bay of Pigs, because he did not want an American Hungary, referring to the Soviet suppression of the Hungarian people in 1956. He also feared that any American action against Cuba would unleash Soviet action against West Berlin.

A force of about 1,400 Cuban exiles landed on Cuban shores on April 17, 1961. The invaders failed to establish a beachhead. Short of supplies and without American military reinforcements, especially air strikes which Kennedy vetoed, the invasion failed. The Cuban people never rose in rebellion against Castro. Nevertheless, Moscow and Cuba had been frightened. However, the new president had looked foolish, weak, and incompetent. Consequently, Cuba now became even more of an obsession for the Kennedy administration. After the Bay of Pigs, Kennedy commented to friends that sooner or later every politician acquired an albatross. "I've got Cuba." The Bay of Pigs fiasco did not prevent Kennedy meeting Nikita S. Khrushchev in Vienna for a summit conference.

Nikita S. Khrushchev. Khrushchev, the son of Ukrainian peasants, was an uneducated coal miner when he joined the Communist

Party in 1918 and clawed his way up the Communist Party apparatus. By 1934 he was helping run the Moscow party organization, and in 1938 he was in charge of the Ukrainian Communist Party. He became a full member of the Politburo in 1939. Following Josef Stalin's death in 1953, Khrushchev eventually defeated all claimants to the top positions in the Soviet Union, becoming the first secretary of the Communist Party in 1953. He became premier in 1958 and head of the Presidium of the Communist Party, called the Politburo, which governed the Soviet Union. Khrushchev shocked faithful communists with his "Secret Speech" on February 24, 1956 when he itemized Stalin's crimes against the party members, listing the names of those whom Stalin had murdered.

As a person, Khrushchev could be warm, humorous and also rude and nasty. His mind was quick but undisciplined. In negotiations he could be tough, blunt and rude. However, he deceived many people, including Josef Stalin who thought him a country bumpkin. Other of Khrushchev's contemporaries underestimated him to their sorrow. He believed sincerely in the promise of the Russian Revolution and that the rotten capitalist world would be replaced by a wonderful new socialist world. Obsessed with the power of the new intercontinental ballistic missiles, he was convinced that these would force the West—the United States—to treat the Soviet Union with respect.

Khrushchev had followed the 1960 presidential campaign closely, rooting for Kennedy whom he preferred over Richard M. Nixon who had clashed with Khrushchev in 1959 in the famous kitchen debate in Moscow over the benefits of capitalism and communism. Kennedy's victory delighted Khrushchev although he knew very little about the president-elect.

The Vienna Summit Conference. At the Vienna Summit Conference, June 3–4, 1961, Cuba was not the main topic, but Khrushchev admonished Kennedy for the Bay of Pigs. He argued that the fiasco had only pushed the Cuban people to greater support of Castro. Kennedy replied that his main fear was Castro's intention to create trouble in the Western Hemisphere. Khrushchev could not understand how six million Cubans threatened the mighty United States. But he was happy that Kennedy had admitted that the Bay of Pigs was a mistake. However, he reminded Kennedy that when the United States placed pressure on Castro, the Soviet Union had come to his assistance. Later in the conference, relations between the two men turned bitter when Khrushchev threatened to sign a peace treaty with East Germany within six months which would end the Western powers' access to West Berlin. "If the U.S. wants war that's its problem," he announced. It was up to the United States whether there would be war or peace. Then said Kennedy: "It will be a cold winter." (*See Document No. 1.*)

In these talks, Kennedy has been described as being weak, vacillating, and failing to stand up to Khrushchev's tirade, but he had not retreated in the face of Khrushchev's bullying. Kennedy had been shocked because he had come to Vienna hoping for a genuine meeting of minds in a statesmanlike effort to discuss issues of mutual concern in the hope of improving Soviet-American relations. But that was not to be. Khrushchev tried to overawe the younger man without regard for mutual courtesies. He deliberately chose to focus on the ineptness of the Bay of Pigs fiasco. But in the argument over Berlin, Khrushchev was at his most menacing, even threatening war. Kennedy learned that in dealing with this communist he would have to be even tougher. Khrushchev's tactics of bluff and bluster had alerted Kennedy to the type of opponent he faced. Actually, Khrushchev's tactics had backfired. But it was classic Khrushchev, playing the role of the bully and resorting to brinkmanship.

During the summer Kennedy ordered a buildup of American forces in Germany. In mid-August another Berlin crisis occurred, when Khrushchev allowed the East German regime to build the Berlin Wall which in itself was a confession of the weakness of the satellite East German government. Kennedy avoided a needless confrontation but sent American troops in armored vehicles along the autobahn from West Germany to West Berlin. Kennedy was showing Khrushchev that he too could be tough.

Kennedy's next step to show Khrushchev that he was tough had results which helped ignite the Cuban missile crisis. For some years Khrushchev had blustered, boasted and even threatened the West with nuclear devastation by numberless Soviet missiles. He had hoped that the threat of nuclear missiles would enable him to reduce conventional military expenditures and invest more funds in the civilian economy. In October 1960 he declared: "We have put missile manufacturing on a production line basis. Recently, I was at one plant and saw that missiles were being churned out like sausages." Gradually the impression developed that there was a "missile gap" and that the Soviet government was outstripping the United States in missile production. During the presidential campaign, Kennedy had lambasted the Republican administration for failing to keep up with Soviet missile production. He called for crash programs to provide weapons to close the missile gap. Early in his administration, Kennedy instituted a massive increase in weapons production.

Meanwhile, Krushchev's brinkmanship in regard to the missile gap, so alarmed American officials that they focused on eliminating the reputed missile gap. By 1960–1961 photographic reconnaissance satellites had shown Khrushchev's bluster and boasts to be a charade. The United States nuclear capability far surpassed that of the Soviet Union. The "missile gap" was actually favorable for the United States. The Soviet Union was not turning out missiles like sausages. Instead the United States had succeeded in out-producing the Soviet Union in nuclear missiles.

After much high-level consultation in the Kennedy administration, it was decided to disclose that United States intelligence sources knew about the limited nuclear forces of the Soviet Union. In a speech on October 21 at Hot Springs, Virginia, the deputy secretary of Defense, Roswell Gilpatric, disclosed that there was indeed a missile gap favorable to the United States. In his speech Gilpatric described the types and numbers of nuclear weapons available to the United States forces— tens of thousands. He announced that the destructive powers of the American forces were so great that even after a Soviet surprise attack, the United States forces would be greater than the total undamaged force which the Soviet Union could launch against the United States in a first strike. The second strike capability of the United States was as great as the Soviet first strike capability.

This announcement was a massive blow to Khrushchev's hopes and plans. No longer could he intimidate the West because his bluff had been called. Now it would be possible for President Kennedy to intimidate Khrushchev who could not free up resources for the much needed development of industry and agriculture. No longer could Khrushchev boast that the Soviet Union was a superpower worthy of respect if not fear. In time Khrushchev would choose to install missiles in Cuba to solve his problem.

Operation Mongoose. In the fall of 1961, the Cuban problem bedeviled the president who complained: "The Cuba thing sits on my desk like a sack of wet potatoes." To members of his staff, Kennedy appeared obsessed with Cuba and Castro. So obsessed was Kennedy that on November 30, 1961 he created Operation Mongoose with the aim of using American resources to help Cubans overthrow the Castro regime. However, this plan was based on the same erroneous assumption as the Bay of Pigs—that in Cuba there was enormous opposition to Castro. Overseeing the operation would be representatives from the State Department, Defense Department and the CIA, as well as the president's brother, Robert, the attorney general of the United States. Known as Special Group (Augmented) or SGA, it would operate in great secrecy To manage this operation, President Kennedy appointed Brigadier General Edward G. Lansdale who had enjoyed a career in spying in the Philippines and in Vietnam. Lansdale's plans included inciting the Cubans to overthrow Castro and preparing for possible direct American military action. The brothers Kennedy were determined that there would not be a repeat of the Bay of Pigs disaster for which they held the CIA responsible.

By February 20, 1962, Lansdale had drafted a plan of action that aimed at a revolt which could take place in Cuba by October 1962. Teams of agents would be sent into Cuba commencing in March, 1962. In April a "Voice" would be set up inside Cuba to broadcast reports on resistance. Through the summer more resistance teams would be infiltrated into Cuba, and bases would be set up for guerrilla operations. By August, Cuban workers would be called upon to begin a work slow down and paramilitary teams would be sent in to engage in harassment and reprisal actions against the government. By September, Lansdale would bring in freedom fighters from Latin America and from East European exile groups. Lansdale planned for a general strike by Cuban workers in October 1962, demonstrations, a declaration of revolution by Cuban people and the establishment of a new government which would be recognized by the United States. Because Lansdale's grandiose schemes alarmed the Special Group (Augmented), he was directed to concentrate on gathering intelligence. (*See Document No. 2.*)

The actual running of Operation Mongoose was turned over to a unit of the CIA, known as Task Force W with its headquarters in Miami on the south campus of the University of Miami. The CIA saw its goal as causing internal dissension leading eventually to the intervention by United States armed forces. Consequently Operation Mongoose soon became the CIA's largest operation with an annual budget of over $50 million and with an estimated 400 agents divided between Washington and the Miami station. There were thousands of Cuban agents, ships and even a small air force.

The activities of the anti-Cubans involved in Operation Mongoose had the barest of cover. Soon they were launching their own attacks on Cuba, even attacks that had been canceled by their CIA handlers. Some of their raids were unauthorized. It was Task Force W, which it is alleged, tried to have Castro assassinated. Some sources claim that a three-man hit team had been dispatched to Cuba to carry out this assassination. Security at the Miami station was lax enough for Castro's agents to gain a fairly clear picture of the goals of Operation Mongoose. All of these activities would indicate that the Americans were gearing up for an attack on Cuba. The invasion should come soon.

To strengthen that belief, in April and May 1962, the United States forces engaged in large-scale operations in the Caribbean. Navy and Marines carried out amphibious exercises in an assault on the island of Vieques off Puerto Rico, code-named Lantphibex 1-62, between April 9–24, 1962. The operation concluded with 10,000 marines hitting the beaches.

Then on April 19–May 11, another exercise, "Quick-Kick" which included 40,000 troops, 79 ships, and 300 aircraft, occurred along the southeastern coast of the United States. The purpose of these exercises was not revealed to the public but they were reported in the press. The operations were designed to test contingency plans for action against Cuba. Certainly Cuban and Soviet agents reported at length on these exercises. Both Cuban and Soviet governments concluded that the United States forces were testing plans in preparation for an invasion of Cuba. Moreover, The commander-in-chief of the Atlantic Fleet (CINCLANT), Admiral Robert L. Dennison, had been ordered to update contingency plans for the invasion of Cuba. The president and his advisers wanted to be able to strike at Castro and his regime if Operation Mongoose offered such an opportunity. There is some evidence that the KGB learned about the order to CINCLANT.

Already the United States, at the January 1962 meeting of the Organization of American States (OAS), had succeeded in having Cuba suspended from membership in the OAS. The Cuban government could only conclude that this action was in preparation for an invasion of Cuba. To step up the pressure on the island, on February 3, Kennedy announced an embargo on all trade with Cuba which meant a prohibition on imports from Cuba as well as all American exports except some medicines and foodstuffs. Other events heightened Cuban fears of an imminent American invasion. Cuban exile groups were engaged in guerrilla attacks which could be interpreted as a prelude to invasion. Cuban invasion fears were not quieted by publicity about large-scale military exercises off the Puerto Rican coast named "Phibriglex-62" scheduled for October and which included an "invasion" of an island, Vieques, to overthrow a mythical leader named Ortsac or "Castro" spelled in reverse. The Cubans also were aware of the loud demands by members of Congress for an attack on the country. Certainly Castro's agents kept him informed about Mongoose. For many Cubans there was a very real fear of an invasion.

Operation Mongoose, the order to CINCLANT, the eviction of Cuba from the OAS and the American military exercises, all reported by intelligence agents to Moscow, must have led to the conclusion that an invasion by the United States would come soon. At the same time, Khrushchev was frustrated because Kennedy was not being accommodating in regard to either Berlin or Cuba. Instead the Kennedy administration appeared tough, uncompromising, boastful of its nuclear advantage and a threat to the Castro regime which Khrushchev had promised to protect. Castro had been asking for additional military help, but he was not always an obedient Soviet satrap. There was the fearful prospect that he might attempt to follow the path of Tito in Yugoslavia and become the leader of an independent Communist state. Moscow also had received reports that Communist Chinese influence was on the rise among some Cuban leaders. Moreover, Castro seemed determined to ignite revolution in other Latin American countries, a move that would certainly push the United States to invade Cuba. As these reports were arriving in the spring of 1962, Khrushchev needed a bold move that would protect Cuba, intimidate the Kennedy administration, end the Soviet missile gap, and demonstrate to the world the power and influence of the Soviet Union. Operation Anadyr seemed the answer: the deployment of nuclear missiles in Cuba.

CHAPTER 2

OPERATION ANADYR

The idea for Operation Anadyr may have originated when Khrushchev was visiting the seashore resort of Varna in Bulgaria. In April 1962, Khrushchev and Defense Minister Rodion Malinovsky were walking along the shores of the Black Sea. Pointing seaward, Malinovsky commented that there were American nuclear bases on the other shore in Turkey. In a matter of minutes, missiles from those bases could devastate cities in the Ukraine and in southern Russia. Should not the Soviet Union have the same right as the Americans, Khrushchev asked Malinovsky? Why should not the Soviet Union deploy missiles in Cuba? In May, while in Bulgaria, "one thought kept hammering away at my brain: what will happen if we lose Cuba?" He believed that it would be "a terrible blow to Marxism-Leninism." If Cuba were to fall, other Latin American countries might reject the Soviet Union. Khrushchev became agitated about the Jupiters (missiles) during visits to the shore of the Black Sea There he would hand binoculars to his guests and asked what they saw. "Nothing," was the reply. When he looked through the binoculars, he announced: "I see U.S. missiles aimed at my dacha". However, there was another viewpoint as Khrushchev wrote later: "The Americans would think twice before trying to liquidate our installations by military means. . . . In addition to protecting Cuba, our missiles would have equalized what the West calls the balance of power." (*See Document No. 3.*)

The Jupiters. The American missiles in Turkey to which Malinovsky referred and which so alarmed Khrushchev, were Jupiter missiles, liquid fueled intermediate range ballistic missiles (IRBMs), inaccurate, vulnerable, outdated and in need of replacement. The decision to place Jupiter missiles in Europe had been made during the Eisenhower administration in an effort to reassure European allies over the missile gap. The decision by the Eisenhower administration to offer IRBMs was the result of the launching by the Soviets of *Sputnik*, the first man-made satellite to orbit the earth on October 4, 1957. This event demonstrated that the Soviet Union had the capability of producing and firing an intercontinental ballistic missile. Because *Sputnik* had undermined the credibility of the United States to provide nuclear deterrent, the Jupiters would have to be a stopgap measure until intercontinental ballistic missiles (ICBMs) could be deployed on the U.S. mainland. Eventually only Italy and Turkey agreed to accept the Jupiters.

When Eisenhower left office in 1961, the missiles had not been deployed but later that year President Kennedy agreed to the installation of the Jupiters. The United States would own and control the warheads; Turkey would own the missiles. The Turkish government desired the missiles because they were political assets which would underscore Turkey's role in NATO and deter Soviet attack.

The Soviet Union, warning that the missiles would strain Soviet relations with those nations which accepted the Jupiters, condemned the deployment of the Jupiters. The Soviet government not only protested publicly but privately complained about being surrounded by United States missile bases. Nevertheless, on March 5, 1962 fifteen Jupiter missiles became operational in Turkey.

By the time that the Jupiters were deployed, they were becoming obsolescent. President Eisenhower complained, "It would have been better to dump them in the ocean instead of trying to dump them on our allies." Within the Kennedy administration there was almost unanimous agreement that the Jupiters were "duds." They were inaccurate and vulnerable. Dean Rusk, secretary of state, claimed that anyone with a .22 caliber rifle firing from a nearby highway could put them out of action. Secretary of Defense Robert McNamara called them "a pile of junk." During the Cuban missile crisis, President Kennedy observed that the Jupiters "had become more or less worthless." On another occasion he called them, "those frigging missiles." Dean Rusk remembered, "We joked about which way those missiles would go if they were fired." At the Vienna summit conference, Khrushchev complained to Kennedy about the Jupiters, but after Khrushchev's tough attitude, it was decided to retain the Jupiters despite the jokes.

Khrushchev, meanwhile, discussed a plan to place missiles in Cuba with Anastas Mikoyan who was considered to be an authority on Cuba. Walking in the garden of Mikoyan's home in Moscow, Khrushchev explained the plan to Mikoyan. The presence of the missiles in Cuba would be announced in a letter to Kennedy, delivered by the Soviet ambassador, Anatoly Dobrynin, in November after the congressional elections. Mikoyan, shocked by Khurshchev's plan, expressed doubt that a secret deployment of missiles in Cuba would be possible. However, he failed to convince Khrushchev that the United States would not accept missiles in Cuba as the Soviet Union had accepted the Jupiter missiles in Turkey. Likewise, Foreign Minister Andrei Gromyko, when informed by Khrushchev about his plans for Cuba, was more doubtful. "It will cause a political explosion in the U.S.A. That has to be taken into account." However, Gromyko did not dare openly oppose Khrushchev.

Moscow Meetings. Back in Moscow, on May 20 Khrushchev met with Andrei Gromyko, Mikoyan, Malinosvky, Frol Kozlov, Khrushchev's heir apparent, and Aleksandr Alekseev, TASS correspondent in Cuba and a KGB agent, whom Khrushchev had appointed as the new Soviet ambassador in Cuba. Khrushchev encountered some resistance when he presented his plan to place medium-range missiles with nuclear warheads in Cuba. Alekseev did not think that Castro would accept the missiles because their deployment would mean a Soviet military base in Cuba when Castro had been calling for the removal of all foreign bases in the Americas. Khrushchev, nevertheless, decided to send a delegation to Castro with his offer of missiles.

In a meeting of the Defense Council on May 21, which included Leonid Brezhnev, Frol Kozlov, Aleksei Kosygin, Mikoyan, and Malinovsky, Khrushchev presented his plan. "In addition to protecting Cuba, our missiles would have equalized what the West likes to call 'the balance of power.' The Americans had surrounded our country with military bases and threatened us with nuclear weapons, and now they would learn just what it feels like to have enemy missiles pointing at you." The debate continued for sometime until these high ranking Soviet officials all accepted Khrushchev's proposal to deploy Soviet forces in Cuba under a Soviet commander. In this meeting, Khrushchev asked Malinovsky how long it would take Soviet armed forces to seize an island ninety miles off the coast of the Soviet Union. "Three to five days. Not more than a week." Those present unanimously approved Operation Anadyr, the name of a river in the northern part of the Soviet Union which flows into the Bering Sea. The code name would imply that Soviet forces were engaged in a strategic exercise in a northern area. Three days later, the Presidium of the Soviet Union unanimously and officially approved the plan. In an effort to disguise the operation, the troops sent to Cuba would be issued felt boots, fleece lined parkas, skis—equipment for the northern latitudes.

It was also agreed to dispatch an "agricultural delegation" to Cuba.

Chosen by Khrushchev, it would be headed by Marshal Sergei Biryusov, chief of the Soviet rocket forces, Sharaf R. Rashidov, a member of the Presidium, Lt. General Sergei F. Ushatov, deputy head of the Air Force's general staff, Major General Pyotr V. Ageyev, from the Operations Directorate, and Aleksandr Alekseev.

Before the Soviet delegation departed for Cuba, the members enjoyed a party hosted by Khrushchev at one of his dachas outside Moscow on May 27. In a farewell speech to the delegation, Khrushchev explained, "An attack on Cuba is being prepared. The correlation of forces is unfavorable to us, and the only way to save Cuba is to put missiles there." He thought John Kennedy was an intelligent man who would not start a thermonuclear war if Soviet warheads were in Cuba just as American missiles were in Turkey which "are aimed at us and scare us." According to Khrushchev, the Soviet missiles in Cuba would "have one purpose—to scare them, to restrain them." He explained that the Soviet scheme must not be disclosed before November 6, election day in the United States. After that date, he planned to visit the United States and to inform Kennedy who would be obliged to accept the missiles. The next day, the delegation left for Havana.

Negotiations in Havana. On May 30 the "agricultural" delegation arrived in Havana. At a reception for the visitors in Havana, Alekseev whispered to Raúl Castro, brother of Fidel Castro. "Our delegation wants to discuss the question of defense and between us Engineer Petrov is not Engineer Petrov. He is Marshal Biryusov of the Strategic Rocket Forces." A meeting was promised with Fidel Castro.

Later that evening, Rashidov handed Castro a letter from Khrushchev in which he expressed the concern of the Soviet government that the United States was about to attack Cuba. Khrushchev offered to "assist Cuba in fortifying its defense capability, even to deploying on its territory Soviet intermediate range missiles, if our Cuban friends consider it useful to them to deter a potential aggressor." Alekseev had not imagined that Castro would accept Khurshchev's offer. After a moment's thought, Castro replied that if it would serve "the socialist camp, and if it would hinder the actions of American imperialism on the continent, I believe that we will agree." But he needed to confer with "my close comrades."

Castro met with the Central Committee which was worried that the presence of Soviet missiles would turn Cuba into "a Soviet military base," damaging its image in Latin America. The Cuban Central Committee thought that Cuba could be more effectively protected by conventional Soviet forces. Nevertheless, the Committee agreed to accept the missiles believing that the missiles would "change the correlation of forces between capitalism and socialism." Castro declared: "We could not refuse; we were already receiving a large amount of assistance from the socialist camp." There was fear of the American reaction when the Americans discovered the missiles, but Castro's confidence in the Soviet Union overcame his fears. He had agreed to Khrushchev's proposal because of his confidence that the Soviet leader knew what he was doing. Castro accepted the offer because of Khrushchev's extravagent claims of nuclear superiority. In 1992, Castro confessed, "I thought that the Soviets had several hundred intercontinental missiles. . . . We imagined thousands, even more, because that was the impression that was created."

In Moscow on June 10, the delegation reported to the Presidium on the results of the mission to Havana. Biryusov assured the Presidium that the missiles could be installed secretly and that after their installation they would look like palm trees to American reconnaissance aircraft. By unanimous vote, the Presidium agreed to confirm the decision taken earlier to dispatch Soviet military forces to defend Cuba with the deployment of medium and intermediate range missiles there within ninety miles of the territory of the United States.

The Treaty. On July 2, Raúl Castro, came to Moscow to negotiate the treaty between the Soviet Union and Cuba. He worked with Malinovsky, Biryusov and Alekseev in drafting a treaty to govern the deployment of the Soviet missiles in the island. Later Fidel Castro made changes in the draft treaty, and in August Che Guevara returned with the draft treaty. The sticking point was secrecy. The Cubans objected to the secrecy because from the outset they wanted a public treaty. Castro argued that they were not violating international law. Cuba had the right to accept missiles. The Cubans told Khrushchev that they feared a violent American reaction when Kennedy learned about a secret treaty. Khrushchev was unconcerned about the Cuban fears. "You don't have to worry, there will be no big reaction from the U.S. And if there is a problem, we will send the Baltic Fleet." Khrushchev may have been merely flippant or ignorant of the history of the Baltic Fleet. The last time that the Baltic Fleet sallied forth was in 1904 when it set sail to battle the Japanese. It was a 18,000 mile ordeal that involved an attack on British fishing fleet in the North Sea which was mistaken for Japanese torpedo boats. Eventually the fleet reached the Pacific where it was defeated by the Japanese in the battle of Tsushima in 1905. The Soviet Baltic Fleet in 1962 would have been completely outmatched in an encounter with American naval forces.

Khrushchev refused to sign the treaty. Apparently he planned to announce it in November, perhaps in Havana or at the United Nations, after the missiles had been fully installed in secret. He may have feared that if the treaty were to be signed, Castro would make it public and needlessly provoke the United States. Nevertheless, had Khrushchev and Castro signed the treaty and made it public, the Kennedy administration would have been restricted in voicing objections to a public commitment. Khrushchev's secrecy would eventually become very costly.

The treaty would be in force for five years, and if not nullified by one of the parties, would remain in force for another five years. The Soviet government would bear all the expenses of the troops deployed in Cuba. Food, vehicles, and supplies and equipment for the Soviet forces would be supplied by the Soviet Union The Cuban government would supply sites of the bases for deployment of Soviet forces without any payment. Garrisons, airport, and all installations would be transferred to the Cuban government whenever the Soviet forces no longer used them. The armed forces of each nation would be under the control of their respective governments who would decide jointly on deploying troops and repelling aggression. When the treaty was no longer in force, the troops from the Soviet Union would be withdrawn.

Missiles in Cuba. Why was Khrushchev so eager and so determined in his plan to deploy missiles in Cuba, ninety miles from Florida? Khrushchev was supremely confident that the presence of the missiles in Cuba would remain a secret until such time as he wished to reveal their presence to the United States. He imagined that after the missiles became operational, the Americans would accept them as a fait accompli. They would think twice before attempting to destroy the Soviet installations. Khrushchev also relied on what he regarded as Kennedy's realization that in a nuclear war there would be no winners. Kennedy had impressed Khrushchev with his caution in the Berlin crisis in 1961. American troops had not challenged Soviet forces when they sealed off

East Berlin from the remainder of the city. Likewise in Cuba, Khrushchev imagined that he could go to the brink of war without any retaliation by Kennedy.

Khrushchev also claimed that he was intent only on defending Cuba from an American invasion. However, altruism was never a force in his policy. Until 1962, no missiles had been deployed outside of the Soviet Union, but now Khrushchev was daring to place the missiles in the backyard of the United States thousands of miles from the Soviet Union. It has been argued that the deployment may have been the result of Soviet determination to repair the gap in the strategic nuclear balance between the United States and the Soviet Union which favored the United States. The deployment of the missiles was also one method of obtaining recognition of the power of the Soviet Union by other nations, in particular, the United States.

Missiles in Cuba would support Khrushchev's long-term objective of reducing Soviet conventional military forces in order to reduce the overall military budget. The money saved could be diverted into the civilian economy. He did not want to spend enormous sums on building up an intercontinental ballistic missiles system. Missiles in Cuba would fill in that gap in the Soviet nuclear arsenal.

Missiles in Cuba would improve the Soviet strategic position in relation to the United States. At the same time Khrushchev would be able to offset the American superiority cheaply. Soviet missiles in Cuba would also vastly improve the Soviet strategic position by placing most of the United States within range of the Soviet missiles in Cuba. Khrushchev wanted missiles in Cuba instead of merely troops and conventional weapons because nuclear missiles aimed at the United States would be the ultimate weapon to deter American action. They would change the strategic balance and make brinkmanship more credibile.

Although Soviet officials have since denied it, Berlin probably played a role in Khrushchev's decision to deploy missiles in Cuba. In the past Khrushchev's bluster and threats had not forced the United States to negotiate over withdrawing troops from West Berlin. Perhaps missiles in Cuba would create new conditions for negotiating over Berlin.

At the same time Khrushchev was in competition with Communist China to show that the Soviet Union was the undisputed leader of the Communist movement. Khrushchev needed an example to prove that the Soviet Union was eagerly supporting world revolution He wanted a socialist state to defend and to prove that his leadership was credible. If he did not support Cuba with the proper zeal he would certainly be attacked by China. As pressure on Cuba increased in 1961–1962, Khrushchev felt compelled to assist Cuba because if the Castro regime were to be overthrown by an American invasion, Chinese denunciations of Khrushchev would be overwhelming.

Finally, Khrushchev knew that if Cuba were to be lost to communism, the Soviet Union would lose face in Latin America. "If Cuba fell," he wrote, "other Latin American countries would reject us, claiming that for all our might the Soviet Union hadn't been able to do any thing for Cuba but make empty protests to the United Nations." In the words of a Soviet general, "It was both an old Bolshevik's romantic response to Castro and to the Cuban revolution." To some of the old Bolsheviks, Castro was a young Lenin whom they could not desert. After the missile crisis, Mikoyan explained Khrushchev's feelings to Secretary of State Dean Rusk: "You Americans must understand what Cuba meant to us old Bolsheviks. We have been waiting all our lives for a country to go Communist without the Red Army, and it happened in Cuba. It makes us feel like boys again."

Khrushchev was unrealistic in his belief that Kennedy would tolerate the missiles. He imagined that Kennedy would accept the missiles in Cuba as Khrushchev had accepted the missiles in Turkey. But the American missiles had been installed in Turkey openly, not secretly. Khrushchev chose to deploy the missiles secretly after promising that missiles would not be sent to Cuba. Khrushchev thought the missiles could be kept secret until they became operational, that is, after November 6. Then the presence of the missiles in Cuba would amount to the status quo with the onus on the Americans if they chose to strike. Khrushchev could not imagine the political impact of missiles in Cuba on the Kennedy administration.

According to Ambassador Alekseev, Khrushchev was fully convinced that Operation Anadyr could be carried out secretly; the Americans could not find out. He advised, "Do everything in such a way that the U.S. public opinion will not be aware of this until November 4 or after November 4th. . . . The Americans are going to have to swallow this the same way we have had to swallow the pill of the missiles in Turkey."

To maintain the secrecy of Operation Anadyr, Khrushchev ordered that all messages concerning the operation would be in writing carried by hand. Radio would not be used. In another move to blind American military intelligence, Khrushchev appointed a General Issa Pliyev to command this expedition to Cuba. Pliyev was famous for leading the last major cavalry charge in history against the Japanese in Manchuria in 1945. He was in artillery, not rockets, but Khrushchev chose Pliyev because he knew he could be trusted. Riots over the price of bread, meat and milk had broken out in Novocherkassk in June, 1962. The commander of the Northern Caucasian military district, Pliyev, obeying Khrushchev's orders, used his troops to quell the riots in which Soviet citizens were killed. Apparently Khrushchev also thought that the appointment of a rocket specialist might alert the Americans. Pliyev, however, knew little about rocket forces, and he lacked diplomatic skills to establish a good relationship with Fidel Castro. He was most unhappy when he received his passport and found that he had been given a pseudonym, "Ivan Aleksandrovich Pavlov." Soon he was at odds with members of his staff who were drawn from the rocket forces; he also had no experience in handling so a large force assembled from all branches of the Soviet army.

Men and Arms. For the Soviets, Operation Anadyr required the movement of a large force overseas, an operation which they had never undertaken before. Originally it was planned to send more than 50,000 troops to Cuba; in September the strength was cut to 45,234, but of that number 41, 902 were actually in Cuba when the movement of troops ceased on October 24, 1962 following the imposition of the blockade. Eventually American intelligence sources estimated the force at about 20,000.

For Operation Anadyr, the Soviet command had put together a diversified force. It included two antiaircraft divisions armed with surface-to-air missiles (SAMs), forty MIG-21 fighter-interceptors, two cruise missiles regiments (FKR) with nuclear warheads—eighty missiles in all. There were also helicopters, a squadron of eleven IL-28 bombers and six IL-28 bombers outfitted to carry atomic bombs. There were six atomic bombs for these bombers. There were four motorized rifle regiments, thirty-one tanks assigned to each regiment plus ten self-propelled cannon, armored reconnaissance vehicles, mortars, antitank guided missiles, antiaircraft machine guns, and three separate Luna rocket units with two launchers and four missiles each. There were also personnel carriers, motorcycles, and over two hundred cars and trucks.

Included in this arsenal were twelve nuclear warheads for the Luna surface-to-suface rockets which would have had a devastating effect on a battlefield. One such rocket could kill everything within a radius of 500 yards as well as all unprotected troops within 1,000 yards. As a result of increased air pressure, survivors would die of radiation poisoning within weeks. Had United States troops landed in Cuba, the beachhead would soon have become an atomic battlefield. In addition, the FKR cruise missile launchers had nuclear warheads one of which could have wreaked havoc on a carrier group. Six atomic bombs were also supplied for the IL-28 bombers. Khrushchev had given General Pliyev oral orders that the battlefield nuclear weapons could be used only if there was an American invasion and communications with Moscow were cut off.

Operation Anadyr also had a naval component. The Soviet navy planned to construct a submarine base in Cuba and to patrol the Cuban waters with a naval force consisting of two cruisers, four destroyers, twelve Komar ships (missile-carrying patrol boats), each of which had two missiles with a ten-mile range. In addition, the Soviet navy planned to send a squadron of eleven submarines, seven of which had nuclear tipped missiles, as well as supply ships, tankers and repair ships. Except for the Komar boats, the naval force was never deployed because of supply difficulties, and, more important, the appearance of Soviet naval units in Cuban waters would only alarm the United States Navy which considered these waters to be its own preserve.

The centerpiece of this force included three R-12 (NATO designation S-4) medium-range-ballistic missile (MRBM) regiments with eight launchers each, two missiles for each launcher and one nuclear warhead for each launcher. The MRBMs had a 1,400-mile range and could threaten sites as far west as El Paso and as far east as Washington, D.C. All of the military installations in the South and Southeast could be targeted There were two other regiments with sixteen longer range R-14 (NATO designation S-5) intermediate-range ballistic missiles (IRBMs) each with eight launchers each, two missiles for each launcher and one nuclear warhead for each launcher. The IRBMs had a 2,800-mile range and the capability of hitting targets in the forty-eight contiguous states. The R-14 missiles were en route to Cuba when the crisis ended and they were shipped back to the Soviet Union. None of the ballistic missiles could be fired without explicit permission from Moscow.

Launching Operation Anadyr. Officially, Operation Anadyr was launched on July 7. Pliyev left on July 10, his staff followed disguised as a group of "technicians"—experts in irrigation, engineering and of course agriculture. Ships carrying the troops left from eight different ports. Eighty-five vessels were used and they would make about 185 trips between Cuba and the Soviet Union. Never before in the history of Russia and the Soviet Union had so large a force been transported so far across the ocean.

None of the ships' captains knew where they were sailing. Before each vessel sailed, the ship's captain and each troop commander received a large envelope and inside each was a smaller envelope. At certain coordinates, the envelope could be opened under the watchful eye of KGB officers. Inside a letter would be an order authorizing the vessel to sail to a specified Cuban port. The letter had to be destroyed after it was read; the troops could be informed and issued civilian clothes to be worn in Cuba.

Troops were moved to embarkation ports under cover of darkness. At the embarkation ports, they were under strict security, cut off from all communication with the outside world. To the surprise of the soldiers, they were required to surrender their Communist Party cards, Communist Youth League cards and military service booklets.

The troopships were freighters with bunks constructed by the troops in the holds. The ships had antiaircraft guns, and in case they had to land at an unfriendly port, there were machine guns as well as submachine guns on board. The troops were packed in the holds which lacked air conditioning and which could not be opened because of observation by American aircraft. The troops could only be allowed up on deck in small groups at night. But when the ships neared areas under surveillance of American planes, these pleasures were ended. These security measures were successful because American planes never discovered that the freighters were carrying troops. Nevertheless, refrigeration too often failed and food spoiled. Storms and sea sickness drove the Soviet soldiers to swear never to set foot on a ship again.

During July, August and September, Soviet freighters carried cargoes from Soviet ports to Cuba. The loading of equipment, supplies and troops would be completed by October 20; the last shipment was scheduled to arrive before November 6, election day in the United States. By the end of September, cargo ships with specially designed holds had transported the R-12 or SS4 medium-range ballistic missiles to Cuba. These missiles were seventy-four feet long and one such missile was the equivalent of one million tons of TNT. Hiroshima was destroyed by a explosion equal to 14,000 tons of TNT. On October 4, the Soviet freighter, *Indigirka,* docked at the port of Mariel. Its cargo included forty-one megaton warheads for the R-12s, thirty-six 12-kiloton warheads for the (FKR) cruise missiles, six 12-kiloton bombs for the IL-28 bombers and twelve 2-kiloton warheads for the Luna rockets. Alexandr Fursenko and Timothy Naftali in *"One Hell of a Gamble" Khrushchev, Castro and Kennedy, 1958–1964,* have estimated that the *Indigirka* carried twenty times the explosive power that Allied bombers dropped on Germany during World War II.

While Soviet missiles and explosives were being unloaded at the docks in Cuba, the Soviet expedition to the island was encountering difficulties. When the first transport arrived on July 26, someone had failed to select passwords to identify those officials in Cuba who had the authority to give the ships' captains routing orders. Without passwords, some of the captains were prepared to return to the Soviet Union.

All equipment which did not resemble agricultural equipment had to be unloaded at night, stored out of sight until it could be moved under cover of darkness on back roads. The sixty-seven-foot trailers which carried the R-12 IRBMs left a trail of downed telephone poles as well as flattened mail boxes as the missiles were moved to their launch sites. Cuban guard detachments accompanied the convoys and consequently all orders had to be in Spanish. Soviet troops had to wear civilian clothes: dark gray pants and short sleeved checked shirts. All communications between Soviet headquarters in Havana and the field units had to be oral and made in person. There was to be total radio silence. Once ashore in Cuba, field commanders soon discovered that sites chosen in Moscow from a map proved to be unsuitable because of terrain or perhaps lack of water.

Camouflage proved impossible When Sharaf Rashidov had reported to Khrushchev after returning from Cuba, he announced that Cuban forests would easily conceal the missiles, an assertion which Khrushchev accepted without question. However, attempting to conceal a missile launch position was not easy because the site was filled with a variety of equipment which could not be easily hidden: fuel tanks, trucks, cables and concrete slabs for the launching. All of these items could be hidden on ground level from a road but not from the air. Cuban forests were thin with only palm trees and dense underbrush which increased the humidity. Even when tractors and trailers were placed under canvas they could be spotted from the air. Apparently no serious consideration had been given to this problem when Khrushchev determined to launch Operation Anadyr.

Soviet troops soon encountered other problems which had been unforeseen back in Moscow. The metal trailers lacked air conditioning and heated up so much during the day that they could not be utilized at night. Tents were stifling as well which was unfortunate because swarms of mosquitoes drove the Soviet soldiers inside them. In some areas, efforts to dig trenches proved difficult when troops hit water just under the surface. Fortifications for surface-to-air (SAM) missile launchers had to be built in blinding heat and rainstorms. When the heat became intense, troops could only work in shifts relieving each other periodically. The rocky Cuban soil resisted Soviet bulldozers and earth-moving equipment. In those circumstances, the soldiers had to dig with pick and shovel which only delayed the completion of the task of fortifying the SAM missile launchers.

Concerned that Operation Anadyr was proceeding too slowly, in October Marshal Malinovsky dispatched an inspection team to Cuba headed by General Anatoli I. Gribkov. When Gribkov and the inspection team arrived in Cuba on October 18, they received the disturbing report from General Pliyev that U-2 spy planes had been flying over the Soviet installations. Gribkov now had the opportunity to see the handicaps under which the Soviet troops had to work. Worst of all, Operation Anadyr had fallen behind schedule which required the R-12 regiments be combat ready by October 25–27. The heat, the terrain, the humidity had all proven too formidable for the Soviet troops so far from home. Gribkov upbraided Pliyev because some of his deputies were lounging in their offices instead of being out in the field overseeing the toiling soldiers. Gribkov insisted that other units, such as rifle regiments, join in with the rocket divisions to bring Operation Anadyr up to schedule. Time was running out for the Soviet forces in Cuba. When Gribkov returned to the Havana headquarters on October 22 after inspecting the troops in their work, he learned that Soviet intelligence had reported that at 19:00 hours President Kennedy would make a very important speech. In all probability it would be about Operation Anadyr.

CHAPTER 3

DISCOVERY

The hope that Operation Anadyr would remain a secret while the buildup continued began to disappear in late July, 1962. By that time, CIA sources in Cuba began to report a noticeable increase in Soviet shipping entering Cuban ports. The increase caught the attention of John A. McCone, director of the CIA, who met with Dean Rusk, secretary of state, General Maxwell Taylor, McGeorge Bundy, Robert McNamara, and Vice-President Lyndon B. Johnson on August 10. McCone had been an industrialist who built and designed oil refineries, factories and power plants. A former chairman of the Atomic Energy Commission, he was a personal friend of Richard M. Nixon for whom McCone had voted in the 1960 presidential election. McCone was not Kennedy's first choice after Allen Dulles had been fired following the Bay of Pigs debacle, but the president believed that McCone would be a competent manager who would subordinate covert operations to Kennedy's foreign policy.

Soviet Shipments to Cuba. McCone reported on August 10 that there had been a sudden increase in the importation of Soviet materiel and personnel. He speculated that the materiel might be electronic equipment or even military equipment, perhaps medium-range ballistic missiles. But McCone offered no proof of his speculation.

By August 20 McCone had more information about the increase in Soviet shipping to Cuba. Since July 1 Soviet personnel had increased by 4,000–6,000, but he had no information about organized military units. They appeared to be Soviet technicians. Soviet ships were being unloaded under great security; the Cuban population had been excluded from port areas. Large crates had been unloaded which could be fuselages or missile components. Trucks had even been lowered into the holds of ships, loaded out of sight, covered with tarpaulins, lifted out and driven off into the countryside. McCone thought these trucks might contain communications or electronic intelligence equipment.

In another meeting on August 21, McCone reported that he had definite information that construction work was underway in Cuba. As to the purpose for the construction, again McCone speculated: communication or electronic intelligence, or ground-to-air missile sites. When someone proposed a possible blockade of Soviet and Soviet bloc shipping to Cuba or a total blockade of the island, Rusk and Bundy opposed any such action because that would produce a blockade of Berlin. If there were any drastic action against a missile site in Cuba, similar action might be taken against American missile sites in Turkey and Italy. No action would be taken, but the president should be briefed.

When McCone briefed the president on August 22, he wanted to continue to monitor and analyze the type of personnel and the equipment being landed in Cuba. How did surface-to-air sites differ from ground-to-ground missile sites? McCone doubted that such differentiation was possible. Kennedy asked what could be done against missile sites in Cuba? Take them out by air or ground offensive? Could guerrillas destroy them? What if the Russians precipitated a crisis over Berlin? There were no answers but everyone present agreed that the Cuban problem must be solved. Following the meeting, McCone left to get married and honeymoon in France.

Another intelligence report contained information indicating stepped up Soviet activity in Cuba. Soviet bloc personnel were engaged in military construction in several locations. Since late July about 1,500 Soviet bloc passengers had debarked under security conditions. An estimated twenty Soviet vessels had arrived with military cargoes since late July. Other Soviet ships had sailed from Black Sea ports loaded with electronic and construction equipment as well as vans, trucks and mobile generators. When these vessels reached Cuba, foreign personnel, not Cubans, unloaded the cargoes. What all of this construction activity implied was as yet unknown. "These developments," the report concluded, "amount to the most extensive campaign to bolster a non-bloc country ever undertaken by the USSR."

More reports were coming in from Cuba. On August 18 *Sovetska Ganauya* docked with large crates on the deck. Their configuration corresponded to Komar guided missile patrol boats. A Soviet passenger ship brought in more "technicians" on August 27 who received a joyous reception. None wore military uniforms or carried weapons. According to other reports, hundreds of young Russians in checked shirts and cheap trousers were spotted sightseeing in Havana.

SAMs in Cuba. In a press conference on August 29, President Kennedy was closely questioned about statements of Republican Senator Homer Capehart of Indiana who had claimed that Soviet troops were on the island. Kennedy stated that the United States had no evidence of Soviet troops in Cuba. In reply to a question about the presence of antiaircraft missiles in Cuba, Kennedy could only state that as yet there was no information. Afterward he was furious with his staff and demanded to know if any information was being withheld from him. Kennedy ordered a review of photographs in regard to surface-to-air missiles (SAM) sites. The review disclosed no SAM sites. The presence of SAM sites was highly significant because on May Day 1960 a Soviet SAM brought down a U-2 piloted by Francis Gary Powers which had been photographing areas of the Soviet Union. The downing of the U-2 and the capture of Powers helped wreck the Paris summit conference.

However, on August 29, a U-2 plane photographed the entire island of Cuba, but clouds obscured the eastern end of the island. Minutes after the photographs were processed, a photo interpreter found a SAM site on the western end of Cuba. After more searching, eight SAM sites were found in various stages of construction. A ninth was found on the east coast. These discoveries sent intelligence analysts back to reexamine agents' reports about construction activity. Many of these reports indicated that Soviet personnel had been observed at these sites.

The evidence showed that work was proceeding on a crash basis. Some sites would be operational within a week's time. The placement of the SAM sites along the northern coast indicated an attempt to provide a defense of the entire island of Cuba. The photographs also showed eight Komar class missile boats which carried two missile launchers each and had a range of fifteen to seventeen miles. In addition, thirty-seven MIG aircraft were discovered. (*See Document No. 4.*)

Cuba in American Politics. Domestic politics next impacted on the Cuban problem. Off-year congressional elections offered Republicans an opportunity to attack President Kennedy, who was vulnerable after the Bay of Pigs debacle and the reported Soviet buildup in Cuba. Senator Richard Russell, Democrat of Georgia, asked McCone, "When is the President going to get off his ass and do something?" Senator Homer Capehart, speaking on August 27, complained about the influx into Cuba of Soviet men and equipment. He claimed that the Russians had been violating the Monroe Doctrine. "Never before have we allowed it to be violated." Capehart advocated an invasion of Cuba.

On the floor of the Senate on August 31, Republican Senator

Kenneth Keating, New York, announced that he had been reliably informed that Soviet ships had unloaded troops. Torpedo boats had also been unloaded along with Soviet naval personnel. "What," he asked "are the Soviets planning to do with their new island fortress?" Keating went on to describe convoys observed carrying amphibious vehicles, tanks, and other equipment. Here was the first in a series of statements which caught the headlines and infuriated President Kennedy. During the next two months, Keating made twenty-five public statements on Cuba in the Senate and on a weekly radio show. In his statements, he offered updated descriptions of the size and buildup of the Soviet force in Cuba. After his August 31 statement, CIA experts evaluated his allegations and found them very accurate. On September 4 he announced to the Senate that the number of Soviet troops had reached 5,000.

Keating never revealed his sources but probably they included Cuban refugees, CIA officials, the Pentagon, and perhaps even John McCone. Keating's motives included his political future, a useful anti-Communist issue, favorable publicity, harming Kennedy in the congressional elections and improving the senator's position within the Republican Party. He was ever mindful of his own reelection campaign coming in 1964 (which he lost.) Keating had become disenchanted with Kennedy after the 1960 presidential campaign when Kennedy seemed to imply that he would somehow topple Castro.

Keating exemplified the political pressure being exerted on the Kennedy administration in regard to Castro's Cuba. Republican senators such as Bourke Hickenlooper (Iowa), Barry Goldwater (Arizona), and Karl Mundt (South Dakota), all urged a blockade of Cuba. John Tower (Texas) demanded the creation of a Cuban government-in-exile which would be armed by the United States for an invasion of the island. Senatorial interest in Cuba led to hearings before a joint session of the Senate Foreign Relations Committee and the Armed Services Committee. As a result of these hearings, on September 20 the Senate passed a resolution which "sanctioned the use of military force" if necessary to "counter Cuban belligerence and subversion in the Western Hemisphere." On September 26, the House of Representatives voted to approve the Senate's resolution.

Keating's campaign infuriated the Kennedy brothers. They believed that they were being badly damaged by something they thought was untrue and at best exaggerated. Administration policies were adjusted to down play Keating's assertions or even disprove them. It took the form of asserting that the Soviet buildup was defensive because it was only surface-to-air missiles.

Partly as a result of the pressure from Keating, on September 4 Kennedy issued a statement. According to the president, information had reached the United States government that the Soviet Union had provided the Cuban government with antiaircraft defense missiles, radar and electronic equipment as well as motor torpedo boats. The number of Soviet technicians reported to be in Cuba or en route amounted to approximately 3,500, a number consistent with helping set up and use this equipment. There was no evidence of an organized combat force in Cuba from a Soviet bloc country, nor military bases being provided to the Russians, nor offensive missiles or offensive weapons under Soviet control. "Were it to be otherwise, the gravest issues would arise." With this statement, Kennedy hoped to assuage his Republican critics and draw the line: no offensive weapons in Cuba. His warning was too late because Soviet offensive weapons were already being emplaced in the island. Had this warning been issued months earlier, history might have been different. However, his warning was so explicit that it left him no option other than to respond to the discovery of missiles in Cuba with a full-blown military confrontation with the Soviet Union.

To Khrushchev, Kennedy's statement seemed to imply that United States forces might soon be moving on Cuba. Consequently on September 7 Khrushchev ordered Luna rockets with nuclear warheads, six IL-28 bombers and six atomic bombs be shipped as soon as possible to Cuba. These weapons, together with the FKR nuclear cruise missiles, meant that Khrushchev was preparing to use nuclear weapons on a battlefield. Never before had a nation prepared to use tactical nuclear weapons in battle. In addition, on September 8, Khrushchev approved an order that the use of nuclear weapons could only be authorized by a signal from Moscow. Upon instructions from Moscow, nuclear missile equipped submarines would prepare to launch missiles on coastal targets in the United States. These orders implied that he was preparing for a possible war between the United States and the Soviet Union.

Three more SAM sites were found in western Cuba on September 5. Two days later a representative of the Defense Intelligence Agency, briefing Kennedy, reported that more study of the August 29 photographs revealed additional surface-to-surface missile sites with a range of twenty to forty nautical miles. The president was furious. He asked if the United States had comparable weapons, and his anger mounted when informed that such was not the case. "Why the hell don't we?" He ordered that this information be tightly restricted and threatened that if any of this information appeared in the next day's edition of the *Washington Post*, those involved would be fired. As a result of this warning, General Marshall S. Carter, deputy director of the CIA, set up a tightly compartmentalized security system, code named PSALM, to disseminate information obtained through Cuban over flights.

Kennedy obtained congressional approval on September 7 for a call-up of 150,000 reservists. The Soviet press denounced his action on September 11, claiming that the armaments and equipment being sent to Cuba were only for defensive purposes. Moreover, the Soviet government declared that the power of Soviet weapons was so great and its missiles so powerful that there was no need to seek a site for them beyond the borders of the Soviet Union.

This information had begun to impact on Kennedy's thinking. At his September 13 news conference, he stated that Soviet technicians and military personnel had been moving into the island in increasing numbers. The movement was under careful surveillance. "But I will repeat the conclusion that I reported last week, these new shipments do not constitute a serious threat to any other part of this hemisphere." He warned that if a Communist buildup were to endanger American security in any way or if Cuba became "an offensive military base of significant capacity for the Soviet Union," then the United States would do what had to be done to protect its security and that of its allies. In answer to a follow-up question, he warned that if Cuba had the capacity to carry out offensive actions against the United States, then the United States would take action. Kennedy was warning Khrushchev that nuclear missiles would not be tolerated on the island of Cuba. Kennedy's warning, however, had come too late.

McCone, who had been in France on his honeymoon, had been kept informed about the Cuban situation, particularly the discovery of the SAM sites. These reports convinced him that the SAMs were intended to protect Cuba from over flights of U-2 planes in order to insure secrecy for MRBMs (medium-range ballistic missiles) to be installed after the completion of the SAM sites. However, on September 19 the National Intelligence estimate issued by the CIA stated that the main purpose of the Soviet buildup in Cuba was to strengthen the Castro regime against what the Soviets and the Cubans considered to be a danger that the United States might attempt to overthrow it. Moreover they

realized that an offensive military base in Cuba might provoke United
States reaction. After this estimate had been issued, CIA agents on the
island reported seeing convoys on September 12 and 17 in which there
were large trailers carrying what one agent described as "large missiles"
about 65–70 feet in length. CIA analysts concluded that the observers
had seen the same convoy and that it might be carrying SS-4 missiles
for MRBMs.

A reluctance to use U-2s over Cuba emerged among some of the
Kennedy administration after a U-2 strayed over the Sakhalin Islands
on August 10 and a Chinese Nationalist U-2 was shot down over mainland China on September 8. These events revived memories of the ill-
fated flight of the U-2 piloted by Gary Powers shot down over the Soviet
Union in 1960. U-2 planes were fragile and limited in number. Secretary of State Rusk and McGeorge Bundy, special assistant to the president on national security affairs, were unhappy with proposals for flights
directly over Cuba, fearing another incident. Only peripheral flights
were authorized no closer than twenty-five miles from the Cuban
shores. Such flights should be beyond the range of the SAMs. However,
the threat from the SAMs was increasing because U-2 flights in September revealed seven more SAM sites plus a cruise missile site near
the Bay of Pigs. Flights on October 5 and October 7 discovered five
more SAM sites. Consequently, it was becoming apparent that a SAM
defense was being constructed which extended the length of the island
of Cuba.

Contingency Plans. The movement of Soviet ships toward Cuba
and the reports from intelligence sources impacted on the Pentagon.
Following a meeting with the Joint Chiefs of Staff on October 1, when
they received a briefing on the latest intelligence reports concerning
Cuba and discussed contingency planning, the onetime Ford Motor
Company executive, Secretary of Defense Robert S. McNamara, directed Admiral Robert Dennison, commander-in-chief of the U.S. Atlantic Command (CINCLANT), "to be prepared to institute a blockade against Cuba." Dennison in turn directed responsible commanders
to take all possible measures necessary to assure maximum readiness to
execute CINCLANT OPLAN (Operations Plan) 312 by October 20.
OPLAN 312 was a contingency plan for various responses by U.S. air
power including air strikes on single targets to widespread attacks
"throughout Cuba." Army commanders were notified to be prepared for

the possible implementation of OPLAN 314 and OPLAN 316 which provided for joint operations in Cuba by Army, Navy and Air Force units. These forces would combine in an amphibious and airborne assault against Havana as well. It was intended that these plans would lead ultimately to the overthrow of the Castro government.

As early as October 3, CINCLANT issued orders for preparations for a blockade if this should become necessary. CINCLANT reminded commanding officers on October 6 of the need to relocate and pre-position troops, aircraft, ships, and supplies. On the same day, Dennison ordered "the development of the highest state of readiness" in order to execute air strike plan OPLAN 312 and invasion plans OPLAN 314 and 316.

The Joint Chiefs of Staff forwarded to CINCLANT on October 8 a memorandum from McNamara regarding the contingencies under which military action against Cuba might become necessary. Among these contingencies, McNamara noted: "Evidence that the Castro regime has permitted the positioning of bloc offensive weapons on Cuban soil or in Cuban harbors." As yet, neither the Pentagon nor the Kennedy administration was fully aware of Operation Anadyr. Nevertheless, CINCLANT was taking every possible step to increase readiness to execute plans against Cuba.

By October there was enough evidence from agents and refugee reports to indicate that in an area west of Havana something unusual was developing, perhaps a MRBM installation. Rusk and Bundy at last conceded, and on October 9 it was agreed to plan a U-2 flight over Cuba to test the operational readiness of the SAM sites and to photograph the area where MRBMs were suspected. At first weather delayed the flights. Then on October 12 operational control of the U-2 flights was transferred from the CIA to the Strategic Air Command of the Air Force. This step was taken to avoid the embarrassment of another "spy" being captured if the U-2 plane were shot down. There must not be another Gary Powers episode.

Mission 3101. Late in the evening of October 13, a U-2 flight, Mission 3101, left Edwards Air Force Base and by 7:31 AM the next morning, October 14, the U-2 was over Cuba. The flight was uneventful—no fighter aircraft and no SAM missiles fired. The plane landed at McCoy Air Force base near Orlando, Florida, and the films were rushed to the Naval Photographic Center in Suitland, Maryland, for processing, and then the processed films were taken under armed naval guard to the Stewart Building in a not so elegant section of Washington, D.C. This building housed the National Photographic Interpretation Center which was controlled, staffed, and funded by the CIA and operated by specialists not only from the CIA but also from the Army, Navy, and Air Force This installation was designed and equipped to handle the interpretation of photographs from U-2 cameras.

There on October 15, interpreters working with photographs of an area fifty miles west-southwest of Havana, discovered canvas covered objects approximately sixty-five to seventy feet in length, as well as trucks and tents in the immediate vicinity The equipment was larger than that found at SAM sites. Nothing so large had been seen in Cuba before. The only conclusion: the canvas covered objects were missile transporters of an unknown system. The staff began to search for answers in large loose-leaf notebooks containing information assembled from many sources: photographs of May-Day parades in Moscow, technical reports, and most important of all, reports and manuals provided by Colonel Oleg Penkovsky of the Soviet Union who had been voluntarily supplying information to the Western intelligence agencies. A search through these "Black Books" showed full-scale views of SS-4 missiles whose dimensions corresponded to those in the U-2 photographs. A three man team of interpreters finally came to the conclusion, "We've got MRBMs in Cuba." Arthur C. Lundahl, the director of the center, was informed; he invoked the PSALM code word to classify the photographs. Lundahl telephoned Ray S. Cline, deputy director for intelligence in the CIA, to inform him that medium range missiles were now in Cuba. These weapons had never before been deployed outside the Soviet Union, not even to the faithful Soviet satellite states. Cline telephoned Bundy and reported cryptically, "Those things we've been worrying about in Cuba are there." Bundy decided not to have any meetings that night and to wait until morning when more information would be available. Nor would he inform the president who was tired from campaigning and could use a good night's sleep. (*See Document No. 5.*)

Meanwhile Lundahl ordered maps prepared showing the range of the MRBMs. The range of 1,100 nautical miles would encompass an area including Washington D.C., Cincinnati, Dallas, New Orleans, ICBM bases, SAC bomber bases and naval bases. Further study of the "Black Books" and the photographs revealed that there was an MRBM launch site and two military encampments. The launch site and one of the encampments contained a total of fourteen canvas-covered missile trailers measuring approximately sixty-seven feet in length and nine feet in width; the overall length of the trailers was thirty feet. The MRBM launch site located in a wooded area contained eight canvas-covered missile trailers and four deployed probable missile launchers. The launch positions were laid out according to manuals supplied by Penkovsky. The second encampment not yet laid out contained six of the canvas-covered missile carriers. The third encampment contained only vehicles, tents and a building under construction. Photographs from over flights on October 15 disclosed that encampment number two was now identified as a definite MRBM launch site and encampment number three was a probable MRBM launch site. The equipment was part of the Soviet ballistic missile system, it was road mobile and could be deployed without requiring construction for launch pads.

These discoveries revealed that the weapons being imported into Cuba were not defensive but could be considered offensive, particularly if they had nuclear warheads. These missiles posed a threat to much of the United States. Operation Anadyr had been discovered.

CHAPTER 4

AIR STRIKE, INVASION OR BLOCKADE?

About 9:00 AM on Tuesday, October 16, McGeorge Bundy, special assistant to the president for national security affairs, broke the news to President Kennedy who was still in bed reading the morning newspapers. "Mr. President," said Bundy, "there is new hard photographic evidence which you will see a little later, that the Russians have offensive missiles in Cuba." Kennedy took the news calmly and began to dictate the names of those with whom he wished to meet later that morning. The list of names included Vice-President Lyndon B. Johnson, Dean Rusk, Robert McNamara, the Attorney General Robert F. Kennedy, General Maxwell Taylor, chairman of the Joint Chiefs of Staff, Lieutenant General Marshal S. Carter, deputy director of Central Intelligence, Roswell Gilpatric, deputy secretary of defense, George Ball, under secretary of State Edwin Martin, McGeorge Bundy, National Security Adviser Theodore Sorenson, C. Douglas Dillon, secretary of the treasury, CIA Director John McCone, Ambassador Charles Bohlen, Llewellyn E. Thompson, ambassador at large, and Kenneth O'Donnell, appointments secretary. Kennedy often chose ad hoc groups to advise him. This group, known to history as the "ExComm," had the full title of Executive Committee of the National Security Council. Its membership would fluctuate with Dean Acheson, former secretary of state in the Truman administration, joining for a time, John McCone, away on his honeymoon, would join later, as would Adlai Stevenson, United States ambassador to the United Nations. The president would make it an official body on October 22 through an executive order. The ExComm met two and three times a day for the next twelve days in total secrecy. However, the members were unaware that their discussions were being taped by President Kennedy.

In the summer of 1962, President Kennedy had the Secret Service install a recording device in the Oval Office. Hidden microphones picked up conversations which were transmitted to a tape recorder in the basement of the White House. The President started the system operating by flipping a hidden switch. His motives for installing this apparatus are unknown but he may have been planning to use the tapes in writing his memoirs. Apparently the existence of this taping system was known only to the president's brother, Robert, Evelyn Lincoln, his secretary, and the Secret Service agents.

The First ExComm Meeting. Using briefing boards on an easel set up at the end of the Cabinet Room on which were set photographs taken by the U-2 cameras, Lundahl used a pointer to indicate trucks, tents and pieces of equipment—launchers, erectors. It was difficult for the members of the ExComm to accept what the photo-interpreters told them. Robert Kennedy later wrote that it appeared to him to be a cleared field for a farm or the basement of a home. President Kennedy came to the point. "Are you sure?" He wanted to know if the experts were certain that these specks on the photographs were missiles. Lundahl replied: "Yes, I am convinced that they are missiles." Again the president asked: "How soon will it be before they can fire these missiles?" A CIA expert gave a conservative answer: more likely days rather than hours. Next McNamara asked about the location of nuclear warheads for these missiles. He received the answer that there was no evidence as to whether warheads were in Cuba.

The president asked Rusk to begin the discussion. The secretary of state wanted a "chain of events" set in motion to eliminate the missile bases. He suggested a quick strike which would not require an invasion. If there was time, stimulate the Organization of American States to take action. They might even get word to Castro. There could be a call-up of certain troop units and reinforcement of Guantanamo as well as forces in southeastern United States. But he found two alternatives: the quick air strikes and alerting allies as well as Khrushchev.

Secretary of Defense Robert McNamara urged air strikes before the missiles became operational. Air strikes would have to be mounted not only against missile sites but also air fields and aircraft. The casualties could total 2,000–3,000. Air strikes could be carried out in a matter of days. Following the air strikes the United States ought to prepare for an invasion by sea and by air. General Maxwell Taylor, recently appointed as chairman of the Joint Chiefs of Staff, promised to have the planning staff begin work that same afternoon. To prevent any additional missiles from entering Cuba, Taylor urged a naval blockade. In addition, Guantanamo should be reinforced and the dependents should be evacuated.

Rusk believed that Berlin was very much a part of this problem. "They may be thinking that they can either bargain Berlin and Cuba against each other, or they provoke us into a kind of action in Cuba which would give an umbrella for them to take action with respect to Berlin." For the first time, someone actually wondered about the reasons for Khrushchev's actions. No one followed up on Rusk's comment.

Kennedy summed up the options: a strike on Soviet bases in Cuba; a broader strike on airfields and SAM sites, and everything else connected with the missiles. Third, do both and launch a blockade. Fourth: consultation. Robert Kennedy added a fifth: invasion. The president wanted to know how soon the armed forces could invade. McNamara replied: seven days after the air strike. Kennedy brought the first meeting of the ExComm to a close. After calling for another meeting that same evening, he ordered the maximum number of U-2 flights over Cuba. Because the strikes would certainly have to take out the missiles, he ordered preparations to achieve that goal as well as preparations for a general air strike and an invasion.

During the meeting, brother Robert sent a note to Sorenson. "I now know how Tojo felt when he was planning Pearl Harbor." He alone had voiced dovish sentiments when he observed that the ExComm had been talking about dropping bombs "all over Cuba." As a result, he warned, "you're going to kill an awful lot of people." For that the ExComm would take a great deal of heat. The Russians would say: "Well we're going to send them in again, and if you do it again, we're going to do the same thing to Turkey."

After the first meeting of the ExComm, Kennedy attended a luncheon in honor of the Libyan ambassador. Adlai Stevenson, the American ambassador to the United Nations, was also a guest. Kennedy had little liking for him, but he would have to be informed. After the luncheon, Kennedy took Stevenson to his study and there showed him the photographs. Kennedy told him that something would have to be done quickly, perhaps an air strike. The president's words alarmed Stevenson. "Let's not go to an air strike until we have explored the possibility of a peaceful solution." He reminded Kennedy that this crisis would eventually end up in the United Nations and it would be "vitally important to go there with a reasonable cause." Later Stevenson sent the president a note urging negotiation before an air strike. In so doing Stevenson became the first high-level official to support negotiations before military action.

After the ExComm assembled that same evening, General Carter reported that with a better readout there was evidence now of a capability of sixteen to twenty-four missiles. These were solid propellant inertial guidance missiles with an eleven-hundred mile range. These missiles would be fully operational within two weeks; they probably had been brought into Cuba in early September. The president pressed Carter as to whether these were really missiles. Carter replied: "In the picture there is an actual missile. They are genuine"

Rusk suggested direct messages to Castro and to Khrushchev but that might lead to reinforcing the missile sites. He was concerned about the reaction in Latin America if there were an air strike and the Russians took some action. If the NATO allies were not warned, the alliance might crumble.

General Taylor reported that the Joint Chiefs of Staff urged that all possible intelligence be obtained, particularly as many photographs as possible. "Then look at this target system. If it really threatens the United States, then take it right out with one hard crack."

McNamara outlined three courses of action. The first was an open approach to Castro, Khrushchev, and the allies. But he thought such an approach would not lead to a satisfactory result. The second course of action was "a declaration of open surveillance": blockade against offensive weapons entering Cuba. The third approach was a limited air attack which the Joint Chiefs of Staff opposed. They preferred 700 to 1,000 sorties a day for five days followed by an invasion. McNamara thought that any form of military action would lead in turn to Soviet military action. Consequently SAC, the Strategic Air Command, should be placed on alert. A large-scale mobilization ought to be considered as well.

On the discussion rambled without any decision. But in these discussions the term "blockade" kept recurring. Except for McNamara, no one took up this possibility. At last Kennedy urged them all to consider the alternatives they had been discussing and whether anything ought to be brought to the attention of Khrushchev. (*See Document No. 6.*)

These two meetings do not support the argument made later that Kennedy was in command, coolly directing the discussion. He neither gave any significant direction to the discussion nor did he make any attempt whatsoever to move the discussions toward a definite conclusion. As yet it seemed that he had not altered his determination to take out the missiles, not because of the Monroe Doctrine, but because of his September pledges to act.

In Moscow that same day, Khrushchev returning from his vacation, had asked to see the American ambassador, Foy Kohler. Khrushchev was quite amiable and apologized for the announcement by Fidel Castro about setting aside a fishing port in Cuba for the Russians. During the three-hour talk, Khrushchev assured the ambassador that all of the Soviet activity in Cuba was defensive.

October 17 the ExComm began meeting in the State Department. The president had decided to absent himself from the meetings because of commitments. Ambassador Bohlen cautioned against military action without warning. The allies would dissent and the United States would be subjected to worldwide criticism. He supported the idea of writing both Khrushchev and Castro first and continued to warn about world opinion if the United States carried out a military strike.

The question of how the allies who had been "under the gun" for years would react when the United States became hysterical over a few missiles in its back yard was debated at length. There were arguments over the McNamara thesis that the appearance of the missiles in Cuba did not change the balance of power. Ambassadors Bohlen and Thompson wondered about the real purpose behind the Soviet action. Perhaps it was preparation for a confrontation with President Kennedy because of overseas bases and Berlin. McNamara and Taylor objected to any talks with the Soviet government because it would give time for the missiles to become operational. Then came an extensive discussion of the advantages and disadvantages of military blockade of Cuba, total or partial, without any conclusion.

Dean Acheson, the mustached, tall, former secretary of state, joined in the discussion for the first time and made the case for a surgical strike without any warning or talking. Acheson objected to the formless nature of the ExComm meetings: people came and went. It reminded him of a "floating crap game." In the evening discussion, Dean Rusk, McCone and Taylor all argued for air strikes. The secretary of state favored informing the allies and then striking. At the end of the day, there was as yet no consensus on what action to follow.

That was not the case with the Joint Chiefs of Staff who advised the secretary of defense that all targets should be hit: MRBMs, combat aircraft and nuclear storage sites. They advocated a naval blockade and preparations for an invasion within sixteen to eighteen days accompanied by air strikes. In preparation for a general war, they recommended dispersing aircraft with nuclear bombs and they urged worldwide military readiness for the United States.

On the morning of October 18 the ExComm learned that the information was now definite: a Soviet regiment with eight launchers and sixteen MRBM ballistic missiles was deployed at two launch sites. Two ICBM sites had been identified in Cuba from photographs. These had a range of 2,200 nautical miles. These were all Soviet manned and Soviet controlled. Three cruise missile sites were now operational as well as twenty-two surface-to-air missiles. The size of the missile force indicated that the Soviet Union intended "to develop Cuba into a prime strategic base, rather than a token show of force."

During the meeting of the ExComm, McNamara supported the Joint Chiefs of Staff arguing against limited strike and insisting on nothing less than a full invasion. Then McNamara insisted that this was not a military problem but a political problem involving holding the alliance together and conditioning Khrushchev for the next move. President Kennedy remarked that whatever action was taken in Cuba most people would consider it a "mad dog act" by the United States.

Ambassador Thompson, the person with the most extensive knowledge of the Soviet Union, favored the blockade plan and a demand to have the weapons dismantled. He believed that Khrushchev was aiming at a summit meeting with President Kennedy to negotiate the missile bases. The president observed that the only offer the United States could make to Khrushchev would be to give him some of the missiles in Turkey. Bundy concurred, stating that he did not think that it would be possible to keep the Turkish bases. George Ball feared negative world opinion if the United States forces struck Cuba without warning as the Japanese had done at Pearl Harbor.

Gradually the discussion turned more and more to the possibility of a blockade and whether a declaration of war would be necessary. Eventually McNamara proposed that air strikes be withheld until October 22 and that meanwhile the ExComm split up into groups. One would discuss the blockade approach and the other group military action. The meeting ended without his suggestion being acted upon. Nevertheless, the consensus appeared to be in favor of the blockade. There were significant comments about the possibility of a trade off—Jupiter missiles in Turkey for Soviet missiles in Cuba. However, neither the president nor the ExComm had yet agreed on what action to take. (*See Document No. 7.*)

Earlier in the day, Dean Acheson had met privately with the president. Acheson repeated his arguments in favor of a surgical strike without warning. As Acheson arose to leave, the president commented, "I guess I better earn my salary this week." Acheson replied: "I'm afraid you have to."

A Meeting with Gromyko. Later that afternoon, the president had a scheduled meeting with the dour-faced Soviet foreign minister, Andrei Gromyko. Kennedy had been advised neither to show Gromyko the photographs nor to demand the removal of the missiles because that would give Khrushchev the initiative. Gromyko opened with Berlin, declaring that if the question were not settled then the Soviet Union would sign a peace treaty with East Germany. Gromyko announced that Khrushchev would be coming to the United Nations in November after the Congressional elections and a meeting with the president would be useful. Turning next to the question of Cuba, Gromyko complained about the "Anti-Cuba Campaign" being waged by the United States. Speaking from notes, Gromyko stated that Soviet aid to Cuba was for the purpose of contributing to the "defense capabilities" and the development of Cuba. Soviet specialists were training Cubans in the handling of armaments which were only defensive and consequently such training did not "constitute a threat to the United States."

Gromyko launched into a defense of Cuba. "What could Cuba do to the United States?" The Cubans only wanted to make their home and country secure. The Soviet Union could not stand by as aggression was being planned. Kennedy argued that there was no intention of invading Cuba but last July the Soviet Union began supplying arms to Cuba which had a profound impact on the United States. He described it as the "most dangerous situation since the end of the war." Gromyko declared that the Soviet government had responded to appeals for assistance only for the purpose of "giving bread to Cuba."

Kennedy then read his September 4 warning against offensive weapons on the island. Gromyko's sour face never changed. "It was incredible to sit there and watch the lies coming out of his mouth," Kennedy said later. The president regretted that he had not shown Gromyko the photographs lying on his desk. (*See Document No. 8.*)

Seymour Hersh, in *The Dark Side of Camelot*, has criticized Kennedy for failing to reveal the U-2 photographs to Gromyko in order to give Khrushchev an escape and to lessen his embarrassment. The photographs were Kennedy's trump card and if he revealed them at this point, he would have lost his advantage. The quarantine was not yet in place; American forces were still being mobilized. Khrushchev would still have had room to maneuver and continue building up the missile bases.

That evening Gromyko met with Dean Rusk and announced that the Cuban issue was caused by the hostile policy of the United States toward Cuba. The United States believed that it must dictate to the Cubans the type of domestic regime that should exist in their country. The Soviet Union, Gromyko insisted, was helping Cuba by providing grain and helping to place the Cuban economy on a sound footing which did not present any danger to the United States. "Soviet specialists are helping Cuban soldiers to master certain types of defensive weapons."

Gromyko's Report. After talking with Kennedy and with Rusk, Gromyko reported to the Central Committee of the Communist Party that everything known about the position of the United States government on Cuba "allows us to conclude that the overall situation is completely satisfactory." There was no reason to believe that the United States was now preparing to intervene in Cuba. The United States was more intent on destroying the Cuban economy in order to cause hunger. The Kennedy administration and the "overall American ruling circles" were amazed "by the Soviet Union's courage in assisting Cuba." The fact that the Soviet Union was giving aid to Castro meant that it was fully committed to repulsing any American intervention in Cuba. He concluded that "it is possible to say that a USA military adventure against Cuba is almost impossible to imagine." (*See Document No. 9.*)

Late in the evening, Kennedy met with some of his closest advisors in the Oval Room on the second floor of the White House instead of the West wing in order that reporters would not become too curious. Nearly everyone agreed that the United States must respond to the missiles because inaction would throw into question the willingness of the Kennedy administration to respond over Berlin, and would divide the allies and the country. They expected a big crunch over Berlin in two or three months. By that time the Soviets would have a large arsenal in the Western Hemphisphere. Using the recording machine after everyone had left, Kennedy concluded: "The consensus was that we should go ahead with the blockade beginning Sunday night [October 21]." The blockade would target offensive weapons, without a declaration of war.

Kennedy and the Joint Chiefs of Staff. President Kennedy's relations with the Joint Chiefs of Staff were at best remote. After the

Bay of Pigs he would not accept the judgment of the Joint Chiefs as holy writ without question. On the morning of October 19 he met with them for the first and only time during the crisis. Taylor announced their opinion: Cuba would not be accepted as a missile base. Eliminate or neutralize the missiles and prevent additional missiles from coming into Cuba. Consequently they wanted a surprise attack, surveillance, and only then blockade. They were united. In reply Kennedy explained that if they were to attack Cuba, it would give the Soviet Union "a clear line to go ahead and take Berlin." They would be considered "trigger-happy Americans who lost Berlin." Then there would be no support among the allies. The West Germans would believe "that we let Berlin go because we didn't have the guts to endure a situation in Cuba." Kennedy argued that Khrushchev was personally committed to Berlin. A quick air strike, according to the president, would neutralize the danger of missiles being used against the United States. In so doing "we increase the chance greatly as I think . . . [of] their just going in and taking Berlin by force." This left him with one alternative which was "to fire nuclear weapons—which is a hell of an alternative—and begin a nuclear exchange." If they blockaded Cuba then Berlin would be blockaded by the Soviet Union.

General Curtis E. LeMay, Air Force chief of staff, crude, often profane and even childish if he could not have his way, announced that there was no choice but attack. If the United States resorted to blockade, "the first thing that's going to happen is your missiles are going to disappear into the woods." Blockade was "almost as bad as the appeasement at Munich."

The other members of the Joint Chiefs of Staff were unanimous in their recommendations. Tall, handsome Admiral George Anderson, chief of naval operations, did not believe that the blockade would lead to an immediate confrontation with the Soviet Union. If the Americans did not take action, the Russians would feel that they were weak. General Earle Wheeler, Army chief of staff, had limited combat service in World War II. He argued for the surprise air strike because it had the lowest-risk course of action in protecting the United States against possible attack. General David Shoup, Marine Corps commandant, who had earned the Medal of Honor on Tarawa in 1943, argued in favor of going in and eliminating the threat in Cuba. Then the United States could take over Cuba and put in a new non-Communist government.

The president observed that the problem was not "so much war against Cuba. But the problem is part of this worldwide struggle with the Soviet Communists, particularly as I say over Berlin." Finally he asked when the Chiefs would be ready for the air strike? LeMay replied that they would be ready at dawn Sunday, October 21, although the best date was October 23. (*See Document No. 10.*)

Following the meeting, Kennedy left on a scheduled campaign trip. He instructed Sorenson and his brother Robert to pull the ExComm together. The president wanted action and soon. Robert should call him whenever he should cut short his trip and return to Washington.

With the president off campaigning in support of candidates for the upcoming election, the ExComm went back to work on October 19. Nicholas Katzenbach, deputy attorney general, provided the ExComm with a legal opinion concerning a blockade of Cuba. He believed that the president had statutory authority to impose a blockade without declaring war. This action could be justified on the basis of self-defense. Then in their discussion the ExComm retraced earlier arguments over imposing a blockade. McGeorge Bundy argued again for an air strike which would be "quick and would take out the bases in a clean surgical operation."

Dean Acheson agreed with Bundy. The missile bases should be cleaned out with an air strike. The missiles were in the hands of a madman. The United States ought to "act and act quickly." General Taylor, reflecting the Joint Chiefs of Staff, warned that the blockade meant abandoning the air strikes. "It was now or never for an air strike." Once more McNamara spoke again in favor of a blockade instead of an air strike.

Robert Kennedy returned to the Pearl Harbor analogy, "A sneak attack was not in our traditions," he reminded his colleagues. He wanted to allow the Soviets room for maneuver in order to pull back from their position in Cuba.

At Dean Rusk's suggestion, the members of the ExComm broke up into two working groups. One would work up a case for blockade and the other group the case for the air strike. Deputy Undersecretary U. Alexis Johnson would head the blockade group and Bundy the strike group. After reconvening at 4 PM, the two groups argued for two hours over the Johnson scenario. The ExComm spent only a half an hour on the Bundy air strike scenario because opinion was turning at last in favor of the blockade. Moreover, the proponents of the blockade realized that it would be a symbolic action indicating to the Soviets that they meant business, but which would not preclude more forceful actions if necessary.

At this point, Adlai Stevenson entered the conference room in the State Department. Asked by Rusk if he had any opinions on the blockade, Stevenson replied that he did and that he favored it. But he believed that the ExComm ought to look beyond the blockade and develop a plan to solve the problem, perhaps a demilitarization of Cuba under international guarantees. At this point the meeting ended with a discussion of when the participants would next meet with the president.

The discussions helped Theodore Sorenson in his task of drafting the speech for the president. They clarified his thoughts and enabled him to return to writing a blockade speech which he finished around 3:00 AM on October 20. For background he had studied the speeches of Woodrow Wilson and Franklin D. Roosevelt when they asked Congress to declare war.

Robert Kennedy was soon on the telephone to the president who was in Chicago fulfilling a promise to Mayor Richard Daley that he would speak in support of Democratic Congressman Sid Yates who was a senatorial candidate running against Everett Dirkson, the Republican leader of the Senate. By this time the president was needed in Washington. The security cover on the missile crisis was beginning to crumble. A few Washington reporters were puzzled by the unusual activity in the White House and in the State Department as well as the Pentagon.

There was much that the president must do in Washington. Consequently he dictated a news release for reporters in Chicago: "Slight upper respiratory infection, 1 and 1/2 degree temperature. Weather raw and rainy. Recommended return to Washington. Canceled schedule." To convince reporters, the president boarded Air Force One wearing a hat. Kennedy had not worn a hat since the silk hat worn at his inauguration. He hated hats.

A Special National Intelligence Estimate had been issued by the CIA on October 19 which had made for somber reading. "A major Soviet objective in their military build-up in Cuba is to demonstrate that the world balance of forces has shifted so far in their favor that the U.S. can no longer prevent the advance of Soviet offensive power even into its own hemisphere." The estimate concluded: "For a pre-emptive or first strike, Cuban based missiles would approach the U.S. with a shorter time-of-flight and from a direction not now covered by U.S. BEWS [Ballistic Early Warning Service]."

On the morning of October 20, according to a CIA Special Intelligence Estimate, there were four MRBM and two IRBM launch sites in various stages of construction. There were sixteen launchers, range 1,100 nautical miles, and eight IRBM launchers with 2,200 nautical mile range. The sixteen MRBM launchers were operational at that time. It was estimated that the four IRBM launchers would be operational within eight to ten weeks. The MRBM missiles could be launched eight hours after the decision to launch. Among the other Soviet weapons identified were twenty-two IL-28 jet light bombers, thirty-nine MIG-21 jet fighters, sixty-two less advanced jet fighters, twenty-four SAM missile sites, three cruise missile sites, and twelve Komar cruise missile patrol boats. For the first time nuclear warhead storage bunkers were identified.

Again the ExComm met in George Ball's office in the State Department on October 20. It amended and approved Sorenson's draft of a speech for President Kennedy. Before McNamara left the conference room, he telephoned an order to the Pentagon ordering four tactical air squadrons to be ready for a possible air strike on Cuba. To a State Department officer who overheard his order, McNamara explained: "If the President doesn't accept our recommendation, there won't be time to do it later."

At 2:30 PM the president, back from Chicago, met with the Ex-Comm. Officially it was a meeting of the National Security Council. Ray Cline, deputy director of intelligence at the CIA, reported that the committee had evidence of MRBMs being deployed that could reach targets from Dallas to Cincinnati and even to Washington, D.C. IRBMS were also being deployed which could reach nearly all of the continental United States. The available evidence indicated the probability that eight MRBM missiles could be fired from Cuba that day.

McNamara presented strong arguments for a blockade of Cuba followed by negotiations for removal of the missiles from the island. General Taylor again spoke in favor of an air strike on October 23, arguing that it would be the last chance to destroy the missiles. The debate turned to the question of an air strike with McNamara warning that it would not destroy all of the missiles and launchers. The president repeated his fear that an air strike would lead to a blockade of Berlin as would a blockade of Cuba. As the discussion continued, gradually more opinions were voiced in favor of the blockade. Even McCone swung over to the blockade side. Taylor argued that the blockade would neither solve their problem nor end the Cuban missile threat. Eventually they would have to use military force. McNamara warned that the air strike involved 800 sorties and would result in several thousand dead Russians as well as chaos in Cuba. The Soviet Union would not take an air strike without a major response. Rusk recommended the blockade as did McNamara.

Maxwell Taylor, representing the Joint Chiefs of Staff, asserted that now was the time to act because this would be the last chance they would have to destroy the missiles. Nevertheless, the consensus was clearly in favor of the blockade. Roswell Gilpatric voiced the opinion of the majority: "Essentially Mr. President this is a choice between limited action and unlimited action, and most of us think that it's better to start with limited action."

Adlai Stevenson's Proposal. As the meeting was winding down, Adlai Stevenson proposed that with the announcement of the blockade, a resolution should be introduced in the United Nations concerning missiles in Cuba. He urged that the United States obtain prior support for the blockade from the Organization of American States. His audience turned hostile when he said that the president should remove the missiles from Turkey and Italy, evacuate Guantanamo and draft a noninvasion pledge for nations in the Western Hemisphere. The immediate reaction was fiercely negative. The president rejected surrendering the base because it would signal "that we had been frightened into abandoning our position." In regard to discussing a withdrawal of the missiles from Turkey, that was a proposal for the future and he would only remove those missiles if Khrushchev raised the subject. Stevenson insisted that Kennedy would eventually have to provide a quid pro quo if he wanted to resolve the crisis, but he failed to convince anyone on the ExComm that it was necessary to find a quick diplomatic solution to the crisis before it escalated into armed conflict.

Later that evening, speaking to Ken O'Donnell, Stevenson said: "I knew that most of those fellows would probably consider me a coward for the rest of my life for what I said today. But perhaps we need a coward in the room when we are talking about nuclear war." Nevertheless, in the end, Stevenson's proposals would eventually become the basis for the final solution of the Cuban missile crisis.

The Decision. At last Kennedy made his decision: he was ready to go ahead with the blockade and take "the actions necessary to to put us in a position to undertake an air strike on the missiles and missile sites by Monday or Tuesday." He was ready to authorize the military forces to make preparations for an invasion of Cuba. In addition he authorized low-level photographic reconnaisance because the blockade would now be instituted. There followed a discussion of the president's speech which would define the objective as halting "offensive millitary preparations in Cuba."

The president observed finally: "The worst course of all would be for us to do nothing. There isn't any good solution. Whichever plan I choose, the one whose plans we're not taking are the lucky ones—they'll be able to say 'I told you so' in a week or two. But this one seems the least objectionable." By the close of the meeting he had converted the supporters of the air strike or the invasion to his decision. There was a final discussion on the draft of the speech that the president would make to the nation. He wanted to deliver it on Sunday, October 21 because secrecy was already commencing to vanish. However, Allied and Latin American governments would have to be notified first. Consequently the speech was scheduled for Monday, October 22, unless reporters broke the story sooner.

Because no one knew if the blockade would be effective, backup plans had been made in case of failure. On the morning of October 21 the president received a briefing from McNamara and General Taylor and from the Commander of the Tactical Air Command, General Walter Sweeney. About 500 bombing sorties would be required to destroy the SAM sites and the MIG air fields, but General Sweeney could guarantee only that ninety percent of the known missile sites would be destroyed. More sorties would be needed leading to an invasion. Nevertheless, the president ordered the Air Force to be prepared to carry out the air strikes any time after the morning of October 22. The president asked brother Robert for his opinion. The attorney general opposed the air strike because "it would be a Pearl Harbor type of attack." It could lead to a general nuclear war. He urged that the Americans start with the blockade and "play for the breaks."

That afternoon, the ExComm met with the president to work on his speech in an effort to toughen it. In the process Rusk proposed that "quarantine" be used for political reasons in an effort to avoid comparisons with the Berlin blockade. Kennedy agreed, observing that later a total blockade could be enforced. After completing their work on the draft of the speech, Admiral George W. Anderson, chief of naval operations, briefed the ExComm on the plan for what was now called a "quarantine" and the procedures that would be followed. As a ship approached the quarantine line, it would be signaled to stop for boarding and inspection. If the ship failed to respond, a shot would be fired across the bow. If the ship did not respond a shot would be fired into the rudder which would cripple the vessel. Kennedy worried that the shot would destroy the vessel but Anderson assured him that would not be the case.

Once more Stevenson tried without any succcess to to get the president to propose a summit meeting with Khrushchev before being forced into such a parley. The president refused to appear as if he were seeking a summit because of Khrushchev's actions. "We should be clear," he said, "that we would accept nothing less than the ending of the missile capability now in Cuba, no reinforcement of that capablity, and no further construction of missile sites."

With the the close of this meeting, the massive machinery of the United States government accelerated its actions. The time for argument and debate had ended. The military and diplomatic branches of the government of the United States were moving into action. The final countdown had begun.

CHAPTER 5

THE FINAL COUNTDOWN

News leaks were increasing. Press Secretary Pierre Salinger had been receiving calls from newspaper reporters. Scotty Reston of the *New York Times* had put it all together and even checked with George Ball and McGeorge Bundy who begged him to hold off. The *New York Times* staff was reluctant to go along with the wishes of the Kennedy administration because they had held off publishing stories about the Bay of Pigs which had turned out to be a disaster. It was necessary for the president personally to telephone the publishers of the *New York Times* and the *Washington Post* and McNamara to telephone the publisher of the *New York Herald Tribune* to ask that they refrain from printing their stories about the crisis.

Mobilization. The reporters and their editors had become aware of the extraordinary military activity—the largest mobilization of American men and equipment since World War II. By October 20 the 82nd Airborne and the 101st Airborne divisions were alerted for immediate movement as were the 1st Division at Fort Reilly and the 4th Division at Fort Lewis. Fighter planes had been deployed to bases in South Florida. High altitude radar picket planes were deployed to an Air Force base near Orlando, Florida. The Air Defense Command had alerted ballistic detection radars and space tracking radars to be aligned for warnings of missile firings from Cuba.

High priority was given to Army air defense battalions equipped with surface-to-air missiles. From bases in Texas, Washington, and Maryland these battalions began to move south to Florida to defend airfields. Little attention had been paid to overloading and as one surface-to-air battalion from Fort Meade, Maryland, traveled south on U.S. Highway No. 1, an alert Virginia state trooper ordered the convoy to follow him to a weighing station. There it became obvious that the convoy had exceeded the weight limit. Despite the convoy commander's complaints that the unit was on a very important mission, the trooper proceeded to write out a citation.

The aircraft carrier *Enterprise* left Norfolk on October 19 ostensibly to escape a hurricane. Soon the *Enterprise* was in waters south of the

Bahamas where radar picket destroyers joined the carrier as escorts. Next the *Independence* joined the *Enterprise* to form Task Force 135. Following the direction of the Joint Chiefs of Staff, Admiral Robert L. Dennison, commander-in-chief Atlantic command, positioned the ships in an arc 500 nautical miles north of Cape Maisi, the eastern most point of land in Cuba. At that distance, the ships would be beyond range of Soviet MIG fighters and IL-28 bombers. From Atlantic coast naval stations, destroyers, cruisers and support ships sailed out to join the quarantine force which now became Task Force 136. Meanwhile, to the north, six of the Navy's new Polaris submarines based in Holy Loch, Scotland deployed to their battle stations under the seas.

The president wanted all dependents taken out of Guantanamo by the time that he would begin speaking to the nation in the evening of October 22. On the morning of October 22, four ships had dropped anchor in Guantanamo bay: *Upshur*, a transport, *Duxbury Bay*, a seaplane tender, *Desoto County*, a landing ship, and *Hyades*, a refrigerator ship. The skippers had been ordered to evacuate the dependents beginning at 11:00 AM and to sail at 5:00 PM. Vehicles with loud speakers drove through the housing area announcing the evacuation. Dependents could bring only one suitcase per person; they were to await buses to pick them up.

An Unusual Voyage. In the case of USS *Hyades,* the skipper, Captain George A. Hagerman, was assigned a quota of 300 evacuees. Consequently the crew had to move into the No. 2 hold, surrendering all of its living space and its bathroom facilities to the women and children. Early in the afternoon, bewildered evacuees began to arrive. They had thought that this was just another evacuation drill and consequently, women showed up in shorts, halters, and sandals, expecting to be released at the end of the drill. They had left their homes without being able to say good-bye to fathers and husbands, leaving all their possessions except for whatever they could cram into their suitcases. Soon 291 mothers, babies and children had crowded on board the *Upshur*. Where to find refrigeration for baby food and infant formulas? Answer: the officers' pantry where a twenty-four hour watch was set up to help mothers with their formulas. Mattresses now covered the deck in the crew's recreational lounge. All of the officers' quarters, except the captain's, were surrendered to some of the new passengers who were ill or very pregnant. Feeding the passengers was time-consuming—the first meal took four hours to serve all of the women and children with sailors helping the children through the mess line.

Twelve crew members were stationed at various locations to assist women and children in finding their way around the unfamiliar territory of a reefer ship. Among the passengers were six pregnant women, one expecting a birth momentarily, 115 toddlers and infants needing supervision. "A Didie Diaper Service" was established in the ship's laundry. The chief engineer installed a nursery in his office with mattresses and two attendants. To wear off excessive energy, the younger passengers were taken on guided tours of the ship. As the reefer sailed north, by October 25 the temperature had fallen and the passengers found themselves unprepared for the colder climate. Early that morning, *Hyades* rendezvoused off Cape Hatteras to receive a transfer of clothing collected from the residents of Norfolk for the passengers who lacked warm clothing. Late in the evening, the *Hyades* deposited her passengers safely at the Norfolk Naval Base, and became once more a refrigerator ship.

Informing the Allies. Before Kennedy made his televised speech, it had become necessary to inform the allies of the United States as well as assorted embassies around the world. Special instructions were sent to twenty-one Latin American embassies as well as personal letters to Latin American chiefs of state. Sixty United States embassies were informed about the president's speech. The State Department warned 134 embassies and consulates to take precautions in regard to hostile demonstrations. Oral briefings were given to ninety-five ambassadors accredited to the United States government. In all, fifteen copies of presidential letters or documents were transmitted to 441 recipients around the world. Briefing teams were dispatched to Harold Macmillan, General Charles de Gaulle, and Konrad Adenauer.

In London on the morning of October 22, the United States ambassador, David K. E. Bruce, briefed Prime Minister Harold Macmillan at No. 10 Downing Street. After the briefing, Macmillan complained that President Kennedy had acted without consulting him first. The prime minister argued that Kennedy should have confronted Khrushchev privately instead of going on television. Macmillan, fearful of damage to his government, insisted that he be permitted to show the British public the photographic evidence because he was under pressure to separate himself from Kennedy. At Macmillan's urging the opposition leader,

Hugh Gaitskill, was also briefed. Gaitskill, annoyed that he had not been informed earlier on the seriousness of the crisis, urged that the situation be negotiated and that the United States withdraw the missiles from Turkey and Italy in return for the Soviet withdrawal of missiles from Cuba.

In Paris on the afternoon of October 22, Dean Acheson, who had agreed to brief General Charles de Gaulle, president of the French Republic, entered the general's office. De Gaulle asked, "Are you here to consult me or to inform me?" Acheson replied that he was there to inform him and proceeded to summarize the crisis; he concluded by presenting de Gaulle with a letter from President Kennedy. Acheson offered to show de Gaulle the photographs of the missile bases but the general countered: "A great nation such as yours would not take such a serious step if there was any doubt. I need no evidence. For our purposes, the missiles are there." Eventually Acheson convinced the general to look at the photographs, When Acheson told him that they had been taken at a height of fourteen miles, de Gaulle exclaimed: "*C'est formidable! C'est formidable!*" At the end of the briefing, de Gaulle assured Acheson that France would stand beside the president in this crisis.

In Bonn, Chancellor Konrad Adenauer promised Ambassador Walter C. Dowling that Kennedy would have the chancellor's full support. The same day in Ottawa, the Canadian prime minister, John Diefenbaker, expressed his belief that President Kennedy would receive support in the Western world, but he turned quite critical when he was shown a copy of Kennedy's speech. Canada would do whatever necessary to bring peace to Cuba including detailing Canadian troops as a United Nations inspection team. Like Britain and France, Canada would not offer the United States any military support.

The Jupiters. There was also the matter of the Jupiters in Turkey. From the very first day of the crisis the Jupiters became a subject of debate in the ExComm. Kennedy's advisers soon recognized the analogy between the missiles in Cuba and the Jupiters in Turkey. If the missiles in Cuba were attacked then the Jupiters would be attacked. Ambassador Thompson observed that Khrushchev could justify his actions because of the Jupiter missiles. The ExComm began to realize that the Soviet missiles and the Jupiters had much in common. Both superpowers were using their missiles to protect their friends. As early as October 17, some of the ExComm argued that a Turkey-Cuba deal might be necessary. By October 21, the general opinion among the ExComm was favorable to a trade.

At this time, the fifteen Jupiters in Turkey were on a higher state of alert than normal. As tension mounted, the president became worried that if commanders of the Jupiters lost contact with a higher command, they would assume that nuclear war had begun and, without orders, launch the Jupiter missiles. Consequently on October 22, President Kennedy ordered the Supreme Allied Commander, Europe, General Lauris Norstad, "to destroy or make inoperable Jupiters if any attempt [was] made to fire them without specific authorization of [the] President." In addition, McNamara sent an order to the Joint Chiefs of Staff, which was passed on to General Norstad, "The President has ordered me to make certain that Jupiters [in Italy and Turkey] will not be fired without his further authorization, even in the event of a selective nuclear or non-nuclear attack on these units by the Soviet Union in response to actions we may be taking elsewhere." These orders indicate that Kennedy was taking precautions against an attack on the Jupiters escalating into nuclear warfare. To the president, these outmoded missiles were not worth the cost of nuclear war. His actions indicate that Kennedy would permit a NATO ally to be attacked by the Soviet Union without retaliation in order to avoid a nuclear holocaust.

At noon on October 22, Pierre Salinger asked the three television networks to supply thirty minutes of network time at 7:00 PM for the president "who wished to speak on a matter of highest national urgency."

In the afternoon of October 22 Kennedy called his advisors together for a final meeting before he announced his policy to the world. Technically this was a meeting of the National Security Council. Kennedy reviewed the reasons for action. Because of his statement in September announcing certain commitments, there had to be action. If there were no action following the secret deployment of Soviet missiles in Cuba, the impression would be conveyed to the Russians "that we would never act, no matter what they did anywhere." In addition, Gromyko had implied that the Soviets would move soon in Berlin. "If they acted in response to the blockade, the Russians would be forced to bring on their Berlin squeeze earlier than expected." The failure to act would harm American interests in Latin America by giving the impression that the Soviet Union's world position was increasing while that of the United States was decreasing. Kennedy returned to the differences between

Soviet missiles in Cuba and United States missiles in Turkey, stressing that the Soviet missiles had been secretly deployed in Cuba where they would have a different effect from missiles positioned in the Soviet Union. Finally, the president explained that he had decided against an air strike because it would not destroy all the missiles, leaving those untouched to be launched against the United States. According to Kennedy, "an air strike had all the disadvantages of Pearl Harbor."

Before he could speak to the nation, Kennedy had to perform some political courtesies. He telephoned former presidents Eisenhower, Truman, and Hoover, met with his Cabinet for the purpose of informing it about what would soon occur, and briefed leaders of Congress who had been called back to Washington from vacations and from campaign trails. It was necessary to ferry some of them back to Washington by Air Force jet planes. Congressman Hale Boggs, Democratic whip, who was deep sea fishing in the Gulf of Mexico, was picked up by a helicopter from an oil rig and then flown to an airfield where he climbed into a jet trainer for the flight to Washington.

Briefing Senators and Congressmen. When the politicians were finally assembled, McCone discussed the information which had been given earlier that day to a meeting of the full National Security Council. Lundahl followed with an explanation of the photographs of the launch sites, discussed their ranges, and the available information relating to Soviet jet bombers, MIG-21 fighters, SAM missiles, and cruise missile sites. The senators and congressmen sat quietly, both surprised and angered. Then the president, Rusk, and McNamara explained the plan for a quarantine. The president reviewed the chronology of the crisis beginning with the revelation of the photos of October 16. He concluded that whatever was done involved a risk. "To do nothing would be a great mistake." A blockade would be undertaken and ships containing offensive weapons would not be allowed to proceed.

To Kennedy's surprise, the senior senator from Georgia, Richard Russell, chairman Senate Armed Services Committee, not only condemned the plan but demanded an immediate invasion of Cuba. The president had warned Khrushchev twice in September. "No further warning was necessary," Russell argued. Khrushchev was rattling his missiles. "We must react," declared Russell. They were at a crossroads. "We're either a first class power or we're not." They were justified in carrying out the announced policy of the United States. "And I think that we should assemble as speedily as possible an adequate force and clean out that situation."

The chairman of the Senate Foreign Relations Committee, J. William Fulbright, who had denounced the Bay of Pigs, called the blockade the worst possible alternative, an affront to the Soviet Union. As soon as a Soviet ship was damaged or sunk, exclaimed Fulbright, "we would be at war with Russia." The senator from Arkansas demanded an attack on the missile bases, but when McNamara reminded him that such a procedure would result in shedding Russian blood, Fulbright retorted that it would not make any difference. Because Cuba was not a member of the Warsaw Pact, Fulbright did not think there would be any reaction if a few Russians were to be killed in Cuba. "I'm in favor, on the basis of this information, of an invasion, an all-out one, and as quickly as possible." Shocked at the reaction he was encountering, Kennedy reminded the senator that an attack on the missile bases would be more provocative and cause more casualties than stopping ships at sea.

Kennedy was shaken by the ferocity of the opposition as other congressmen joined with Russell and Fulbright in attacking the blockade idea. The president's defenders were few. Senator Everett Dirksen, Republican leader in the Senate, voiced his support for the president. Finally the meeting ended because Kennedy had to prepare for his speech to the nation. Later he complained to Sorenson, "If they want this job, they can have it. It's not great joy to me." (*See Document No. 11.*)

As Kennedy was preparing to speak, diplomatic representatives of NATO, SEATO, and CENTO received a briefing from George Ball. About the same time, a smiling Anatoly Dobrynin, the Soviet ambassador, entered the office of Dean Rusk. He left with a copy of Kennedy's speech and a short message for Khrushchev which began with a stern "Sir." When Dobrynin walked out of Rusk's office, his face was ashen. Khrushchev had never informed Dobrynin about Operation Anadyr. The ambassador had been told that the Soviet government was supplying Cuba only with defensive weapons.

In Moscow, the American ambassador, Foy Kohler handed in similar documents at the Soviet Foreign Office an hour before Kennedy spoke on television. In his message, Kennedy reminded Khrushchev that at their Vienna meeting he had told him the United States would not tolerate "any action on Khrushchev's part which in a major way disturbed the existing over-all balance of power in the world." Moreover, Kennedy said that he had publicly stated that if certain developments in

Cuba occurred, the United States would do whatever was necessary to protect its security. In view of the development of long-range missile bases and offensive weapons systems in Cuba, the United States was determined that this threat to security of this hemisphere would be removed.

Scarcely noticed in Washington that day, out in Turkey the first U.S. Jupiter missiles were formally turned over to the Turkish Air Force to operate and to maintain. Certainly Soviet military intelligence was well aware of this event.

A President Speaks. Promptly at 7 PM speaking from the Oval Office, President Kennedy told the nation and the world about the offensive missile sites being prepared in Cuba. There were medium-range ballistic missiles capable of striking Washington, D.C. and every city in the southeastern United States. There were also long-range missiles capable of hitting most major cities in the Western Hemisphere. These actions contradicted the Soviet assurances that this buildup was defensive in nature.

United States strategic missiles had never been "transferred to the territory of any other nation under cloak of secrecy and deception." The Soviet clandestine decision to station strategic weapons outside of the Soviet Union was "a deliberately provocative and unjustifiable change in the status quo which cannot be accepted by this country."

Action was required and so Kennedy announced that a quarantine on all offensive military equipment being shipped to Cuba was being initiated. The armed forces were directed to prepare for any emergency. The United States would regard the launching of any nuclear missile from Cuba against any nation in the Western Hemisphere as an attack on the United States by the Soviet Union.

Kennedy asked Khrushchev to remove this threat to world peace. He called the leaders of Cuba "puppets and agents of an international conspiracy." Finally he told the American people that this was a "difficult and dangerous effort on which we have set out." He warned that "the greatest danger of all would be to do nothing." (*See Document No. 12.*)

As Kennedy began to speak, twenty-two interceptor aircraft carrying nuclear weapons were airborne off the coast of Florida to guard against any Soviet aircraft flying from Cuba. At the same time a message to all branches of the United States armed forces ordered the establishment of Defensive Condition 3 (DEFCON 3). In the five-stage DEFCON system, DEFCON 3 required that military forces assume a condition of readiness beyond normal conditions and prepare to move to the next stage, DEFCON 2 if necessary. This was the highest stage of readiness for a nuclear war ever assumed by United States forces.

At SAC (Strategic Air Command) bomber bases alert operations increased from twelve to sixty-six sorties a day. These B-52 bombers flew three preassigned routes. Along one route bombers flew across the Atlantic Ocean, then refueled over Spain and on over the Mediterranean Sea. A second bomber route lay north across Canada to Hudson Bay and then orbited over Thule, Greenland. The third route was north to Newfoundland, across Greenland, then over the Arctic Ocean, Alaska, and then down the Pacific Coast to bases in the western United States.

All bomber planes not in the air had a full load of fuel and bombs. Fighter bombers in Great Britain, Italy, France, Turkey, Germany, South Korea, Japan and the Philippines were all armed, fueled, and prepared to strike targets behind the Iron Curtain. Atlas and Titan missiles in the United States were prepared for firing. Five divisions were alerted and the First Armored Division was on the move to Fort Stewart, Georgia, in preparation for a landing in Cuba if necessary.

The alert and the mobilization of United States forces was intended to reinforce Kennedy's words that the United States would react to any nuclear strike launched from Cuba with full retaliatory attack on the Soviet Union. The United States now awaited the response from the Soviet Union.

CHAPTER 6

CONFRONTATION

Dean Rusk had stayed late at the State Department and did not get home until 2:00 AM, October 23. At daylight he awoke. "Ah," he thought, "I am still here. This is very interesting." Obviously Khrushchev had not replied with a nuclear attack. When he slipped into George Ball's office, Rusk found the undersecretary asleep on the couch because he had been up all night monitoring reports from United States outposts around the world. Rusk woke up Ball and grinned. "We have won a considerable victory. You and I are still alive!"

Reaction in Moscow. In Moscow during the night of October 22/23, Colonel Oleg Penkovsky had been arrested. Only then did the Soviet High Command learn exactly what information he had disclosed to British and American intelligence services. In his last coded telephone signal to his handlers shortly before his arrest, Penkovsky sent a message that a Soviet attack was imminent. However, his handlers after some thought suppressed the message. Even the ExComm was not informed.

There is every indication that all of the Soviet leaders were caught by surprise. Neither Dobrynin nor Gromyko had any warning of the intent of the president's speech. Gromyko left the United States on the afternoon of October 22. Before his departure, he gave a routine statement to reporters. Soviet officials in New York, Washington, Moscow, and Havana claimed that they had no information that the United States had discovered the missiles nor had they realized that a United States military alert was imminent.

In Moscow, Khrushchev knew only that Kennedy would make a public statement about the Soviet position in Cuba. He assembled the Presidium to discuss the possibility of war over Cuba. Malinovsky dismissed Kennedy's television speech as a "preelection trick." Khrushchev was both angry and downcast. They had never intended to unleash war, he said, just intimidate them. He and his colleagues realized that now a United States invasion of Cuba was possible as well as a nuclear exchange between the United States and the Soviet Union. Khrushchev never left the Kremlin that night; he slept on a couch in his office expecting alarming news at any moment.

Even before the contents of Kennedy's speech were known in Moscow, Soviet Defense Minister Rodion Malinovsky ordered all leaves canceled and all personnel scheduled to be released retained on active duty. The commander of the Warsaw Pact Forces ordered increased combat readiness. However, in contrast to the United States armed forces, the Soviet High Command did not order an alert for the Soviet strategic missile forces. Most important of all, there were no threatening moves by the Soviet forces in Berlin.

During the night, the Soviet commander in Cuba, General Pliyev, received a message from Malinovsky ordering him to prepare to repulse any invasion. However, Khrushchev and his colleagues had been troubled about reducing the risk of a conflict in Cuba. Consequently the same night, Malinovsky also sent Pliyev ("Comrade Pavlov") an order reconfirming the standing orders that MRBMs could be fired only with the explicit permission from the Kremlin. At the same time, the right to use tactical nuclear battlefield weapons was rescinded. In July, Khrushchev had personally given Pliyev the authority to use the tactical nuclear weapons if he could not contact Moscow in the midst of battle. At the time, Malinovsky had refused to send a written order to that effect. Now even Khrushchev's oral order had been rescinded. Moscow was taking no chances because only the tactical nuclear weapons were ready for battle. Castro was of course not informed of the restrictions. Nevertheless, he ordered full mobilization of the Cuban armed forces and a war alert throughout the entire island.

On October 23 the State Department took particular care to obtain the consent of the Organization of American States (OAS). All-day negotiations were necessary until Dean Rusk obtained unanimous agreement to the demand that the Soviet Union withdraw missiles from Cuba and to the authorization of a limited blockade.

From Moscow came a message from Khrushchev to President Kennedy denouncing the quarantine as a "threat to peace and the security of peoples." It was "naked interference in the domestic affairs of the Cuban Republic, the Soviet Union and other states." The armaments in Cuban were exclusively for "defensive purposes, in order to secure the Cuban Republic from attack of [an] aggressor."

In the ExComm meeting on October 23, President Kennedy discussed the Proclamation of Interdiction of Ships to be issued later that day. In addition, contingency plans were approved in case there were incidents involving U-2 overflights. There would be an immediate retaliation against the SAM sites involved if a U-2 plane were shot down, and planes were to be placed on alert to hit the nine missile sites. Kennedy approved six low-level reconnaissance flights over Cuba in order to obtain better photographs of Soviet missile sites. Taylor gave the orders for them to leave immediately. President Kennedy expressed concern about conditions on airfields in Florida where planes might be lined up row upon row as at Pearl Harbor, an easy mark. He ordered these airfields to be photographed because if there were reprisals after a U-2 shootdown, Florida airfields would be a tempting target. As it turned out, planes were indeed lined up in rows on Florida airfields as the president feared. This condition was swiftly changed.

In the afternoon in New York, at a special meeting of the United Nations Security Council, Stevenson followed the administration line in arguing that the United States had adhered to the ideals of the United Nations since 1945, but that the Soviet Union had been aggressive. Cuba was "an accomplice in the Communist enterprise of world domination." The Soviet U.N. ambassador, Valerie Zorin and the Cuban delegate, Mario Garcia-Inchaustegui, replied with denunciations of the United States action.

Later in the day, the ExComm approved the proclamation of the quarantine after some last minute changes. At 6:00 PM President Kennedy signed the proclamation establishing the quarantine to go into effect on October 24 at 10:00 AM when the Commander-in-Chief, Atlantic Fleet would begin enforcing the quarantine. In the past, Kennedy had used a number of pens in signing important documents, but he thought that practice inappropriate this time and so he signed with only one pen. He placed the pen in his pocket announcing, "I am going to keep this one."

In an evening meeting of the ExComm there was much discussion over the procedure to be followed when dealing with ships trying to run the blockade which refused to stop when challenged. How to make the vessel stop? Open fire? What if the ship were then disabled? What to do if a boarding party were not allowed on board the vessel? McNamara warned that they ought to avoid "shooting a ship, a Soviet ship carrying wheat to Cuba or medicine." The president was worried that if the Americans tried to board a ship the Soveit crew would use machine guns. "And we're going to have one hell of a time trying to board that thing and getting control of it because they're pretty tough." They might have soldiers or marines on board. He thought that taking a Soviet vessel would be a major operation. "We may have to sink it rather than take it." McNamara reported that a submarine had been observed moving westward. There was concern that it might attempt to sink an aircraft carrier.

The discussion turned to civil defense. The president was concerned about the consequences if the United States launched an invasion of Cuba and missiles were fired at the mainland. A Department of Defense spokesman reported that within the 1,100 mile radius of the MRBMs on Cuba lived ninety-two million United States citizens. Kennedy wondered if the cities could be evacuated before an invasion of Cuba. It was soon apparent that very little could or would be done in such a crisis. (See Document No. 13.)

In Moscow that evening, Khrushchev received a message from Kennedy replying to his earlier letter to the president. Kennedy reminded Khrushchev that the actions of his government furnishing armaments to Cuba had set in motion the chain of events. The president was concerned that they both would "show prudence and do nothing to allow events to make the situation more difficult to control than it already is." He expressed his hope that Khrushchev would issue instructions to Soviet ships to observe the terms of the quarantine which had been endorsed by a vote of the OAS that afternoon.

A Meeting with Dobrynin. Back in Washington the same evening, at the suggestion of his brother, Robert Kennedy slipped into the Soviet embassy to meet with Soviet Ambassador Anatoly Dobrynin in his office. Robert Kennedy wanted Dobrynin to know how Soviet duplicity had contributed to the crisis. Six weeks earlier, Kennedy complained, Dobrynin had told him that the Russians had not placed long-range missiles in Cuba. Based on that information, President Kennedy had informed the American people that weapons furnished by the Soviets to the Cubans were defensive. This information had been confirmed by a TASS statement and by Gromyko when he met with President Kennedy on October 18. In the light of these assurances, said Robert Kennedy, the Soviet actions were "hypocritical, misleading and false."

Dobrynin asked why the president had not told Gromyko the known facts when they had met? Robert Kennedy claimed that there was nothing that the president could have told Gromyko that he did not already know. Why did not Gromyko inform the president of the truth? Dobrynin did not think that Gromyko knew the truth about the missiles in Cuba. As their talk ended, Robert Kennedy asked about the Soviet orders for their ships. According to Dobrynin, they would continue on course to Cuba. "I do not know how this will end for we intend to stop your ships," said Robert Kennedy as he left the embassy.

The next day, October 24, there were early reports that Soviet ships capable of carrying military cargoes on the way to Cuba appeared to have slowed down. Some even seemed to have altered course.

Khrushchev's Meeting with Knox. In Moscow on a business trip, William Knox, the president of Westinghouse International Company, received a call at his hotel informing him that Khrushchev wanted to see him. Later when he was ushered in, Khrushchev surprised Knox by engaging in a long conversation which began with a denunciation of Kennedy for the blockade. In trying to convince Knox that the missiles were defensive, Khrushchev admitted for the first time that there were nuclear warheads on the missiles. Khrushchev assured Knox that all of the equipment was under Soviet control and would only be fired on his personal orders. He swore that they would never be fired except in defense of Cuba or the Soviet Union. If Soviet ships were sunk, Soviet submarines would go into action. Then he came to the purpose of the meeting: Khrushchev proposed a personal meeting with President Kennedy. They could meet in Washington, Moscow, a neutral country or at sea. Khrushchev warned: "If the United States insists on war, we'll all meet in hell."

As they were speaking, on the high seas the quarantine went into effect. The line of interception had been changed from 800 to 500 miles because at 800 miles the interception would come too quickly.

Confrontation on the High Seas. The quarantine would go into effect at 10:00 AM on October 24. Before the ExComm meeting that morning, the president talked briefly with his brother. "It looks really mean, doesn't it?" said the president. "But then, really there was no other choice. If they get this mean on this one in our part of the world, what will they do on the next?" Brother Robert replied, "I just don't think there was any choice, and not only that, if you hadn't acted, you would have been impeached." The President thought for a moment and replied: "That's what I think—I would have been impeached."

The ExComm meeting on October 24 was tense. What would the Soviets do? Intercept? Announce withdrawal? The photographic evidence indicated that work on the missile sites was still continuing. McNamara announced that two Soviet ships were nearing the quarantine line. Interception would come very soon. The next report was more chilling: two Soviet submarines had moved into position between the two Soviet ships. McNamara explained that practice depth charges would be used to warn the submarines and force them to surface. Robert Kennedy remembered: "These few minutes were the time of greatest worry by the president. His hand went up to his face and covered his mouth and he closed his fist. His eyes were tense, almost grey, and we just stared at each other across the table." In this confrontation, Soviet ships might be sunk and lives lost. President Kennedy warned that if there was a confrontation and a ship was sunk they could assume that Berlin would be blockaded. Tension mounted. The president asked if there was not some way to avoid this confrontation. McNamara explained that there was too much danger to the other vessels. This had to be done and they had to expect it.

At 10:25 AM, McCone was handed a note. "Mr. President, we have a preliminary report which seems to indicate that some of the Russian ships have stopped dead in the water." McCone left to confirm the intelligence report. Minutes later he returned and announced: "The report is accurate." Six ships had stopped or had turned back. President Kennedy insisted that if the ships had turned back, give them every opportunity to do so.

Dean Rusk whispered to Bundy: "We're eyeball to eyeball, and I think the other fellow just blinked."

The Soviet ships were turning back because Khrushchev had decided not to test the quarantine with ships carrying weapons. He did not wish the Americans to obtain control of Soviet weapons and thus learn more about Soviet weapons technology.

DEFCON 2. At the direction of McNamara and the Joint Chiefs of Staff, the Strategic Air Command (SAC) went to DEFCON 2 which meant an increase in the alert bomber forces to 1,430 planes capable of responding. ICBMs were increased to 145, DEFCON 2 was one step removed from DEFCON 1—war. It was believed that such a high degree of alert for SAC would signal American resolution and make it unlikely that Soviet forces would retaliate.

Shortly after the DEFCON 2 was announced, General Thomas S. Power, commander of the Strategic Air Command, sent a message to all SAC wings, in a clear, uncoded, voice transmission which was reportedly picked up by Soviet intelligence. Power has been criticized for this transmission, but his message stressed calm judgment in a tense period. If there were any questions concerning instructions, he ordered SAC personnel to use the telephone for clarification. "If you are not sure what you should do in any situation, and if time permits, get in touch with us here." In such a crisis, Power's concern for safety was vital during dangerous operations.

Safety was of concern also to Robert McNamara who saw the crisis as political not military. By October 24 McNamara, who practically lived at the Pentagon, feared that the Navy did not understand that the quarantine was an exercise in communications, not a military operation. In a briefing in the Navy's Flag Plot Room, McNamara asked Admiral George W. Anderson, Jr., chief of naval operations, to review the procedures to be followed when a Soviet ship reached the quarantine line. McNamara wanted to know what Anderson planned to do.

"When that ship reaches the line, how are you going to stop it?" he asked Anderson.

"We'll hail it," replied the admiral.

"In what language—English or Russian?"

"How the hell should I know?" answered Anderson.

"What will you do if they don't understand?"

"I suppose we'll use flags."

"Well," asked McNamara, "what if they don't stop?"

"We'll send a shot across the bow," replied Anderson.

"Then what if that doesn't work?"

"Then we'll fire into the rudder," was the answer.

"What kind of a ship is it?"

"A tanker, Mr. Secretary," answered Anderson.

"You are not going to fire a single shot at anything without my express permission, is that clear? Do you understand that?"

Red faced, the admiral retorted: "The Navy has been running blockades since the days of John Paul Jones and if you and your deputy will go to your offices, the Navy will run the blockade." As he turned to leave, McNamara told the Admiral that this was a means of communicating with Khrushchev and no force would be used without his permission.

"Don't worry Mr. Secretary, we know what we are doing here," replied the Admiral. McNamara had the last word: Anderson was not reappointed chief of naval operations.

The secretary of defense was attempting to practice what came to be called "crisis management" by using the quarantine as a means to send Khrushchev a political message. McNamara feared that someone misunderstanding how the crisis was being managed could turn it into a nuclear war.

In an effort to lessen the chance of a confrontation that might lead to a nuclear war, U Thant, the acting secretary general of the United Nations, under pressure from nonaligned U.N. delegations, intervened in the crisis. He proposed that the United States suspend the quarantine and the Soviet Union suspend shipping weapons to Cuba for two or three weeks in order to provide a block of time for a settlement. Khrushchev accepted with enthusiasm. President Kennedy replied that the existing threat lay in secretly introducing offensive weapons into Cuba. The answer lay in removing those weapons.

During the evening of October 24, Kennedy received a message from Khrushchev, both rude and threatening but at the same time it was a plea not to humiliate Khrushchev with a dangerous confrontation on the high seas. "Who asked you to do this?" He implied that Kennedy had acted under pressure from imperialists, militarists, and capitalists. Kennedy had no right to impose a quarantine which was intended to intimidate the Soviet Union. He accused Kennedy of taking this action not only out of hatred for Cuba but also because of the election campaign in the United States. Khrushchev's accusations included "outright banditry" toward Cuba and "degenerate imperialism." The quarantine was an "act of aggression" and Soviet ship captains had instructions to ignore the orders of the American blockading naval forces. Finally he warned that the Soviet Union would take the means necessary to protect its rights. "We have everything necessary to do so." (*See Document No. 14.*)

Late in the evening a reply had been drafted and polished for dispatch to Moscow. Kennedy reminded Khrushchev of his statements in September which warned that shipping weapons to Cuba would create "the gravest issues." At that time the United States government had received explicit assurances publicly and privately that the Soviet government was not shipping offensive weapons to Cuba. The president had urged restraint on those in the United States who demanded action. Next he learned that the Soviet assurances were false because "your military people had set out recently to establish a set of missile bases in Cuba." Khrushchev had to recognize that "it was not I who issued the first challenge." Kennedy hoped the Soviet government would act to restore a more peaceable condition.

Sooner or later it would become necessary to implement the quarantine. A Soviet tanker, *Bucharest*, had been steaming closer to the quarantine line. The first order had been not to allow her through the quarantine Then after discussion in the ExComm the order was changed. In the morning of October 25, as *Bucharest* passed through the quarantine line the ship signaled, "my name is the *Bucharest* bound for Cuba." As the vessel slowed an American destroyer photographed the deck cargo and she was not boarded.

In the Joint Chiefs of Staff meeting, Admiral Anderson brought up a CINCLANT request for the Air Force to help "pinpoint the location" of Soviet shipping in the Atlantic. General LeMay immediately volunteered SAC and announced that the Air Force could locate the Soviet ships in a matter of hours. However, the only SAC force that could be deployed immediately was the tanker aircraft stationed in the Azores and Bermuda. At the orders of LeMay the tanker aircraft flew off over the Atlantic with crews who knew little or nothing about identifying specific merchant ships or vessels carrying weapons. A number of ships were reported to be Russian because they had a red star on the on their stacks. A red star identified tankers belonging to the Texaco oil company. SAC identified other British, Greek or American ships as Soviet shipping.

Lippman and the Jupiters. In the pages of American newspapers that morning, the syndicated columnist, Walter Lippman, proposed that as a "face saving" understanding, the United States agree to remove the Jupiters from Turkey. In return the Soviet government would remove the missiles from Cuba. Lippmann observed that Cuba was comparable to Turkey. The Soviet missile bases in Cuba like the NATO bases in Turkey had little military value. "The Soviet military base in Cuba is defenseless and the base in Turkey is all but obsolete." There was no discussion of this development in the ExComm on October 25, but Ambassador Dobrynin regarded it as a trial balloon sent up by the Kennedy administration.

In Prague on October 25, screaming, shouting Czechs demonstrated in front of the American embassy. Banners proclaiming "Hands Off Cuba" hung from balconies across the street from the United States Embassy. In New York City, the fire commissioner appealed for 50,000 volunteers to assist in fire control in the event of an attack. Pickets at the White House urged the president to get tougher with Cuba while others called for keeping the peace at any price.

In the ExComm on October 25, McNamara argued for low-level reconnaisance flights over all of Cuba. Such flights were justified, he argued, because the Soviet troops were camouflaging weapons and buildings. If the flights showed that the MRBMs were eight hours from launch, then the planes could be armed for attack. President Kennedy agreed and the Joint Chiefs of Staff were informed of the new tactic.

The debate continued over the the hailing and stopping of ships. The members of the ExComm were seeking a means of pressuring Khrushchev without sinking a vessel. When would the Americans stop a Soviet ship and board it? Robert Kennedy observed that they should stop one which carried something other than baby food. The president did not want to sink a ship and so he decided that they ought to await an answer from Khrushchev in reply to a proposal that he keep Soviet ships away from the quarantine line during preliminary negotiations.

Confrontation in the United Nations. There was also confrontation in the Security Council where Soviet ambassador Valerian Zorin asked why the president had not confronted Gromyko on October 18 with the "so-called" evidence. The reason Zorin announced was that the United States had only "falsified evidence." Zorin had played into Stevenson's hands because by that time he had permission to display the U-2 photographs.

Stevenson answered Zorin. "Well, let me say something to you, Mr. Ambassador—we do have the evidence. . . . and let me say something else—these missiles must be taken out of Cuba!"

"Let me ask you one single question. Do you, Ambassador Zorin, deny that the U.S.S.R. has placed and is placing medium and intermediate range missile sites in Cuba? Yes or no? Don't wait for the translation. Yes or no?"

"I am not in an American courtroom, sir," Zorin answered, "and therefore I do not wish to answer a question that is put to me in the fashion in which a prosecutor puts questions. In due course, sir, you will have your reply."

Stevenson roared back. "You are in the courtroom of world opinion right now and you can answer yes or no. You have denied that they exist and I want to know whether or not I understood you correctly." In reply Zorin said that Stevenson should continue his statement—Zorin was taking his turn as council president. In due course of time Stevenson would get his answer.

"I am prepared to wait here for my answer until hell freezes over, if that is your decision," Stevenson announced. Zorin tried to recognize the Chilean representative who preferred to yield the floor to Zorin. But Stevenson came back. "I have not finished my statement. I asked you a question, Mr. President and I have not had a reply to that question. I will now proceed, if I may, to finish my statement." He finished by having aides bring in easels and briefing boards with three panel foldouts. There were photographs of two missile sites in various stages of construction and photographs of IL-28 bombers being assembled on an airfield. Using a prepared script, Stevenson explained the photographs to his rapt audience and the television audience as well. When he finished his lecture, Zorin questioned the authenticity of the photographs, reminding Stevenson that at the time of the Bay of Pigs he had (unknowingly) produced fake photographs. Unabashed, Stevenson proposed that the Soviet Union ask the Cuban delegate to permit a U.N. team to inspect the sites. "Our job, Mr. Zorin," he concluded, "is to save the peace. And if you are ready to try, we are." It was great theater but it did not break the impasse. The missile crisis continued.

Why then did Zorin fall into the trap? Was it a failure on the part of his superiors in Moscow to keep him informed? Partly so. It may also have been his own laziness in failing to adjust to the changing events. It may also have been his health. Within a short time he was withdrawn from the Security Council. Toward the end of his life, Stevenson regretted his tactics with Zorin. Yet his performance delighted President Kennedy who understood the impact of theatrics in politics. The president observed, as he watched on television, "I never knew Adlai had it in him."

False Alarms. While Zorin and Stevenson confronted each other in the Security Council, American soldiers and airmen were on guard against sabotage during the night of October 25. Sabotage operations were expected to precede the launching of a nuclear first strike against United States command centers and military units. If war broke out, sabotage was expected first.

Near midnight October 25, a guard saw an apparent saboteur climbing a base security fence at the Duluth, Minnesota, Direction Center. The guard fired at the saboteur and set off a sabotage alarm connected to alarm systems at other bases. Throughout the area guards set off into the night to look for saboteurs. In Wisconsin at Volk Field, a defective alarm system resulted in a klaxon going off signaling an immediate launching of aircraft. Alerted by the signal, pilots ran to their nuclear equipped F-100A intercepteors, started the engines, and began taxiing down the runway. This could not be a practice drill because the pilots were on a DEFCON 3 alert. A nuclear war must have begun. As the planes taxied down the runway, a car flashing its lights drove out on the runway and an Air Force officer signaled the pilots to stop their planes. There was no nuclear attack. The saboteur, who had caused the alert, was only a bear.

Confrontation on the High Seas. The next day, October 26, a different confrontation came on the high seas. By now it was necessary to stop a ship in order to show the Soviet Union that the United States was taking the quarantine seriously after the *Bucharest* had not been halted. The ExComm and the president finally decided on *Marucla*, owned by a Panamanian company, flying the Lebanese flag and chartered by Russians. It was an old Liberty ship built in Baltimore during World War II and it carried a varied cargo. United States intelligence sources knew that the Soviet government never shipped weapons in a neutral or western owned ship. Stopping this vessel would not antagonize anyone.

The destroyer, USS *Joseph P. Kennedy, Jr.*, selected to stop the *Marucla*, had been named after the president's brother killed in World War II. The night before, the *Marucla* had been advised by radio that she would be boarded. At dawn the old freighter stopped dead in the water and a boarding party came aboard. The Greek skipper who spoke English was most cooperative. Naval officers in dress whites examined the cargo manifest. The ship's crew moved the deck cargo and removed the hatch covers in order for the boarding party to examine the boxes in the cargo holds. The hatches were closed and the *Marucla* was soon on her way to Cuba. The United State had demonstrated its intention to enforce the quarantine.

Panic Buying. While the U.S. Navy enforced the quarantine, in Poland there was so much panic buying in food stores that purchases of flour, sugar, rice, and salt were limited. There were protest rallies against "reckless and lawless" United States policy toward Cuba. Steel-helmeted police were stationed to guard the American embassy in Warsaw. In the southeastern United States there was strict security at all military bases. The Florida National Guard was on twenty-four hour alert. In these states there was an increase in the sale of a variety of items: batteries, flashlights, radios, water purification pills, and first aid supplies. In Miami there was heavy buying of canned goods. The Dade county manager advised the public to lay in two weeks' supply of food and stay off the highways. However, there was not any noticeable exodus of tourists from Miami Beach hotels.

In other sections of the United States, customers hurried to purchase a variety of items they believed would be needed during the crisis. In Los Angeles canned goods, powered milk, and bottled water were in demand. In Washington, D.C., the most sought after item was bottled water. Radio stations gave out information on stocking fallout shelters. In an army surplus store in Washington, D.C., on Pennsylvania Avenue, the largest seller was pemmican, a food concentrate containing dried meat, nuts, raisins and the like, in pocket-sized cans. Mess kits sold well as did halozone tablets, K rations, and small alcohol stoves.

As a safeguard against sabotage, the Benjamin Franklin Bridge across the Delaware River linking Philadelphia and Camden was closed to pedestrian traffic by the Delaware River Port Authority for an indefinite period.

In the ExComm on October 26, McNamara proposed night reconnaisance flights complete with the dropping of flares as in World War II. The President vetoed that idea. Much of the day's discussion revolved around tactics in the United Nations The aim was to seek some commitment from the Russians to stop further construction of missile sites, to bring an end to Soviet military shipments, to defuse weapons in Cuba and to have United Nations representatives on the ground in Cuba as observers. The quarantine would continue until a United Nations quarantine was in place. President Kennedy was concerned that if the quarantine were to be lifted and a United Nations quarantine substituted, the United States would be unable to reestablish a quarantine. "We will get the Soviet strategic missiles out of Cuba only by invading Cuba or by trading." The president doubted that the quarantine alone would produce a withdrawal of the missiles.

A Proposal from Khrushchev. Kennedy's reply to Khrushchev's last letter had been disappointing because it required capitulation. Consequently Khrushchev called members of the the Presidium to the Kremlin on October 25. He told them that recent intelligence reports indicated that Kennedy would not yield. If the Soviet Union kept missiles in Cuba, the result would be a war that Khrushchev never intended. Now he was considering asking Kennedy for a pledge not to invade Cuba in return for a removal of the missiles from Cuba. His change of mind resulted from bits and pieces of information indicating the weakness of the Soviet forces in Cuba and the strength of the United States. After obtaining the support of the Presidium for this change in policy, Khrushchev suggested to his colleagues that they go to the Bolshoi Theater to hear the American bass, Jerome Hines, in *Boris Goudounov*. It was Khrushchev's first public appearance since the crisis had begun.

The next day Khrushchev received more information including the move of SAC (Strategic Air Command) to DEFCON 2 as well as a report that American hospitals had been instructed to receive casualties. Another source reported that Warren Rogers of the *New York Herald Tribune* had claimed that Kennedy had decided to "finish with Cuba," and that plans were completed for an attack on the island. Even the KGB had reported that the Kennedy administration was on the brink of war. Shaken by this information, Khrushchev began to dictate another letter to Kennedy which he then sent to members of the Presidium for their comment. They had already approved his change in strategy.

In the evening of October 26, another letter came from Khrushchev which seemed long, rambling, and repetitive. He denied that there were any offensive weapons in Cuba. Weapons were only defensive, shipped there at the request of the Cuban government. He accused Kennedy of resorting to "piratical measures." If Kennedy and the American government would give assurances that the United States would not participate in an attack on Cuba, restrain others from such action, recall the United State Navy, such measures would change everything. Moreover, if Kennedy would declare "that the United States will not invade Cuba with its troops and will not support any other forces which might intend to invade Cuba, then the necessity for the presence of our military specialists in Cuba will be obviated." (*See Document No. 15.*)

What did it mean? Llewellyn Thompson who had served in Moscow, believed that Khrushchev himself had written the message, not Moscow bureaucrats. The copy handed in to the American embassy in Moscow appeared to have been written hastily with corrections made in violet ink apparently in the same hand as the signature. Words had been crossed out and others written in. The letter seemed to indicate that Khrushchev was under great strain. If Kennedy would lift the blockade and promise not to invade, Khrushchev offered only to stop bringing in more weapons but said nothing about removing ones already there. Was this the offer which the ExComm had been looking for? General Taylor regarded the letter as a stalling tactic. LeMay dismissed it with obscenities. Rusk wondered if Khrushchev was disturbed, perhaps losing his cool. Robert Kennedy, however, was encouraged: here was the beginning of an agreement.

There was a new twist. During the afternoon, John Scali, diplomatic correspondent for ABC, had met in a restaurant with Alexander Feklisov (alias Fomim), counselor of the Soviet Embassy and a KGB colonel. Feklisov proposed that a way could be found out of the crisis if the Russians promised to remove missiles from Cuba under U.N. supervision, and Khrushchev promised never to introduce offensive weapons into Cuba again. Would President Kennedy be willing to promise not to invade Cuba? Zorin would be interested if Stevenson suggested such a settlement in the U.N. Security Council. Feklisov asked Scali to use his State Department contacts to learn if Kennedy would make such a promise.

It is not generally agreed that Feklisov was acting on his own initiative. Nevertheless after Dean Rusk heard Scali's story he went to the president in order that Scali could report that an answer came from the highest level of the United States government. Later Scali informed Feklisov, following instructions from Rusk, that the United States saw "real possibilities" in the offer but time was urgent.

Krushchev's letter may have been prompted by a report by Dobrynin on October 25 that President Kennedy was a "hot tempered gambler" seeking reelection, consequently the possibility of an invasion of Cuba could not be excluded. According to Dobrynin, some diplomats and journalists considered that the probability of an armed invasion of the island was great. The Kennedy administration needed only a plausible excuse to justify an invasion of Cuba. Khrushchev also received a letter from Castro declaring that an invasion would come within the next twenty-four or seventy-two hours.

Within the administration there was reluctance at this time to forswear the invasion. Work continued on the missile sites at a faster pace. The assembling of the IL-28 planes continued.

Official Washington did not know that on October 26 at Vandenberg Air Force Base an Atlas ICBM, ready for a test launch, was indeed launched without any orders from Washington at 4:00 PM. At this writing, it is unknown if Soviet intelligence picked up the ICBM launch. Certainly no one in the ExComm had any knowledge of this launch and its potential for convincing Soviet intelligence that it was part of a genuine attack. And then came Black Saturday.

CHAPTER 7

BLACK SATURDAY

On Saturday, October 27, about 2:00 AM Washington time, a message from General Pliyev in Havana reached his superiors in Moscow. According to recent intelligence, the United States had located the positions of the MRBMs and the IRBMs; the Strategic Air Command was on full alert. The Cubans expected an air strike during the night of October 26/27 or at dawn October 27. Castro had ordered Cuban antiaircraft batteries to fire on American planes in the event of an American invasion. If there were to be an attack on Soviet installations, General Pliyev, commander of the Soviet forces, intended to use all means of defense. In Moscow, Malinovsky and Khrushchev approved. However, the prohibition against using nuclear weapons without the Kremlin's permission was still in force.

A Nuclear Strike? Castro had gone to the Soviet embassy to the ambassador's apartment. He was convinced that an attack by the Americans would come within days if not hours. To encourage Khrushchev, Castro began dictating a letter to him. He wrote that the attack upon Cuba was "almost imminent within the next 24 or 72 hours." According to Castro, the most likely possibility was an air attack; the second, an invasion. The Cubans would resolutely resist the attack whatever it might be. The danger which this attack would pose "for humanity is so great that following that event the Soviet Union must never allow the circumstances in which the imperialists could launch the first nuclear strike against it." If the imperialists invaded Cuba "that would be the moment to eliminate such a danger forever through an act of clear legitimate defense however harsh and terrible the solution would be, for there is no other." Alarmed by Castro's words, Soviet ambassador Alekseev asked if Castro meant for the Soviet Union to be the first to launch a nuclear strike. Although later he denied that, Castro asserted that "we must not wait to experience the perfidy of the imperialists, letting them initiate the first strike and deciding that Cuba should be wiped off the face of the earth." In so many words, Castro was urging Khrushchev to launch the first nuclear strike on the United States.

In London on October 27, thousands of demonstrators were turned back from the United States embassy in Grosvenor Square. They had intended to show the Yanks that Britain disapproved of the blockade of Cuba. Policemen blocked off the embassy while demonstrators waved signs: "Hands Off Cuba" and "Up Fidel, Kennedy to Hell." About 150 demonstrators were arrested. The British government refused permission to use Trafalgar Square for a demonstration against the blockade by erecting railings around the Nelson Monument.

Missile Exchange. In Moscow on the morning of October 27, there was relief that the expected American attack had not come to pass, but Kennedy had not offered any concessions. Khrushchev, however, realized that he was in no position to take action in the Western Hemisphere. Obviously his message to Kennedy had not succeeded and now he must send another message. "If at the same time," he told members of the Presidium, "we could achieve additionally the liquidation of the bases in Turkey we would win." He had received what he thought were hints suggesting the possibility of an exchange: Soviet missiles in Cuba for United States missiles in Turkey. Here was an opportunity to win a victory when he was staring at defeat. In the presence of the members of the Presidium, Khrushchev dictated another letter to Kennedy that would startle and confuse the ExComm. Because it had taken six hours for his previous message to reach Kennedy, after the letter had been typed and translated, it was decided to broadcast it on Radio Moscow to save time, a procedure that would further confuse the ExComm.

In going public with this message, Khrushchev had signaled his willingness to negotiate. He had backed away from using the missiles to threaten war. In the past, when he was bluffing, he had threatened nuclear war. Now his bluff had been called. Khrushchev had no wish to threaten nuclear warfare when such a war might actually erupt. He did not realize that the American Air Force would soon suffer its first casualty in the Cuban missile crisis.

A U-2 Shot Down. In Cuba, about 10:00 AM, Cuban antiaircraft guns had commenced firing on reconnaissance planes in response to Castro's orders. Only one was hit and it returned safely to the mainland. To Soviet troops, this sounded as if invasion had commenced. A SAM unit received a report that a U-2 had been sighted. The radar had locked on the target. The SAM commander contacted Pliyev's headquarters for instructions, but he was absent. The U-2 might soon be out of range, and the photographs from the U-2 might help the American invasion. There had been reports that such an invasion was imminent. Pliyev's deputy, Lt. General Stepan Grechko, who commanded the Soviet air defense, gave the order to fire at 10:22 AM. The U-2 flying at 70,000 feet, piloted by Major Rudolph Anderson, was hit. The plane crashed and Anderson's body was found in the wreckage. Grechko believed that combat had begun and reacted in a military manner. Despite Khrushchev's efforts to control his forces in Cuba, he had failed to prevent a casualty.

The report of the downing of a U-2 alarmed Khrushchev and for a time he blamed Castro. Gretchko, however, received only a mild rebuke. Concerning the incident, Khrushchev later wrote Castro: "The fact that an American plane was shot down over Cuba turned out to be a useful measure, since the operation was successfully executed. This is a lesson to the imperialists."

In Washington, the first news on Saturday morning, October 27, was disquieting. J. Edgar Hoover, director of the Federal Bureau of Investigation, informed Robert Kennedy that Soviet diplomats in New York City, in expectation of war, were preparing to burn documents.

The latest report from the CIA to the ExComm was just as disturbing. Work on the missile sites in Cuba continued without any letup. Five MRBM sites were considered fully operational and the sixth site would become operational by October 28. This report meant that there would be a capacity to launch up to twenty-four MRBM missiles within six to eight hours of the decision to launch. However, no new missile sites had been identified.

A New Message. That morning the ExComm was concerned about a Soviet tanker, *Grozny*, which was about 100 miles from the quarantine line. Suddenly President Kennedy read out loud a news ticker report handed to him. "Premier Khrushchev told President Kennedy yesterday he would withdraw offensive weapons from Cuba if the United States withdrew rockets from Turkey." Bundy exclaimed: "No he didn't." Someone asked: "He didn't really say that, did he?" Kennedy asked: "That wasn't in the letter we received was it?" Assured that it was not, the discussion resumed on the number of reconnaissance missions. Then back to Turkey. "We're going to be in an unsupportable position on this matter if this becomes his proposal," Kennedy observed. More came in over the ticker. Kennedy read from the ticker:

"Mr. Khrushchev said that in the Security Council, the Soviet Union would solemnly pledge not to use its territory as a bridgehead for an attack on Turkey, called for a similar pledge from the United States not to let its territory be used as a bridgehead for an attack on Cuba."

"Well this is unsettling now," said Kennedy, "because he's got us in a pretty good spot here." As he saw the situation, Khrushchev was saying " 'If you'll get yours out of Turkey, we'll get ours out of Cuba.' I think we've got a very touchy point here." At last a full copy of the letter was available.

Khrushchev stated that "we were willing to remove from Cuba those missiles you regard as offensive." In turn the United States would remove its missiles from Turkey. Representatives of the U.N. Security Council could make on-the-spot inspections to determine if the pledges had been fulfilled, providing the Cuban and Turkish governments would permit these inspections. The U.S.S.R. would promise not to invade Turkey, interfere in Turkish internal affairs, or make Soviet territory available for a base of attack on Turkey. The United States government would make similar statements about Cuba, promise to respect the inviolability of Cuban borders and sovereignty, pledge noninterference in internal affairs, and promise not to invade Cuba. (*See Document No. 16.*)

Who had written the letter? The tone was more accusatory than the previous message. One possibility, Bundy suggested, was that Khrushchev's "hard nosed people" had overruled him. McNamara asked: "How can we negotiate with somebody who changes his deal before we even get a chance to reply, and announces publicly the deal before we receive it?" Thompson suggested that Khrushchev had written the previous letter and sent it off without clearance.

U-2 Over Soviet Russia. Early in the afternoon came a report that a U-2 on an air sampling mission had strayed into Soviet air space over Chukotski Peninsula in Siberia. Soviet MIGs scrambled. The U-2 pilot was ordered to return immediately. His fuel exhausted, the plane flamed out over Siberia. U.S. interceptors were soon airborne to save the U-2 and prevent Soviet fighters from entering American airspace. These planes were armed with air-to-air nuclear missiles. Near the Bering Strait, the U-2 pilot established visual contact with U.S. interceptors who escorted the plane to a nearby landing site. One deputy recalled that McNamara turned white and yelled: "This means war with the Soviet Union!" President Kennedy commented, "There is always some son-of-a-bitch who doesn't get the word." McNamara immediately ordered the suspension of air sampling fights. Worse was yet to come.

From the Pentagon, McNamara learned that a U-2 flying over Cuba was thirty to forty minutes late. Next came a report that reconnaissance planes over Cuba had been fired upon; one plane had been hit but returned safely. The ExComm went back to drafting a letter to U Thant, and most important, a message to Khrushchev.

President Kennedy complained that Khrushchev had sent the second message in order that it would cause maximum embarrassment. It was not a private proposal and he had made it in a way that the Turks were bound to say that they disagreed. Robert Kennedy reminded his elder brother that the Turkish bases had nothing to do with security in the Western Hemisphere. But the president feared that the Turks might refuse to withdraw the Jupiters. The Turks, he contended, must understand the peril for the United States if it were to take action in Cuba.

In discussing the letter to Khrushchev, Kennedy proposed that Khrushchev be told that in Cuba, if work on the missiles ceased, only then could Turkey be discussed. The president wanted some indication from Khrushchev in the next twenty-four hours that he would "stand still and disarm those weapons." Then under those conditions the United States would be glad to discuss Turkey. Moreover, the president was worried that if the deal were to be turned down by the Soviets then the United States would be put into the position of having to do something. "What we are going to be faced with," he stated, "is that because we wouldn't take the missiles out of Turkey we are either going to have to invade or [have] a massive strike on Cuba which may lose Berlin." Soon there could be a minimum of 500 sorties in air strikes and seven days later an invasion of Cuba "all because we wouldn't take the missiles out of Turkey."

Paul H. Nitze (assistant secretary of state for international affairs) reminded the president that the Turks would not agree to take out the Jupiters unless under pressure from NATO. Kennedy insisted that they could not accept Khrushchev's latest proposal unless the Turks would agree. If there were Turkish and NATO opposition, Khurshchev's latest proposal could not be accepted.

Llewellyn Thompson, the former ambassador to the Soviet Union, disagreed with the president, insisting that they could get Khrushchev to take the missiles out of Cuba because he had already proposed to remove them for a pledge not to invade Cuba. Thompson argued that it was important for Khrushchev to say: "I saved Cuba. I stopped an invasion." The president feared that a pledge not to invade Cuba would mean "a hell of a fight." Brother Robert joined with Thompson in arguing that they should say that they accepted Khrushchev's offer in his letter of October 26. "He's made an offer and you're in fact accepting it." He argued that the letter that was then being drafted for Khrushchev should say: "You made an offer to us, and we accept it. And you've made a second offer, which has to do with NATO, and we'll be glad to discuss that at a later time." Robert Kennedy continued: "I think we must say: He made an offer. We accept the offer." He considered it silly to bring up NATO at this time.

General Taylor, who had returned from a meeting of the Joint Chiefs of Staff, announced that they recommended that Operation Plan 312 (OPLAN), the air strike, be executed Monday morning (October 29), unless there was irrefutable evidence that offensive weapons were being dismantled, and followed seven days later by Operation Plan 316, invasion of Cuba. "Well that was a surprise," commented Robert Kennedy as laughter erupted. The discussion moved on to whether to send reconnaissance planes over Cuba the next morning.

U-2 Down. Then came the confirmation: The U-2 plane was down and the pilot's body was in the wrecked plane. "How do we interpret this?" asked McNamara. "I don't know how to interpret it." A shocked president asked: "How can we send a U-2 fellow over there tomorrow unless we take out all the SAM sites?" Someone exclaimed: "They've fired the first shot!" Reacting to the hawkish comments of his colleagues, Dean Rusk's eyes began to brim with tears. Dean Acheson brought him up sharply: "Pull yourself together, Dean, you're the only Secretary of State we have!"

Throughout that beautiful October afternoon, as the ExComm labored over the letter to Khrushchev, it did so without the knowledge that nuclear warheads and nuclear bombs were already in Cuba. Nor did the ExComm know that when the American invasion force landed on the Cuban shores it would face a total of 42,000 Soviet soldiers combined with 270,000 Cuban troops which meant a combined force of more than 300,000.

At last Kennedy directed Sorenson and Robert Kennedy to finish drafting the reply to Khrushchev. They would ignore the second message and answer only the October 26 letter. There would be no promise about the Jupiters, but there would be a pledge not to invade Cuba.

Earlier in the week, Kennedy had agreed to retaliate by attacking the SAM site involved in the action, but he chose not to do so, fearing that it would only escalate to something much worse. He authorized low-level reconnaisance flights for October 28, and if planes were fired upon, the SAM sites would be taken out by air action. President Kennedy also agreed to consider increasing pressure on Khrushchev by adding POL (petroleum, oil, and lubricants) to the list of prohibited goods.

As the long session of the ExComm came to an end, President Kennedy commented: "We can't very well invade Cuba with all the toil and blood it's going to be, when we could have gotten them [Soviet missiles] out by making a deal on the same missiles in Turkey. If that's part of the record, then I don't see how we'll have a very good war." McNamara remembered the beautiful sunset on October 27 as the ExComm finished meeting and the uncertainty as to which message Khrushchev would answer. "I wondered if I'd ever see another Saturday sunset like that." (*See Document No. 17.*)

The Message To Khrushchev. That evening the message was sent off to Khrushchev. As drafted, in the new message Kennedy replied to the October 26 letter but ignored the October 27 message. As a first step, the Soviets must cease all work on offensive missile bases in Cuba and render all weapons system in Cuba inoperable under U.N. supervision. Khrushchev should have the weapons systems removed from Cuba under U.N. supervision and halt the introduction of additional weapons into Cuba. The United States agreed, that after arrangements had been made through the U.N. to carry out these measures, to end the quarantine and to give assurances against invading Cuba. If the threat continued it could lead to intensification of the crisis. The message omitted any mention of the Jupiters and Turkey. The ExComm had to convince the president that any open trade of Jupiters for the Cuban missiles must be avoided because it could rupture NATO. (*See Document No. 18.*)

Later in discussion with a small group of the ExComm, it was agreed to give Dobrynin a copy of the letter and a very personal message from the president to be conveyed by his brother. Robert Kennedy would tell the ambassador that if there were no reply by October 29, military action would commence against Cuba. An oral message would be given to

Dobrynin: Turkish missiles must not stand in the way between peace and war.

Kennedy-Dobrynin Meeting.

Dobrynin came to the Justice Department about 7:45 PM that same evening. Robert Kennedy informed the ambassador that work was continuing on the missile bases in Cuba. American planes flying over Cuba had been fired upon and a U-2 plane shot down and the pilot killed. "This was an extremely serious turn of events." If the Cubans fired on American planes, "then we are going to shoot back," which could only result in additional incidents. In regard to Dobrynin's complaint that United States airplanes were violating Cuban air space, Kennedy argued if they had not violated the air space, Dobrynin and Khrushchev's statements that there were no missiles bases in Cuba would still be believed. According to Kennedy, Khrushchev had been misleading when he proclaimed that the Soviet Union would never establish missile bases in Cuba. As a result, Kennedy insisted that the missile bases had to go and "they had to go right away." If they were not removed by tomorrow, "we would remove them." If the Soviet forces retaliated, Kennedy warned that there could be dead Americans and dead Russians before it was over. Robert Kennedy commented that "there were unreasonable heads among the generals who were 'itching for a fight'." The situation could get out of control. (*See Document No. 19.*)

A letter was being transmitted to Khrushchev asking that the missile bases be dismantled and weapons removed from Cuba. Then the quarantine would be repealed and assurances would be given that there would not be any invasion of the island. When Dobrynin asked about the Turkish proposal, according to Kennedy's record of the meeting, he declared, "there could be no quid pro quo—no deal of this kind could be made." NATO had to make the decision because a unilateral announcement would wreck NATO. Four to five months would be needed in order to accomplish the withdrawal from Turkey. If Khrushchev were agreeable, he could exchange opinions with Kennedy through Dobrynin and himself. Nothing could be mentioned publicly about Turkey. This information was so confidential that it was known to only two or three people in Washington. Kennedy insisted that "this matter could not wait." Dobrynin should contact Khrushchev and by the next day have a commitment to withdraw the missiles from Cuba under U.N. super-

vision. "Otherwise," Kennedy warned, "there would be drastic consequences." Dobrynin promised to relay this information to Khrushchev
immediately. To Dobrynin, Kennedy appeared very upset and kept re-
peating that time was of the essence. (*See Document No. 20.*)

The Jupiter deal had to remain secret because if it became known the
Republicans would denounce it as "appeasement." It would antagonize
the Joint Chiefs of Staff who already had little regard for the president.
There were also militant members on the ExComm who would vigor-
ously oppose such an arrangement.

According to Dean Rusk's recollections in 1987, after Robert Kennedy had left the Oval Office for his talk with Dobrynin, Rusk and
President Kennedy agreed privately that if Khrushchev rejected the
terms in Kennedy's letter by October 30, then U Thant would be asked
to propose a Turkey-Cuba deal and Kennedy would accept it. Rusk telephoned Andrew Cordier, former U.N. undersecretary, and dictated a
statement which he would hand to U Thant after receiving a signal from
Rusk.

That night McNamara issued a statement announcing the call-up of
twenty-four troop air reserve carrier squadrons involving 14,000 personnel to man 300 troop carriers which would drop paratroops and supplies to units that would land on Cuban shores on October 29. Preparations were underway for the invasion. Through the night United States
naval vessels maintained the quarantine. All night SAC bombers flew
their appointed routes through the Arctic skies and Polaris submarines
patrolled the seas while Washington awaited Khrushchev's reply.

CHAPTER 8

THE END OF THE MISSILE CRISIS

During the night of October 27/28, Khrushchev had been meeting with a Presidium that was divided: stand firm or seek accommodation. By morning, the Presidium feared that the United States would attack both the Soviet Union and Cuba. The Dobrynin-Kennedy talk on the night of October 27 signaled that the United States was determined to get rid of the missiles, even by bombing. From Soviet intelligence sources came reports that bombing raids on Cuba would begin on October 28 or 29. Castro, fearing an attack within twenty-four to seventy-two hours, had dispatched a message to Khrushchev which the Soviet leader interpreted as call for a nuclear attack on the United States.

Other reports both true and false frightened Khrushchev and his colleagues. President Kennedy was supposed to be scheduled for a television talk (he was not) during which he would declare war. Soviet generals interpreted the report of the U-2 sampling flight over Chukotski Peninsula to mean a last minute intelligence mission preparatory to a nuclear attack. Then came the downing of Anderson's plane which horrified Khrushchev. The Politburo was in session the night of October 27/28 at Khrushchev's dacha. Upon receiving the report of Dobrynin about his meeting with Robert Kennedy, Khrushchev said, "Comrades, now we have to look for a dignified way out of this conflict."

Khrushchev and the Presidium were convinced that Kennedy had made his last concession and that the United States was preparing to invade Cuba in retaliation for the Bay of Pigs. They believed that the Soviet missiles had prevented that event which would have meant the defeat of a Communist nation. It would be a good exchange if they would be rid of the Jupiters as well as receiving a pledge not to invade Cuba.

In the afternoon of October 28, Dobrynin received a cable from Gromyko instructing him to get in touch with Robert Kennedy at once and to inform him that the contents of his conversation with Dobrynin had been conveyed to Khrushchev who in turn was sending an urgent reply. "The suggestions made by Robert Kennedy on the president's instructions are appreciated in Moscow. The president's message of October 27 will be answered on the radio today, and the answer will be highly positive." Immediately Dobrynin arranged a meeting with Robert Kennedy and relayed Khrushchev's message. Robert Kennedy thanked the ambassador. He would go immediately to the White House to inform the president. "At last," said Kennedy, "I'm going to see my kids. Why I've almost forgotten my way home." For the first time since the crisis had begun, Dobrynin saw Robert Kennedy smile.

Dispatching The Message. Khrushchev and the Presidium knew by Sunday morning, October 28, that speed was essential. However, in 1962 dispatching an official message from Moscow to Washington was a slow process which often took hours. Consequently, two messages were prepared: one by radio for speed and the other for delivery through the normal channels. The usual message from the Foreign Ministry in Moscow was first drafted, then it had to be encrypted. Next the message was dispatched to the United States via Western Union. After it had been received in Washington, a man on a bicycle carried the message through traffic to the Soviet embassy. There it was decrypted and then translated into English before being carried to the State Department by messenger.

To save time, Khrushchev sent a message by radio announcing that the Soviet government had ordered the missiles to be dismantled, crated, and returned to the Soviet Union. He accepted Kennedy's pledge that there would be no attack on Cuba and no invasion. The Soviet Union was prepared to seek an agreement with the United States to work out the dismantling process.

Khrushchev would have preferred a public exchange of missiles. Instead he had been forced to accept a secret exchange; publicly he had accepted a defeat. Moreover, the missiles would not be removed simultaneously. By insisting on delaying the removal of the Jupiters from Turkey, President Kennedy would avoid the appearance of trading missiles in Cuba for missiles in Turkey. Worst of all for Khrushchev, there was nothing to prevent Kennedy from reneging on the promise to withdraw missiles from Turkey. Khrushchev had to pull his missiles out of Cuba without any means of compelling Kennedy to dismantle the Jupiter missiles in Turkey.

Castro's Anger. Meanwhile, in Cuba, Castro who had not been consulted by his Soviet ally, was furious. He cursed Khrushchev calling him "son-of-bitch, bastard" and other obscenities. Khrushchev had talked him into accepting the missiles and then he had agreed to remove them without consulting Castro. To Castro, the missiles had been a sign of Soviet commitment to the Cuban cause. He had considered them as substitutes for membership in the Warsaw Pact which he desired. Now the missiles were to be removed at the demand of the accursed United States. Not to be outdone, Castro soon issued his demand, his "Five Points."

1. End the economic blockade of Cuba.
2. End subversive attacks against Cuba.
3. Halt attacks on Cuba carried out from United States military bases in Puerto Rico.
4. Cease aerial and naval reconnaissance flights over Cuban air space.
5. Return Guantanamo naval base to Cuba.

Moscow paid lip service to Castro's Five Points, but Washington ignored them.

While the Soviets were awaiting Kennedy's reply to the radio message, the KGB reported that Kennedy was going to church. Within the Presidium there was agitated discussion. Had he gone to church to pray before ordering a nuclear attack? Or was this report merely disinformation to mislead the Soviet Union?

Upon receiving Khrushchev's radio message, Kennedy issued a statement calling the Soviet decision "a constructive contribution to peace." Later, in a message to Khrushchev, the president stated that he considered his letter of October 27 and Khrushchev's reply "firm undertakings" on the part of the American and Soviet governments which should be promptly carried out.

Not everyone in Washington was elated over the news of Khrushchev's concession. When the Joint Chiefs of Staff were brought to the White House in the afternoon for the president to thank them for their advice and help in the crisis, he was surprised at their reaction. Admiral Anderson exclaimed: "We've been had!" General LeMay roared: "Why don't we go in there on Monday and make a strike anyway?" Intelligence reports seemed to indicate that the Chiefs were indeed correct. Photo reconnaissance flights on October 29 indicated that no dismantling had taken place. The advice of the Joint Chiefs on October 29 was to destroy all Soviet offensive weapons in Cuba: nuclear delivery systems, bombers, surface-to-surface missiles, warheads, supporting and operating equipment and missile fuel. Not until November 1 was there photographic evidence that the MRBM bases were actually being dismantled.

Khrushchev's Letter. On October 29, Dobrynin brought Robert Kennedy a letter from Khrushchev addressed to the president in which he confirmed the conversation between the attorney general and Dobrynin during the night of October 27. Then the attorney general had said it would be difficult for the president to engage in a public discussion about eliminating the American missile bases in Turkey because of the NATO connection. Robert Kennedy had stated that the removal of the bases from Turkey might take four to five months. Any exchange of views would continue confidentially through Robert Kennedy and the ambassador. Because Khrushchev understood the delicacy and the complexity of the issues involved, he had not mentioned them in his letter to the president on October 28 in which he had consented to removing the missiles from Cuba. According to Khrushchev, the proposals in that message were based on Kennedy's agreement to resolve the question of missiles in Turkey as Robert Kennedy had informed Dobrynin on October 27. Khrushchev hoped that agreement on this matter would help to relax international tensions. Robert Kennedy accepted the letter without comment. (*See Document No. 21.*)

The following day, the attorney general again met with Dobrynin and returned Khrushchev's letter. According to Robert Kennedy, the president confirmed the understanding regarding the removal of the American missile bases in Turkey. This understanding would be fulfilled within the time period indicated but without mentioning any connection with the events in Cuba. However, there could not be any formal written understanding, even "the most confidential letters" regarding so delicate an issue. Robert Kennedy would not be involved with transmitting such a letter because no one knew where or when such letters might be published. "The appearance of such a document could cause irreparable harm to my political career in the future," Kennedy declared. For these reasons the Kennedy brothers requested that the letter be taken back. They would live up to their promises even if given in oral form. Their word would be the guarantee. Only Dean Rusk and Llewellyn Thompson had any knowledge of this understanding. The Khrushchev letter should be taken back without delay. (*See Document No. 22.*)

Dobrynin took the letter back because he realized that President Kennedy wanted to avoid exchanging documents on such a delicate issue which could leave a trace. Moreover, the ambassador knew that if he insisted on leaving the letter, it would damage any future prospects of doing business with the Kennedy brothers. In his memoirs, Dobrynin noted that "Robert Kennedy added that someday—who knows?—he might run for president and his prospects could be damaged if the secret deal about the missiles in Turkey were to come out." (The last Jupiter came down April 24, 1963).

Eventually Khrushchev realized that this unwritten, private agreement would benefit both sides. He would not have to argue the question with Castro who would object to being treated as a bargaining chip equivalent to a minor member of NATO. For President Kennedy, the secret deal was necessary in order to avoid a crisis within NATO and denunciations as an appeaser from the Republican opposition in an election year. Knowledge of the deal would antagonize not only the Joint Chiefs of Staff but also the more militant among the ExComm. The American public would not learn about the secret deal until years after the death of the Kennedy brothers.

Moscow-Havana Relations. Relations between Moscow and Havana now turned chilly. In his message of October 30, Khrushchev pointedly criticized Castro's cable of October 27 in which he urged the Soviet Union to launch the first nuclear strike against the United States. "You of course, realize where that would have led," wrote Khrushchev. "Rather than a simple strike, it would have been the start of a thermonuclear world war." Although the United States would have suffered, so would "the Soviet Union and the whole socialist camp." Khrushchev insisted that they had reached the goal that had been sought when the missiles had been sent to Cuba. "We have wrested from the United States the commitment not to invade Cuba and not to permit their Latin American allies to do so." Khrushchev reminded Castro that it had been done without a nuclear strike.

A furious Castro berated Khrushchev reminding him that "countless eyes of Cuban and Soviet men, who were willing to die with supreme dignity, shed tears upon learning about the surprising sudden and practically unconditional decision to withdraw the weapons." Castro admitted that they would have been annihilated in a nuclear war. "However, that didn't prompt us to ask you to withdraw the missiles, that didn't prompt us to ask you to yield." Castro claimed that he had not called for the Soviet Union to launch the first nuclear strike. Instead he meant that after the American invasion had begun, only then should the Soviet Union have launched a nuclear strike against the United States. Nevertheless, he did not dare break with Khrushchev because the entire economic life of Cuba depended on the Soviet Union.

U Thant's Mission. A new player entered the contest when Castro, on October 28, invited U Thant, acting secretary general of the United Nations, to visit Cuba for discussions on the crisis. By the time of his departure on October 30, U Thant had no plan for action other than a proposal of Vasily Vasilyevitch Kusnetzov, the Soviet first deputy foreign minister, dispatched to New York to take over from the ineffective Zorin. Kuznetzov proposed that the Red Cross inspect Soviet ships carrying missiles back to the Soviet Union. It was a brilliant ploy because few if any Red Cross personnel would be knowledgeable about Soviet military equipment. On hearing the news, General LeMay exclaimed: "Jesus Christ! What the hell do gray ladies know about missiles?" Before leaving New York for Cuba, U Thant insisted that the quarantine and reconnaissance flights over Cuba be suspended while he was there. Kennedy complied with his request.

Once in Cuba, U Thant presented several proposals to Castro in order to verify that the process of dismantling the missiles was being accomplished. Castro summarily rejected all of U Thant's proposals: inspection by a U.N. team, aerial inspection by U.N. reconnaissance planes (although the United Nations lacked such aircraft), and verification by the Red Cross. Castro denounced all of the proposals on the grounds that they were intended to humiliate Cuba. However, at the second meeting on October 31, he agreed to return the body of Major Rudolph Anderson. (For years afterward, visitors to Havana would be taken to see the wreckage of his U-2.) After U Thant and his eighteen-member delegation left Cuba on October 31, Kennedy ordered the resumption of the reconnaissance flights and the quarantine, but not the U-2 flights.

By November 1, aerial photographs finally indicated that the missile sites were being dismantled and bulldozed; the IRBM sites were partially dismantled but nothing had been done with regard to the IL-28 bombers. In his letter of October 22, Kennedy had called not only for the removal of the missile bases but also "offensive weapons in Cuba." Khrushchev stated in his letter of October 28 that he would remove "those weapons you describe as offensive." By November 2, Kennedy and the ExComm had classed the IL-28 bombers as "offensive." Although their range was limited, they could reach mainland United States. They were believed to have nuclear capability but Washington did not know that there were six atomic bombs available for them.

The fate of these bombers became one of the problems that had to be debated by another Soviet negotiator, First Deputy Premier Anastas Mikoyan, a genuine old Bolshevik. He had visited Cuba in 1960 and negotiated economic and trade agreements with Castro whom he acclaimed as "a young Lenin." When the old Bolshevik left Moscow, his wife of forty years was dying and even though she passed away while he was in Havana, he continued the negotiations with Castro and did not return for her funeral.

Mikoyan and Castro. Khrushchev sent Mikoyan to patch up the strained relations with Castro and to negotiate the Cuban role in the settlement of the crisis. At first Castro refused to see him. Occasionally Castro simply went out into the countryside leaving Mikoyan to await his return. Consequently Mikoyan remained in Cuba for twenty-two days before completing his assignment.

Relations indeed became impossible. On November 7 a dinner celebrating the forty-fifth anniversary of the Russian Revolution was a total disaster. In the usual abundance of toasts, the Soviet military command made no mention of Fidel Castro. The chief of Cuban military intelligence tried to insult the Soviet guests by proposing a joint toast to Castro and to Josef Stalin which infuriated Khrushchev when he heard about it.

Because Castro refused all on-site inspections, the only recourse for Kennedy was to rely on photographic reconnaissance, with the hope that no planes would be fired on by Castro's gunners. By November 1, the ExComm had received reports that all of the MRBM sites had been bulldozed and equipment removed. Construction of the IRBM sites had been halted. By November 2 the quarantine was maintained by hailing vessels entering the quarantine line but there was no boarding. Mikoyan succeeded in convincing Castro to agree to the removal of the missiles after receiving assurances that the Soviet government would maintain a brigade on the island of Cuba.

Kuznetsov-McCloy Negotiations. In New York the newly appointed envoy, Vasily V. Kuznetsov, first deputy minister of foreign affairs, took over negotiations replacing the incompetent Zorin. His American counterpart, John J. McCloy, former high commissioner to Germany, had been asked to serve as a special advisor to Adlai Stevenson because Robert Kennedy did not believe that Stevenson would be vigorous enough in negotiating with the Soviet diplomats. On November 4, Kuznetsov and McCloy had a pleasant Sunday lunch at McCloy's home in Stamford, Connecticut. When they got down to business, McCloy stated his concern over the matter of verification of the removal of Soviet equipment from Cuba. Kuznetsov advised McCloy that Castro's agreement to inspection was not at all certain. Instead Kuznetsov assured McCloy that all of the sites had been dismantled as of November 2; shipping schedules would be provided in order that American ships could inspect Soviet vessels at sea and count the missiles. He also mentioned a formal protocol of guarantees against invasion of Cuba by the United States, and he tried to bring in Guantanamo, but McCloy ruled that out.

Meanwhile, by November 5 Soviet ships were beginning to return MRBMs and the launch equipment to the Soviet Union. Because Castro refused all on-site verification, the only possible method of verification was to have the Soviet vessels inspected at sea. American ships moved along side the Soviet ships and the covers were removed from the deck cargo in order that the cargo could be observed and photographed.

IL-28 Bombers. Negotiations were deadlocked over the IL-28 bombers. The ExComm debated various methods to force their removal from Cuba. In New York there were endless meetings with Kuznetzov over the issue. The Soviet negotiators wanted to remove the bombers after the quarantine had been lifted, but the American negotiators refused. Once more President Kennedy used his brother as the go-between with Ambassador Dobrynin. November 5, when the ambassador brought another letter from Khrushchev, Kennedy informed him the Soviet Union had agreed to get rid of those weapons which were considered offensive. It was very clear that the IL-28 bombers had to go.

In the letter from Khrushchev which Dobrynin handed over, Khrushchev complained that Kennedy was only complicating the situation by placing defensive weapons in the category of "offensive" weapons. He could not see what could be gained by such demands which could not lead to the betterment of Soviet-American relations. Khrushchev believed that the Soviet Union had met President Kennedy's demands consequently the two leaders ought to complete their understanding. Khrushchev and the Presidium argued that the IL-28 bombers were obsolete in view of their low ceiling and low speed. They were fifteen years old, were useful only in coastal defense, and could not be used in combat over enemy territory.

President Kennedy immediately rebutted Khrushchev's argument about the IL-28 bombers. They were not a minor question, Kennedy insisted. Indeed, although they were not modern, they were distinctly capable of offensive use against the United States and other countries in the Western Hemisphere. The presence of these bombers in Cuba, he claimed, would require military defense response capabilities. Moreover, he contended, these bombers could carry offensive weapons for long distances, and they were not needed any more than missiles for purely defensive purposes on the island of Cuba. He was not trying to complicate the situation but only stating what had been meant in their understanding of October 27–28. In Washington, the ExComm tried without any success to devise methods to force Castro to give up the bombers. However, on November 9, the last of the Soviet ships carrying MRBM missiles from Cuba finally left the island.

Stevenson informed the ExComm that on November 12 that the negotiations in New York over the IL-28 bombers were now deadlocked. The Soviet diplomats refused to give in on the withdrawal of the IL-28 bombers and they even insisted on Castro's five points. Stevenson offered a package of proposals which he thought the Soviet would reject. McCloy suggested that if the Russians would agree to take out the IL-28 bombers by a fixed future date, the quarantine would be lifted immediately. McCloy believed that Khrushchev was under great pressure. He urged that the Cuban problem be dealt with from a world point of view as a U.S./U.S.S.R. problem, not United States and Cuba. At last the ExComm agreed that Khrushchev should be told to give the order to remove the bombers, and when they were observed leaving Cuba on Soviet ships, the quarantine would be lifted.

In a mesage to President Kennedy on November 12, Khrushchev informed him that "our obligations with regard to dismantling and removal of both missiles and warheads have already been fulfilled." He still resisted removing the IL-28 planes, arguing that the planes were of no value as combat weapons. He offered "a gentleman's word" that the planes and all personnel and equipment would be removed at a future date when "the conditions were ripe."

Once more brother Robert was appointed to convey the messages between the president and the Soviet ambassador. In the Soviet embassy on the evening of November 12, he explained to Dobrynin that for domestic policy reasons the president needed a firm agreement on the removal of the IL-28 planes. It was a matter of great concern because of criticism in the United States. Dobrynin, however, used Khrushchev's arguments to rebut Robert Kennedy's proposal. Robert left the embassy, and after conferring with the president, returned later the same evening with a proposal that Khrushchev and the president agree on the removal of the planes by a specific date, and the United States would lift the quarantine, even the next day. The president would not insist on publicizing the date if there were objections. Perhaps the planes could be removed within thirty days. For domestic public opinion, Robert asked if they could at least report that some planes had been dissembled or if removed from containers they had been replaced. Dobrynin agreed to inform Khrushchev.

After their talk, Robert Kennedy joined a party in the embassy for the Bolshoi Ballet. Before he left the party, he kissed a ballerina born on the same day, month, and year as he had been. (*See Document No. 23.*)

In Havana, Mikoyan had been encountering more resistance from Castro. Again Mikoyan on November 12 met with Castro and launched into a long flowery monologue which Castro finally cut short. "What does the Soviet government want?" Mikoyan answered: "If we will agree to remove the IL-28 bombers from Cuba, then we can wrest a formal agreement from the Americans." He admitted that the bombers were militarily insignificant. Castro retorted: "And later won't they put the question to you of on-site inspections?" The United States would call for the inspection and continue the blockade. The next day Castro insisted to Mikoyan that the naval blockade must end and the overhead reconnaissance at the same time that the bombers were withdrawn.

Castro decided to shock the Soviets. On November 14 he ordered antiaircraft batteries to shoot down United States reconnaissance planes. It was Wednesday; the firing would begin by the end of the week. Khrushchev was infuriated when he received this news. Mikoyan was instructed to make clear to the Cubans that the responsibility would be theirs.

In a letter to Khrushchev on November 15, Kennedy repeated the offer: remove the IL-28 planes within thirty days and the quarantine would end. In conclusion, he warned that if there were any interference with the reconnaissance flights "We shall take the necessary action in reply."

Invasion Rehearsal. The next day the largest amphibious landing since World War II took place in Onslow Beach, North Carolina, a full-scale rehearsal for the invasion of Cuba. The Joint Chiefs met with the president and reported the readiness for an invasion of Cuba; 40,000 marines, 100,000 Army troops and 14,500 paratroopers were ready with planes and naval vessels. The Chiefs recommended that if the IL-28 bombers were not removed, they should be taken out by an air strike.

President Kennedy even notified de Gaulle, Konrad Adenauer, and Harold Macmillan that if the IL-28s were not withdrawn the United States would be forced to extend the quarantine to include petroleum products and attack Cuba if American reconnaissance planes were fired upon.

Negotiations on Long Island. At the Soviet residence in Locust Valley on Long Island, on a pleasant Sunday, November 18, McCloy, his wife, and son, together with Kuznetsov, Zorin, and his wife played Russian billiards and enjoyed a good lunch. Over coffee the diplomats got down to business. Kuznetsov accused the Americans of stalling. McCloy then reviewed the problem of the bombers. He explained that President Kennedy had waived a precondition: United Nations observers in Cuba. If there were no removal of the bombers, the president, according to McCloy, would have no choice but to reimpose the full quarantine. The president would hold a news conference on November 20 and he would have to say something about the bombers. Moreover, the president would not sign any document containing conditions demanded by Castro. Nor would he agree to any document requiring two or three signatories which would amount to a treaty requiring 2/3 vote of the Senate. The president would not assent to Castro's demand for a reciprocal United Nations observation in the United States as well as in Cuba. McCloy warned that the United States was not contemplating stopping the over flights of Cuba until it was certain that there would be no reintroduction of weapons. Finally, American planes would return fire if Castro's guns fired at them.

Castro Concedes. Fearful of what Castro might do next, on November 16, the Presidium authorized Khrushchev to give an oral promise to Kennedy that the IL-28s would be removed within a month. On November 19, Castro, aware that Kennedy would be holding the press conference on November 20 and afraid that a more dangerous period would follow, dispatched a letter to U Thant in which he conceded that the planes were the property of the Soviet government brought to Cuba to defend against aggression. If the Soviet government considered it desirable to remove the bombers, the Revolutionary Government of Cuba would not object to this decision.

Khrushchev informed President Kennedy on November 20 that the Ilyushin (IL-28) bombers would be removed within thirty days. After learning of Khrushchev's decision, Kennedy announced the ending of the quarantine. The Joint Chiefs of Staff ordered the end of the SAC alert. On the same day, SAC forces lowered their alert status from DEFCON 2. In the other military commands, the alert returned to DEFCON 4. The next day John Kennedy officially lifted the naval quarantine of Cuba. (*See Document No. 24.*)

Then the Cuban government almost torpedoed the agreement between Moscow and Washington. The nuclear warheads for the tactical weapons and the six atomic bombs still remained in Cuba where Cuban officials wanted to retain them to repel any possible American attack. Mikoyan realized that Kennedy had announced on November 20 that all nuclear weapons had been removed from Cuba. Knowledge that such nuclear devices remained in Cuba could easily unravel the Khrushchev-Kennedy agreement of November 20. Acting on his own initiative, Mikoyan, insisting that there was a Soviet law which forbade turning over nuclear weapons to other countries, demanded that the Cuban government return the nuclear devices to the Soviet Union. Reluctantly the Cubans conceded by November 23.

In a meeting with President Kennedy and Dean Rusk on November 29, Mikoyan tried once again to obtain clarification of the United States pledge not to invade Cuba. Kennedy would not concede and rejected any formal guarantee.

In a final negotiation with McCloy, however, Kuznetzov warned: "All right, Mr. McCloy, we will get the IL-28s out as we have taken the missiles out. But I want you to tell you something, Mr. McCloy. The Soviet Union is not going to find itself in a position like this ever again."

CHAPTER 9

CONCLUSION

In the aftermath of the Cuban missile crisis, the belief emerged that the crisis had demonstrated the ability of President Kennedy and the ExComm to handle crisis management. By carefully using the threat of force in bargaining, Soviet expansionism could be curbed. Instead of allowing diplomats in striped pants to handle the negotiations, they would be replaced by expert managers who would use the threat of force and politics to micromanage crises. Such, it has been argued by Kennedy admirers, was the technique used during the missile crisis. The management of the crisis was not as adroit as has been imagined when the transcripts of the ExComm meetings are examined. The crisis managers were very human and very lucky.

The Cuban missile crisis became the first example of the new method of controlling military operations from the White House and the Pentagon thanks to major advances in communications technology. From his desk in the Oval Office, President Kennedy was able to control the direction of military operations. The president and McNamara could monitor the deployment of American forces as they were mobilized to move on Cuba. As a result, professional military men were relegated to a secondary role by Kennedy and McNamara. It can be argued that micromanaging a crisis from the White House situation room, which became so pronounced during the Johnson administration, was first practiced in the Cuban missile crisis. Years later, Johnson and McNamara attempted to manage a war half a world away in Vietnam just as Kennedy and McNamara, so it was believed, had managed the Cuban missile crisis. The results, as far as Vietnam were concerned, would be disastrous.

Crisis hawks believed that Khrushchev was so deterred by the nuclear superiority of the United States that the Soviet Union would not have attempted to use force anywhere even if the U.S. naval vessels had halted Soviet ships at the quarantine line or American troops had invaded Cuba. Such a belief influenced those who advocated an air strike during the crisis. The single greatest deterrent was the fear of both Khrushchev and Kennedy that aggressive action could lead to nuclear conflict, and so neither would make a premeditated decision to launch a nuclear strike. Despite their reluctance to initiate a nuclear war, there was always the possibility of mistakes which crisis management could miss when disaster was near and crisis management was lacking.

Mistakes and Near Misses. There were enough mistakes or near misses to prove the danger of brinkmanship when nuclear forces are involved. The list includes Penkovsky's coded signal for an imminent Soviet attack, the launching of an ICBM from Vandenberg Air Force Base, as well as a U-2 flight into Soviet air space, and later a fighter group scrambling armed with nuclear weapons. Operation Mongoose was not suspended until October 30 by Robert Kennedy as an afterthought. Clandestine units were wandering around Cuba with little or no control. A CIA-sponsored covert action team blew up a factory on November 8. Had such a group attacked Soviet installations, attempted to assassinate Soviet officers, or fired at Soviet missiles, the results could have been far reaching. There was also the Minnesota bear turned saboteur whose antics triggered a false alarm and nearly sent interceptors into the skies. Low-level depth charges were used to force a Soviet submarine to the surface. There were also the Luna rockets with their nuclear warheads which if fired could have wrecked American landings and started the first nuclear battle. Finally perhaps the greatest danger came when Cuban antiaircraft batteries open up on October 27 and the Soviet commander ordered a SAM missile fired at Major Anderson's plane, the only casualty of the crisis.

These SAM missiles and antiaircraft fire could well have become "The Guns of October." According to Robert Kennedy, his brother had been deeply impressed by Barbara Tuchman's book, *The Guns of August,* the story of the European crisis in the summer of 1914 when Europe went to war following the assassination of the heir to the Austro-Hungarian throne. President Kennedy's fears of another 1914 came close to reality on October 27 when firing commenced at Anderson's plane just as it had in August 1914. Had Kennedy retaliated for the downing of Anderson's plane, events could easily have escalated into war. By refraining from retaliation, President Kennedy avoided action that might have started a war and perhaps prompted another book, *The Guns of October.*

Crisis Management. To avoid such a catastrophe, Robert McNamara tried to practice crisis management by using the quarantine to send Khrushchev a political message. However, in the view of revisionist historians, crisis management would perhaps have not been necessary had not Kennedy overreacted and risked the first nuclear war to save his reputation. By forcing the removal of the missiles before the November congressional elections, Kennedy would gain a political advantage. If he had backed down, he was concerned that Khrushchev would never take him seriously again, particularly in Berlin. By refusing to permit missiles ninety miles off the Florida coast, Kennedy would appear tough, even macho to American voters. Revisionist historians have also accused Kennedy of preferring confrontation to seeking quiet, secret negotiations with Khrushchev. Such a tactic was not as easy as it may have appeared. The usual method—a letter to Khrushchev—would have alerted him and given him the opportunity to go public first. The letter could easily have become an ultimatum or have allowed Khrushchev to delay replying while the installation of the missiles proceeded even faster. Khrushchev could also have revealed the communication before the ExComm could decide on an appropriate strategy. Another possibility would have been for Kennedy to have confronted Andrei Gromyko in their meeting on October 18, but there was doubt that Gromyko could have been trusted to keep the matter private. Moreover, he had been assuring the Kennedy administration that there were no offensive missiles in Cuba. This argument neglects Khrushchev's favorite method of operation which was a form of brinkmanship that relied on bluff and bluster while he continued to construct the missile bases. Moreover, the Kennedy administration would have encountered strong political repercussions had the story of private communication leaked to the press. There would have been less room to maneuver because of intense public pressure.

The Crisis and Domestic Politics. Kennedy was indeed concerned over the domestic political ramifications of the Cuban missile crisis. During the presidential campaign, he had exploited the issue of Cuba and Castro, denouncing the Republicans for being soft on this issue, implying that if he were elected president he would settle the Cuban problem. Instead of settling the problem, Kennedy had allowed Cuba to become a Soviet offensive missile base. Had he not forced the removal of the missiles from Cuba, he would have faced a powerful reaction not only from Republicans but also from some fellow Democrats. Moreover, Kennedy had assumed the role of a warrior fighting the Cold

War particularly where Cuba was concerned. In this role, if he failed to force the Soviets to remove their missiles he could jeopardize his presidency, so he thought. As he told brother Robert, "I would have been impeached." Whether he would have been impeached is indeed problematical, but he would most certainly have had to endure an intense political firestorm. The Cuban missile crisis was a domestic political threat for the Kennedy administration.

At the same time, Kennedy was quite aware that if Cuban and Soviet resistance produced American casualties, Republicans and Democrats alike would have been quick to condemn him. CICLANT had estimated that by D+10 United States casualties would have totaled 18,484. President Harry Truman had faced a similar problem in the Korean War, when Republicans and some Democrats deserted him after casualties had been reported. Certainly this was one reason that Kennedy did all that he could to avoid hostilities. As an example, he avoided any retaliation after Major Rudolph Anderson was killed when it would have been so easy to order an attack on the responsible SAM battery.

Revisionist historians also contend that in all probability Kennedy was on the verge of attacking Cuba but that the missile crisis saved Cuba from an invasion. There were indeed operational plans—OPLAN 312, 314 and 316—but despite the existence of these plans, there is no evidence that Kennedy had decided to order an invasion of Cuba. Most probably he sanctioned measures which he hoped would destabilize the Castro regime. Robert McNamara has since admitted that if he had been a Soviet leader or a Cuban he would have concluded that the United States was planning to invade Cuba. Certainly Castro, Khrushchev, and the Presidium were convinced that an American invasion of Cuba was imminent.

Khrushchev's Responsibilities. From the study of this crisis, the traditional argument praising Kennedy's brilliant handling has now been rebutted by the revisionist contention that he needlessly risked nuclear conflict when Khrushchev was only acting defensively in trying to save Cuba from invasion and at the same time trying to reverse the strategic imbalance in nuclear power. Nevertheless much of the responsibility still lies with Khrushchev because he failed to comprehend fully what the effect would be on Kennedy when he learned about the presence of missiles in Cuba. Nor did Khrushchev understand that he had created a most unpleasant political problem for Kennedy. To know about the missiles and to take no action was nothing more than political suicide. Khrushchev was accustomed to secrecy as a way of life in the Soviet Union, but he never imagined that Kennedy, after careful planning, would announce to the American public that Soviet nuclear weapons were ninety miles from Florida in Cuba.

Khrushchev was at fault, along with his military advisors, for imagining that the presence of the nuclear weapons in Cuba could have remained secret despite the over flights of the U-2 planes which had photographed the Soviet Union. Khrushchev may have thought that when the missiles were discovered, Kennedy might use an agent to contact Khrushchev about negotiating their removal instead of going public. Khrushchev had only revealed his ignorance of the basics of American political life.

He was also probably fooled by Kennedy's attitude when West Berlin was sealed off by the wall. Then Kennedy had been careful to signal to Khrushchev that the United States would not overreact. Khrushchev could not imagine that missiles in Cuba would move Kennedy to order the most extensive mobilization of American forces since World War II.

President Kennedy's Responsibilities. Kennedy must be faulted for failing to warn Khrushchev against placing nuclear missiles in Cuba until September 1962. Kennedy had been ill-served by his advisors who actually doubted that Khrushchev would go so far as to install the missiles. Kennedy's failure to warn Khrushchev may have been accepted by Khrushchev as license to install the missiles.

The Kennedy brothers can be criticized for initiating Operation Mongoose, a hysterical reaction to Castro. This covert action only intensified Cuban and Soviet expectations that the United States would eventually mount a full-scale military operation aimed at overthrowing the Castro regime. Despite the enormous expense and the hit-and-run attacks, Operation Mongoose was a failure. Certainly Operation Mongoose served to convince Khrushchev that an American invasion of Cuba was imminent.

After the missiles had been withdrawn, President Kennedy never publicly assured the Soviets and the Cubans that United States forces would not intervene in Cuba. However, at the height of the Cold War such a public assurance after the Bay of Pigs would have been a political disaster in an election year. Perhaps Kennedy hoped that by leaving open the possibility of an invasion he would deter the Soviet Union and

Cuba from any action inimical to American interests in the Western Hemisphere.

Jupiters and the Crisis. The decision to remove the Jupiters, from Italy as well as Turkey, was central to the resolution of the missile crisis This arrangement was in total contrast to the public perception that the Kennedy administration had maintained a tough, no concession attitude in managing the missile crisis, and that as a result Khrushchev had decided to remove the missiles from Cuba. To maintain this image there was a cover-up intended to deceive the public, Congress and the NATO allies as to the secret agreement by the Kennedy brothers to withdraw the Jupiters from Turkey. Months later, when some congressmen and senators became suspicious, members of the administration were vehement in their denials that there had not been any trading of missiles. Ironically, the Jupiters, which had helped create the missile crisis, had never been put to any good use until President Kennedy sacrificed them to end the Cuban missile crisis.

In addition, the claim was made that what amounted to an ultimatum had forced Khrushchev to concede in his October 28 message to Kennedy. But in the meeting with Dobrynin the night of October 27, Robert Kennedy had assured the ambassador that the demand for a withdrawal was not an ultimatum.

There was a striking difference between the public perception of John Kennedy as a hard-nosed, cold warrior, unafraid of Khrushchev, and his plan to use the Cordier option to negotiate a peaceful end to the missile crisis. As recounted earlier, Andrew Cordier of Columbia University, would give U Thant a statement dictated by Dean Rusk proposing the removal of the missiles from Cuba and Turkey. At a signal from Rusk, Cordier would hand the statement to U Thant. Here was Kennedy's last resort: a public trade proposed by an impartial party. If everything else failed, Kennedy would turn to the United Nations.

In contrast to this statesmanlike action by Kennedy, he went out of his way to disparage Adlai Stevenson who had been the first in the administration to propose trading the Jupiters. John Kennedy was apparently a source for an article in the *Saturday Evening Post* in December 1962 written by Stewart Alsop and Charles Bartlett which charged Stevenson with wishing "to trade the Turkish, Italian and British bases for the Cuban bases." The attack may have been the result of the Kennedy brothers fear that Stevenson's bravura performance in the Security Council on October 25 might enhance his popularity and revive his presidential potential. At the same time it was a method of covering up the missile trade which the Kennedy brothers feared could endanger their political future.

Positive Results. As Philip Nash has pointed out in *The Missiles of October*, the missile trade, including Turkish as well as Italian Jupiters, became the first arms reduction agreement between the United States and the Soviet union. Moreover, for the first time in the history of the arms race, both nations dismantled a portion of their operational nuclear delivery systems.

There were other positive results of the Cuban missile crisis. In June 1963 both governments agreed to create a direct "hot line" communications link between Moscow and Washington. A limited test ban treaty was signed in August 1963. According to the terms of this treaty, both governments agreed "to prohibit, to prevent and not to carry out any nuclear test explosions or any other nuclear . . . in the atmosphere." In September 1963, the Soviet and American governments agreed to back a United Nations resolution to ban the placing of nuclear weapons of mass destruction in space.

Certainly the most important result of the Cuban missile crisis was not just that the Soviet government had removed nuclear missiles from Cuba but that the United States never attempted an invasion, and most important, promised not to invade Cuba. However, at the time there was no formal agreement which the Soviet government dearly wished to obtain.

Kennedy on Intervention in Cuba. Even after the crisis had ended, President Kennedy was still concerned about intervening in Cuba. On November 21, George Ball, pointed out to him that in the event of a war the United States had the right to move into Cuba under the terms of the Rio Pact of 1947. After Ball explained his interpretation of the pact, Kennedy, commented, "We would [do] it any way if we have to."

In 1963 after the missiles had been dismantled and removed, in a meeting of the National Security Council on January 22, Kennedy revealed his thinking about Cuba. He expected that the time would come when the United States would have to act in Cuba in response to some future situation. "We should be prepared to move on Cuba if it should be in our national interest." Cuba could be used to limit Soviet actions "just as they have had Berlin to limit our actions." Kennedy would never have the opportunity to act in Cuba. (*See Document No. 25.*)

Although the threat of an American invasion of Cuba had ended, nevertheless efforts to undermine and overthrow the Castro regime continued for some time. No significant effort appears to have been undertaken in the years since 1962 to wean Cuba away from the Soviet Union. Such a process would have required concessions which American politicians dare not propose.

Cuba and Kennedy's Successors. When President Lyndon Johnson met Mikoyan on November 26, 1963, the president stated that "There would be no change in the Kennedy policy. . . . We had no plans for invasion."

A more formal confirmation came in the Nixon administration when the National Security Adviser, Henry Kisssinger, on August 7, 1970 assured the Soviet Chargé, Yuli M. Vorontsov, that the United States regarded the 1962 understanding as still in effect and voiced his satisfaction that the Soviet government regarded the understanding as still in force. Apparently the Soviet government had sought American reaffirmation because of Cuban worry over a possible American attack. Through a TASS statement on October 13, 1970, the Soviet government reaffirmed that it would do nothing to contradict the understanding reached between the Soviet Union and the United States in 1962. The first public confirmation from the United States government came on November 13, 1970 through a State Department spokesman that Kennedy's statement of November 20, 1962 and the TASS statement on October 13, 1970 were the basis for concluding that the two governments had reached an understanding on the limits of their action with regard to Cuba.

This diplomatic activity stemmed from Soviet preparations to establish a submarine base in Cienfuegos Bay on the southern coast of Cuba, a development had again been revealed by photographs from a U-2 reconnaissance plane on September 16, 1970. Instead of taking strong diplomatic action, Kissinger had used a press leak and a press briefing to review Kennedy's November 20, 1962 statement. At that time, Kissinger warned that the U.S.S.R. should be under no doubt that the United States government would view "the establishment of a strategic base in the Caribbean with the utmost seriousness." The crisis was resolved quickly with another TASS statement on October 13 denying that the Soviet Union was building a submarine base and confirming that the Soviet Union would adhere to the 1962 understanding.

The Soviet government again tested the understanding in May 1972 when a nuclear ballistic Golf II class submarine visited Cuba. When the submarine left port on May 6, it quickly submerged. A United States surveillance patrol, after making sonar contact, forced this submarine to surface repeatedly until well out in the Atlantic Ocean.

During the Carter administration, in November 1978 a mini-crisis broke out over the shipment of MIG-23 fighter-bombers to Cuba. In a press conference, President Carter assured reporters that the terms of the 1962 agreement had not been violated and that there was no evidence of nuclear weapons in Cuba. Then in June 1979 the State Department issued a statement that the MIG-23 planes did not violate the 1962 agreement because they were not adapted to deliver nuclear weapons.

Yet another mini-crisis appeared in 1979 when a Soviet "combat brigade" was discovered in Cuba. These troops did not constitute a violation of the 1962 understanding because the Soviet government in 1962 had promised to remove all military personnel "associated" with nuclear weapons.

During the Reagan administration there was no formal statement regarding the 1962 agreement. However, Reagan informed reporters on September 14, 1983 that "as far as I'm concerned, that agreement has been abrogated many times by the Soviet Union and Cuba bringing in what can only be considered offensive weapons, not defensive, there."

The missile crisis and the 1962 understanding did provide Fidel Castro with years of safety. Alarmed at the prospects of a nuclear war, the Soviet Union and the United States were frightened into a truce which became Castro's salvation. Had there not been a missile crisis, Castro would never have been able to acquire a promise that the United States would refrain from an invasion. However, the collapse of the Soviet regime meant that Castro had lost his economic security. Without the Soviet Union, Castro lacked a sponsor to join in guaranteeing the security of Cuba against invasion by United States forces. At the same time, the collapse of the Soviet Union meant that there was no threat of a nuclear conflict over Cuba. Moreover, the American people lost interest in an armed attack to overthrow Castro. Ironically Castro is secure from an American invasion thanks to the Cuban missile crisis.

The Impact on the Warsaw Pact Members. Strangely enough the Cuban missile crisis had a major impact on the Warsaw Pact nuclear operations. The October events underscored Soviet concerns about maintaining control over nuclear weapons and their unauthorized use. Apparently Khrushchev was unnerved by Castro's request that the Soviet Union launch a nuclear assault on the United States if the United States invaded Cuba. At one point in the Cuban-Soviet negotiations, Khrushchev had considered the possibility of giving Castro some control over Soviet forces, including the IL-28 bombers and the Luna tactical nuclear rockets. Instead he changed his mind and the military forces in Cuba were left under the command of their respective governments. However, Castro's letter of October 26 indicated the danger of delegating responsibility for nuclear operations to Castro. Moscow was more alarmed when the local Soviet commander, Pliyev, asked to have restrictions removed on control of nuclear warheads. Then Khrushchev was frightened by the downing of the U-2 by local Soviet commanders on their own initiative after Cuban troops began firing antiaircraft guns. Soviet troops in Cuba were not permitted to down American planes except those carrying out an attack. Khrushchev initially thought that Castro had ordered the troops to fire on Anderson's plane. Additional accidents could cause Khrushchev to lose control of the situation. Such an incident indicated that the Soviet government must retain complete authority over Soviet forces. The Cuban missile crisis effectively determined that Moscow would exert unlimited control and command of the use of nuclear weapons by Warsaw Pact nations. Efforts to have the Soviet government grant its Warsaw Pact allies any say in the use of nuclear weapons were vetoed thanks to the lessons learned in the Cuban missile crisis.

Kennedy, Khrushchev, and Castro. The Cuba missile crisis had a profound effect upon the three major figures in this drama. John Kennedy was never reconciled to a modus vivendi with Fidel Castro. Ironically, Kennedy's assassin was an energetic worker for the pro-Castro organization, Fair Play for Cuba, who claimed to be a great admirer of Fidel Castro.

Nikita Khrushchev remained in power until a conspiracy of his colleagues resulted in his overthrow in 1964. Although not the chief reason for removing him from office, his Cuban adventure was held against him. In a speech drafted for Khrushchev's prosecutors, Dimitri Polyanski, a Presidium member, denounced Khrushchev for the Cuban confrontation because he had insisted that Soviet missiles be deployed in

Cuba. This action had provoked a crisis which carried the world to the brink of war. Polyanski attacked Khrushchev for the humiliation which the Soviet Union had to endure. Because there was no other way out, it had to accept every demand and condition dictated by the United States, even going so far as permitting U.S. planes to inspect Soviet ships. Polyanski condemned Khrushchev because at the insistence of the United States, the missiles and most of the Soviet forces were withdrawn from Cuba. It was a victory for the United States. Moreover the Cuban missile crisis, according to Polyanski, damaged the international prestige of the Soviet government, the Communist Party, the Soviet armed forces, and at the same time helped increase the authority of the United States.

Had Khrushchev succeeded in his Cuban adventure and had he been able to appear at the United Nations in November 1962, as he had hoped, with a signed treaty embodying a Cuban-Soviet alliance and with the missiles all in place, his position in Moscow would have indeed been more secure. Nevertheless, his failure in Cuba did not by itself bring him down but it certainly helped in his downfall.

Fidel Castro, alone of this trio, survived, outliving his archenemy and his patron. The Cuban missile crisis saved him from being toppled. With the Soviet Union ended, there was no danger that Soviet machinations in Cuba could escalate into a nuclear war. Castro, thanks to the Cuban missile crisis, need not fear that an American invasion force will land on Cuba shores. Few Americans have any interest in overthrowing his regime if the price means the loss of American lives. It is indeed the supreme irony, that Fidel Castro with his scraggly beard and interminable speeches is now a relic of the Cuban missile crisis.

PART II

DOCUMENTS

DOCUMENT NO. 1

THE VIENNA SUMMIT CONFERENCE, JUNE 3, 1961[1]

The only face-to-face meeting between Nikita S. Khrushchev and John F. Kennedy occurred at the Vienna Summit Conference in June 1961. Among the subjects they discussed was the Cuban question.

γ γ γ

The President said that he agreed with Mr. Khrushchev. . . . The second point he wanted to make, the President said, was that he held no brief for Batista. The disagreement between the United States and Castro is not over monopolies; this question could be subject to discussion. The main point is that Castro has announced his intention to act in that general area, using Cuba as a base. This could eventually create a peril to the United States. A further point is, the President said, that the United States recognizes that it has bases in Turkey and Iran. However, these two countries are so weak that they could be no threat to the USSR, no more than Cuba to the US. The President reminded Mr. Khrushchev of the announced policy of the USSR that it would not tolerate governments hostile to it in areas which it regards as being of national interest to it. He inquired what the USSR's reaction would be if a government associated with the West were established in Poland. The United States stands for the right of free choice for all peoples and if Castro had acted in that spirit, he might have obtained endorsement. The United States has never taken any action with regard to such countries as . . . because the governments in those countries were freely elected and their policies are regarded by the United States as the judgment of their leadership. The President concluded by saying that it was critical to have the changes occurring in the world and affecting the balance of power take place in a way that would not involve the prestige or the treaty commitments of our two countries. The changes should be peaceful. Finally, the President said, if certain governments should fail to produce better living for their people, if they failed to give better education, higher standard of living, etc., to their people, and if they worked in the inter-

[1] Copyright © 1992 *The Cuban Missile Crisis*, By Laurence Chang and Peter Kornbluh. Reproduced by permission of The New Press, NY, pp. 12–13.

est of only a small group, their days would be doomed. But in all these developments, the President reiterated, we should avoid direct contact between our two countries so as not to prejudice the interests of their national security.

Mr. Khrushchev said he agreed with the President's conclusion. Likewise, there were some points of agreement between him and the President with regard to Cuba, although there was still considerable disagreement. For instance, Mr. Khrushchev said, he agreed that the right of free choice should be ensured to all peoples but the question of choice should be solely up to the people themselves. If Castro has not held any elections, this is an internal affair and it grants no one the right to intervene. If Castro fails to give freedom to his people he will detach himself from them and he will be removed just as Batista was. It would be a different situation if our two countries took it upon themselves to decide this question. Mr. Khrushchev then said that he had noted some inconsistency in US policy. He specified that he did not mean the policy of the President personally, because he had been in the White House only since quite recently, but rather US policy in general. He said that the United States places great emphasis on democracy.

DOCUMENT NO. 2

OPERATION MONGOOSE, FEBRUARY 20, 1962[2]

In November 1961, President Kennedy initiated Operation Mongoose with the intention of using American resources to help Cubans overthrow the Castro regime. Brigadier General Edward Lansdale, appointed to manage Operation Mongoose, reviewed the program and the basic plan for Operation Mongoose.

γ   γ   γ

SENSITIVE   20 February 1962

Program Review
by Brig. Gen. Lansdale

THE CUBA PROJECT

The Goal. In keeping with the spirit of the Presidential memorandum of 30 November 1961, the United States will help the people of Cuba overthrow the Communist regime from within Cuba and institute a new government with which the United States can live in peace.

The Situation. We still know too little about the real situation inside Cuba, although we are taking energetic steps to learn more. However, some salient facts are known. It is known that the Communist regime is an active Sino-Soviet spearhead in our Hemisphere and that Communist controls inside Cuba are severe. Also, there is evidence that the repressive measures of the Communists, together with disappointments in Castro's economic dependency on the Communist formula, have resulted in an anti-regime atmosphere among the Cuban people which makes a resistance program a distinct and present possibility.

Time is running against us. The Cuban people feel helpless and are losing hope fast. They need symbols of inside resistance and of outside interest soon. They need something they can join with the hope of starting to work surely towards overthrowing the regime. Since late November, we have been working hard to re-orient the operational concepts within the U.S. government and to develop the hard intelligence and operational assets required for success in our task.

The next National Intelligence Estimate on Cuba (NIE 85-62) promises to be a useful document dealing with our practical needs and with due recognition of the sparsity of hard facts. The needs of the Cuba project, as it goes into operation, plus the increasing U.S. capability for intelligence collection, should permit more frequent estimates for our guidance. These will be prepared on a periodic basis.

Premise of Action. Americans once ran a successful revolution. It was run from within, and succeeded because there was timely and strong political, economic, and military help by nations outside who supported our cause. Using this same concept of revolution from within, we must now help the Cuban people to stamp out tyranny and gain their liberty.

On 18 January, the Chief of Operations assigned thirty-two tasks to Departments and Agencies of the U.S. government, in order to provide a realistic assessment and preparation of U.S. capabilities. The Attorney General and the Special Group were apprised of this action. The answers received on 15 February provided the basis for planning a realistic course of action. The answers also revealed that the course of action must contain continuing coordination and firm overall guidance.

The course of action set forth herein is realistic within present operational estimates and intelligence. Actually, it represents the maximum target timing which the operational people jointly considered feasible. It aims for a revolt which can take place in Cuba by October 1962. It is a series of target actions and dates, not a rigid time-table. The target dates are timed as follows:

Phase I, Action, March 1962. Start moving in.

Phase II, Build-up, April-July 1962. Activating the necessary operations inside Cuba for revolution and concurrently applying the vital political, economic, and military-type support from outside Cuba.

Phase III, Readiness, 1 August 1962, check for final policy decision.

Phase IV, Resistance, August-September 1962, move into guerrilla operations.

Phase V, Revolt, first two weeks of October 1962. Open revolt and overthrow of the Communist regime.

Phase VI, Final, during month of October 1962. Establishment of new government.

Plan of Action. Attached is an operational plan for the overthrow of the Communist regime in Cuba, by Cubans from within Cuba, with outside help from the U.S. and elsewhere. Since this is an operation to prompt and support a revolt by the people in a Communist police state, flexibility is a must for success. Decisions on operational flexibility rest with the Chief of Operations, with consultation in the Special Group when policy matters are involved. Target actions and dates are detailed in the attached operational plans, which cover:

> A. Basic Action Plan Inside Cuba
> B. Political Support Plan
> C. Economic Support Plan
> D. Psychological Support Plan
> E. Military Support Plan
> F. Sabotage Support Plan
> G. Intelligence Support Plan

Early Policy Decisions. The operational plan for clandestine U.S. support of a Cuban movement inside Cuba to overthrow the Communist regime is within policy limits already set by the President. A vital decision, still to be made, is on the use of open U.S. force to aid the Cuban people in winning their liberty. If conditions and assets permitting a revolt are achieved in Cuba, and if U.S. help is required to sustain this condition, will the U.S. respond promptly with military force to aid the Cuban revolt? The contingencies under which such military deployment would be needed, and recommended U.S. responses, are detailed in a memorandum being prepared by the Secretaries of State and of Defense. An early decision is required, prior to deep involvement of the Cubans in this program.

DOCUMENT NO. 3

NIKITA KHRUSHCHEV'S MEMOIRS[3]

After he had been forced from power, Nikita Khrushchev had to endure an unwelcome retirement. Friends urged him to tape-record his memoirs which he began to do in 1967, continuing until his death in 1971. The tapes were smuggled out of the Soviet Union, transcribed, translated and edited for publication. In this excerpt, Khrushchev offers his account of the origins of the Cuban missile crisis.

γ   γ   γ

The fate of Cuba and the maintenance of Soviet prestige in that part of the world preoccupied me even when I was busy conducting the affairs of state in Moscow and traveling to the other fraternal countries. While I was on an official visit to Bulgaria, for instance, one thought kept hammering away at my brain: what will happen of we lose Cuba? I knew it would have been a terrible blow to Marxism-Leninism. It would gravely diminish our stature throughout the world, but especially in Latin America. If Cuba fell, other Latin American countries would reject us, claiming that for all our might the Soviet Union hadn't been able to do anything for Cuba except to make empty protests to the United Nations. We had to think up some way of confronting America with more than words. We had to establish a tangible and effective deterrent to American interference in the Caribbean. But what exactly? The logical answer was missiles. The United States had already surrounded the Soviet Union with its own bomber bases and missiles. We knew that American missiles were aimed against us in Turkey and Italy, to say nothing of West Germany. Our vital industrial centers were directly threatened by planes armed with atomic bombs and guided missiles tipped with nuclear warheads. As Chairman of the Council of Ministers, I found myself in the difficult position of having to decide on a course of action which would answer the American threat but which would also avoid war. Any fool can start a war, and once he's done so, even the wisest of men are helpless to stop it—especially if it's a nuclear war.

[3] From *Khrushchev Remembers* by Nikita Khrushchev. Copyright © 1970 by Little, Brown and Company. By permission of Little, Brown and Company, pp. 493–496.

It was during my visit to Bulgaria that I had the idea of installing missiles with nuclear warheads in Cuba without letting the United States find out they were there until it was too late to do anything about them. I knew that first we'd have to talk to Castro and explain our strategy to him in order to get the agreement of the Cuban government. My thinking went like this: if we installed the missiles secretly and then if the United States discovered the missiles were there after they were already poised and ready to strike, the Americans would think twice before trying to liquidate our installations by military means. I knew that the United States could knock out some of our installations, but not all of them. If a quarter or even a tenth of our missiles survived—even if only one or two big ones were left—we could still hit New York, and there wouldn't be much of New York left. I don't mean to say that everyone in New York would be killed—not everyone, of course, but an awful lot of people would be wiped out. I don't know how many: that's a matter for our scientists and military personnel to work out. They specialize in nuclear warfare and know how to calculate the consequences of a missile strike against a city the size of New York. But that's all beside the point. The main thing was that the installation of our missiles in Cuba would, I thought, restrain the United States from precipitous military action against Castro's government. In addition to protecting Cuba, our missiles would have equalized what the West likes to call "the balance of power." The Americans had surrounded our country with military bases and threatened us with nuclear weapons, and now they would learn just what it feels like to have enemy missiles pointing at you; we'd be doing nothing more than giving them a little of their own medicine. And it was high time America learned what it feels like to have her own land and her own people threatened. We Russians have suffered three wars over the last half century: World War I, the Civil War, and World War II. America has never had to fight a war on her own soil, at least not in the past fifty years. She's sent troops abroad to fight in the two World Wars—and made a fortune as a result. America has shed a few drops of her own blood while making billions by bleeding the rest of the world dry.

All these thoughts kept churning in my head the whole time I was in Bulgaria. I paced back and forth, brooding over what to do. I didn't tell anyone what I was thinking. I kept my mental agony to myself. But all the while the idea of putting missiles in Cuba was ripening inside my mind. After I returned to Moscow from Bulgaria I continued to think about the possibility. Finally we convened a meeting and I said I had some thoughts to air on the subject of Cuba. I laid out all the considerations which I've just outlined. I presented my idea in the context of the counterrevolutionary invasion which Castro had just resisted. I said that it would be foolish to expect the inevitable second invasion to be as badly planned and as badly executed as the first. I warned that Fidel would be crushed if another invasion were launched against Cuba and said that we were the only ones who could prevent such a disaster from occurring.

In the course of discussions inside the Government, we decided to install intermediate-range missiles, launching equipment, and Il-28 bombers in Cuba. Even though these bombers were obsolete, they would be useful against an enemy landing force. The Il-28 was too slow to fly over enemy territory because it could easily be shot down, but was well suited for coastal defense. The Il-28 was our first jet bomber. In its time it had been god of the air, but by the time we gave military assistance to Cuba, the Il-28 had already been taken out of production.

Soon after we began shipping our missiles to Cuba, the Americans became suspicious. Their intelligence told them that the number of our ships going to Cuba had suddenly and substantially increased and that our own people were unloading the ships once they reached Cuban ports. We didn't allow the Cubans to do any of the unloading or installation of the missiles themselves. While the Americans had no direct information about what we were delivering, they knew that whatever we were doing, we were doing with our own hands. It was not long before they concluded on the basis of reconnaissance photographs that we were installing missiles. They also knew about our Il-28 bombers which had been flown to Cuba.

The Americans became frightened, and we stepped up our shipments. We had delivered almost everything by the time the crisis reached the boiling point.

There are people who argue with the benefit of hindsight that antiaircraft missiles should have been installed before the ballistic missiles so as to close the airspace over Cuba. This doesn't make sense. How many surface-to-air missiles can you fit on a tiny sausage-shaped island? There's a limit to the number of missile installations you can put on an island as small as Cuba. Then, after you've launched all your missiles, you're completely unprotected. Moreover, antiaircraft missiles have a very short range. Antiaircraft batteries can easily be knocked out from the sea and air.

I want to make one thing absolutely clear: when we put our ballistic missiles in Cuba, we had no desire to start a war. On the contrary, our principal aim was only to deter America from starting a war. We were well aware that a war which started over Cuba would quickly expand into a world war. Any idiot could have started a war between America and Cuba. Cuba was eleven thousand kilometers away from us. Only a fool would think that we wanted to invade the American continent from Cuba. Our goal was precisely the opposite: we wanted to keep the Americans from invading Cuba, and, to that end, we wanted to make them think twice by confronting them with our missiles. This goal we achieved—but not without undergoing a period of perilous tension.

DOCUMENT NO. 4

CIA INTELLIGENCE MEMORANDUM, SEPTEMBER 3, 1962[4]

Using agents' reports, periodically the CIA reported on Soviet activities in Cuba. As this report indicates, by early September 1962 there was signifi-cant Soviet military activity in Cuba, including a growing number of SAM sites and an increase in the delivery of Soviet military equipment but as yet there was no indication of MRBMs.

γ　　　　　　γ　　　　　　γ

Washington, September 3, 1962.

SUBJECT

Recent Soviet Military Activities in Cuba

1. U–S photography of 29 August confirms extensive Soviet mili-tary deliveries to Cuba in recent weeks. Surface-to-air missile (SAM) sites, guided missile boats, and additional land armaments were ob-served.

2. The photography shows eight SAM sites being set up. One prob-able assembly area has been identified and SAM equipment has been located at one additional site.

A. The small amount of permanent construction at these sites and the speed of the work indicate the program is proceeding on a crash basis.

B. Some of these sites could be operational within a week or two.

C. A minimum of 125 technically trained personnel will be required to operate each site.

1. This figure excludes security and support personnel.

2. No indications that Cubans are trained for SAMs. Soviet person-nel doubtless will man the sites for at least the 9 to 12 months while Cubans are being trained.

3. Additional SAM sites probably will be set up in the near future.

[4] Department of State, *Foreign Relations of the United States 1961–1963*, Volume X, *Cuba, January 1961–September 1962* (Washington, D.C., 1996), pp. 950–953.

A. All sites now confirmed are in the Western one-third of the island.

1. The one area of SAM activity in Oriente province probably will be followed by several others in the vicinity.

2. Defector and clandestine reports from Las Villas province indicate that at least two sites will be located there, but no confirmation or definite locations thus far.

B. The pattern now emerging suggests as many as 24 sites may eventually be set up—enough to blanket the entire island.

4. At least 8 Komar-class missile boats have been delivered to Cuba in recent weeks.

A. These PT-like boats carry two missile launchers each, with the radar guided missile effective against surface targets to ranges of between 15 and 17 miles. The missile carries a 2,000 lb. HE warhead.

B. Some Cuban naval personnel have received training in the USSR, but it is not known if this included Komar training.

C. These boats are in addition to 13 or more torpedo boats and 6 submarine chasers delivered by the USSR earlier this year.

5. The photography shows that current deliveries to Cuba also contain land armaments, including tanks and possibly self-propelled guns.

A. Reports indicate other shipments have contained artillery, tanks, and possibly combat aircraft, but these are not confirmed.

B. The photography of 29 August turned up the highest number of MIG aircraft yet noted, some 37.

1. We believe Cuba's aircraft inventory includes approximately 60 MIG jet fighters, including at least a dozen MIG-19s.

2. No MIG-21s or any type of bomber have been noted.

6. Soviet shipments of military equipment and personnel to Cuba show no sign of letting up.

A. About 16 Soviet dry-cargo ships are now en route to Cuba, of which at least 10 probably are carrying military equipment.

1. Total number of military or military-related shipments to Cuba since the current deliveries began in mid-July may be as high as 65.

2. Routine Soviet deliveries of economic aid and trade goods are being made largely on Western ships.

B. At least 1,700 Soviet military technicians arrived in Cuba in late July and early August in connection with these military activities.

1. Most of these Soviets appear to be involved in setting up SAM

facilities but thus far we cannot conclude that this is their only objective.

C. At least 1,300 more Soviets are arriving unannounced this week; no reports on their activities so far.

1. Still additional bloc personnel probably have arrived on some of the cargo ships.

DOCUMENT NO. 5

CIA MEMORANDUM, OCTOBER 16, 1962[5]

On October 14, 1962, a U-2 spy plane returned from a flight across Cuba with photographs which indicated that Soviet military forces had erected MRBMs in two sites. The photographs became the hard evidence which ignited the Cuban missile crisis. The memorandum contains a description of the two sites as well as speculation on the link between Cuba and Berlin.

γ   γ   γ

16 October 1962

CENTRAL INTELLIGENCE AGENCY

MEMORANDUM: Probable Soviet MRBM Sites in Cuba

1. Photography of 14 October 1962 has disclosed two areas in the Sierra del Rosario mountains about 50 n.m. west southwest of Havana which appear to contain Soviet MRBMs in the early stages of deployment. A third area, about five and ten miles east of the first two, respectively, appears to be a military encampment. The first site includes 14 large tents, 15 smaller tents and 75 vehicles of a number of different types. The most significant vehicles at this site are six canvas-covered trailers of 80 feet in overall length which are of the general size and configuration of those used to transport the Soviet SS-3 (700 n.m. ballistic missile) and SS-4 (1100 n.m. ballistic missile). These trailers, of which eight more are located at the second site, are believed to be larger than those required to transport the Soviet SS-2 (350 n.m. ballistic missile).

2. The second site is 5 n.m. east of the first, and in addition to the eight trailers, contains four specially configured vehicles or pieces of equipment which could be used for missile erection in a field environment. At the time of photography, one of the trailers was in juxtaposition with one of these possible erectors. This site also contains 17 large tents, 20 small tents, 10 large trucks, 16 small trucks and 12 unidentified pieces of large equipment. No other missile associated equipment,

[5] CIA Staff, editors, *The Secret Cuban Missile Crisis Documents/Central Intelligence Agency.* (New York: Brassey's Inc. 1994), pp. 140–141.

such as instrumentation or propellant storage, have been detected. No facility to store nuclear warheads can be identified at any of these three installations.

3. The dimensions of the trailers indicate that either the SS-3 or SS-4 ballistic missile systems are involved. Both of these systems are road-mobile and can be deployed with no heavy construction work for launch pads, etc. Both the SS-3 and SS-4 are single stage vehicles which will carry a 3,000 lb. warhead to a maximum range of 700 n.m. and 1100 n.m. respectively. The SS-3 system requires liquid oxygen as an oxidant, while the SS-4 employs storable propellants. From a logistic and operational standpoint it would be more advantageous to deploy the SS-4 system to Cuba.

4. We do not have evidence from shipping coverage or other sources to indicate definitely when the missile units arrived in Cuba. From the extensiveness of the present activity, we judge that equipment may have begun to arrive during September. At the time of the 14 October photography, a column of trucks and equipment was visible on a road within one of the installations. Although we cannot be sure, it seems likely that the bulk of the personnel and equipment were shipped from the USSR as an integrated road mobile unit, suitable for field deployment. The time required to reach operational readiness could thus be quite short. Assuming that the necessary fueling and handling equipment is available, that communications are being installed, and that warheads are in Cuba or en route, an operational MRBM capability could probably exist in Cuba within the next few weeks.

5. The Soviet leaders' decision to deploy ballistic missiles to Cuba testifies to their determination to deter any active US intervention to weaken or overthrow the Castro regime, which they apparently regard as likely and imminent. This estimate of US intentions prompted Moscow's statement of 11 September which warned that an attack on Cuba would lead to a general nuclear conflict. The Soviets presumably believe that the presence of these missiles, which they expect would quickly become known to the US government, will significantly increase the costs and risks of any US action against the Cuban regime. They also probably believe that the missiles will reinforce the deterrent link between Cuba and Berlin which was implicit in the 11 September Soviet statement and in subsequent private conversations. Moscow clearly is seeking to portray Berlin as a hostage for Cuba.

DOCUMENT NO. 6

EXCOMM MEETING, OCTOBER 16, 1962[6]

On October 16, President Kennedy called a meeting of his senior advisers, known as the Executive Committee of the National Security Council or ExComm, who received a briefing and examined the photographs taken from the U-2 plane on October 14, 1962 over Cuba. Then the ExComm and the president began to debate how best to deal with the Cuban missile crisis.

γ　　　　　γ　　　　　γ

McNamara: I would recommend, Mr. President, that you authorize such flights as are considered necessary to obtain complete coverage of the island. Now, this seems to be ill-defined. But I purposely define it that way because we're running into cloud cover on some of these flights, and I would suggest that we simply repeat the flight if we have cloud cover and repeat it sufficiently often to obtain the coverage we require. . . .

President Kennedy: Well, here's . . . Let's look, tonight. It seems to be we ought to go on the assumption that we're going to have the, course number two we've called it, which would be a general strike [and] that you ought to be in position to do that, then, if you decide you'd like to do number one.

Bundy: I agree.

Robert Kennedy: Does that encompass an invasion?

President Kennedy: No. I'd say that's the third course.

Let's first start with, I'd have to say first find out, the air, so that I would think that we ought to be in position to do one or two. One would be just taking out these missiles. If there were others we'd find in the next 24 hours . . . Number two would be to take out all the airplanes. And number three is invade.

Carter?: Well, they'd have to take out the SAM sites also, Mr. President.

---

[6] Reprinted by permission of the publisher from *The Kennedy Tapes* by Ernest R. May and Philip D. Zelikow, Cambridge, MA: Harvard University Press, Copyright © 1997 by the President and Fellows at Harvard College, pp. 52, 94–99.

President Kennedy: Okay, but that would be in two, included in number two.

[Several people start talking.]

Taylor: In order to get in to get the airfields, there's a good number we'd have to get.

Gilpatric or Alexis Johnson?: Well, isn't there a question whether any of the SAM sites are operational?

Taylor: We're not sure yet.

President Kennedy: Okay. Well, let's say we've decided we got to go in the whole way. So let's say that number two is the SAM sites plus the air.

Bundy: It's actually to clear the air, to win the air battle.

President Kennedy: Yeah, well, whatever it is. [Unclear.]

Now, it seems to me we ought to be preparing now, in the most covert way, to do one and two, with the freedom to make the choice about number one depending on what information we have on it—what kind of moves that requires, and how much is that gonna . . .

McNamara: Mr. President, it requires no action other than what's been started. And you can make a decision prior to the start, Saturday or any time thereafter.

President Kennedy: Well, where do we put all these planes?

Taylor: You recall we have this problem, Mr. President. We're going to get new intelligence that will be coming in from these flights [the President agrees] and that's gonna have to be cranked into any strike plans we're preparing. So there is that factor of time. The Secretary has given you the minimum time to make a decision, so that we can brief the pilots and then crank in the new intelligence. I would point out . . .

McNamara: To answer the question you asked: We don't have to decide how we're gonna do it. All we have to decide is if we want Sweeney* to be prepared to do it.

Taylor: That's correct.

McNamara: And Sweeney has said that he will take the tape that comes in tomorrow and process it Thursday and Friday [October 18 and 19] and prepare the mission folders for strikes on Saturday [October 20] or earlier, every day thereafter.

Taylor: Yes. The point is that we'll have to brief pilots. We're holding that back. And there'll be, I would say, 400 pilots will have to go to be

*General Walter Sweeney, Commander in Chief, Tactical Air Command

briefed in the course of this. So I'm just saying this is widening the whole military scope of this thing very materially, if that's what we're supposed to do at this time.

President Kennedy: Well, now, when do we start briefing the pilots?

Taylor: They'll need at least 24 hours on that, when this new intelligence comes in.

President Kennedy: They will . . . In other word, then, until tomorrow. All I was thinking of—at least until . . .

Bundy: Can they be briefed in such a way that they're secure, [so] they have no access to—

McNamara: The President does not have to make any decision until 24 hours before the strike, except the decision to be prepared. And the process of preparation will not, in itself, run the risk of overt disclosure of the preparation.

Bundy: Doesn't [it] imply briefing, the preparation?

Taylor: It does, but—

McNamara: It implies the preparation of mission folders.

Taylor: Say, 24 hours before they go, they start a briefing.

I'd like to say this, Mr. President, the more time you can give, the better. Because they can then do a lot more rehearsing and checking out of all the pilots. . . .

McNamara: Mr. President, we need to do two things, it seems to me.

First, we need to develop a specific strike plan limited to the missiles and the nuclear storage sites, which we have not done. This would be a part of the broader plan, but I think we ought to estimate the minimum number of sorties. Since you have indicated some interest in that possibility, we ought to provide you that option. We haven't done this.

President Kennedy: Okay.

McNamara: But that's an easy job to do.

The second thing we ought to do, it seems to me, as a government, is to consider the consequences. I don't believe we have considered the consequences of any of these actions satisfactorily. And because we haven't considered the consequences, I'm not sure we're taking all the action we ought to take now to minimize those.

I don't know quite what kind of a world we live in after we've struck Cuba, and we've started it. We've put, let's say, 100 sorties in, just for purposes of illustration. I don't think you dare start with less than 100. You have 24 objects. Well, you [have] 24 vehicles, plus 16 launchers, plus a possible nuclear storage site, but there's the absolute minimum that you would wish to kill. And you couldn't possibly go in after those with less than, I would think, 50 to 100 sorties.

Taylor: And you'll miss some.

McNamara: And you'll miss some. That's right. Now, after we've launched 50 to 100 sorties, what kind of a world do we live in? How do we stop at that point? I don't know the answer to this. I think tonight State and we ought to work on the consequences of any one of these courses of action, consequences which I don't believe are entirely clear to any of us.

Ball: At any place in the world.

McNamara: At any place in the world, George. That's right. I agree with you.

Taylor: Mr. President, I should say that the Chiefs and the commanders feel so strongly about the dangers inherent in the limited strike that they would prefer taking *no* military action rather than to take that limited strike. They feel that it's opening up the United States to attacks which they can't prevent, if we don't take advantage of . . .

President Kennedy: Yeah. But I think the only thing is, the chances of it becoming a much broader struggle are increased as you step up the . . . Talk about the dangers to the United States, once you get into beginning to shoot up those airports. Then you get a lot of antiaircraft. And you got a lot of . . . I mean, you're running a much more major operation, therefore the dangers of the worldwide effects are substantial to the United States, are increased. That's the only argument for it [the limited strike].

I quite agree that, if you're just thinking about Cuba, the best thing to do is to be bold, if you're thinking about trying to get this thing under some degree of control.

Rusk: In that regard, Mr. President, there is a combination of the plans which might be considered, namely the limited strike and then, or simultaneously, the messages to Khrushchev and Castro which would indicate to them that this was none other than simply the fulfilling [of] the statements we have made all along.

President Kennedy: Well, I think we . . . In other words, that's a matter we've got to think about tonight. I don't . . .

Let's not let the Chiefs knock us out on this one, General, because I think that [what] we got to be thinking about is: If you go into Cuba in the way we're talking about, and taking all the planes and all the rest, then you really haven't got much of an argument against invading it.

McNamara: It seems to me a limited strike, plus planning for invasion 5 days afterwards to be taken unless something untoward occurs, makes much more sense.

Taylor: Well, I would be personally . . . Mr. President, my inclination is all against the invasion, but nonetheless trying to eliminate as effectively as possible every weapon that can strike the United States.

President Kennedy: But you're not for the invasion?

Taylor: I would not be, at this moment. No, sir.

We don't want to get committed to the degree that shackles us, with West Berlin.

McNamara: This is why I say I think we [have] to think of the consequences here. I would think a forced invasion, associated with assisting an uprising following an extensive air strike, is a highly probable set of circumstances. I don't know whether you could carry out an extensive air strike of, let's say, the kind we were talking about a moment ago, 700 sorties a day for 5 days, without an uprising in Cuba. I really . . .

Martin: In this morning's discussion we went into this, talked to some of your people, I believe, a little bit. And we felt an air strike, even of several days, against military targets primarily, would not result in any substantial unrest. People would just stay home and try to keep out of trouble.

McNamara: Well, when you're talking about military targets. We have 700 targets here we're talking about. This is a very damned expensive target system.

Taylor: That was in number [unclear], Mr. Secretary. But that's not the one I recommended.

McNamara: Well, neither is the one I'd recommend.

President Kennedy: What does that include? Every antiaircraft gun? What does that include?

Taylor: This includes related defenses, all sorts of things.

McNamara: Radar sites, SAM sites, and so on. But whether it's 700 or 200, and it's a least 200 I think . . .

Taylor: More in the order of 200, I'd say.

McNamara: It's at least 200. You can't carry that out without the danger of an uprising.

Robert Kennedy: Mr. President, while we're considering this problem tonight, I think that we should also consider what Cuba's going to be a year from now, or 2 years from now. Assume that we go in and knock these sites out. I don't know what's gonna stop them from saying: "We're gonna build the sites 6 months from now, bring them in [again]."

Taylor: Nothing permanent about it.

Robert Kennedy: Where are we 6 months from now? Or that we're in any better position? Or aren't we in [a] worse position if we go in and knock them out, and say: "Don't do it." I mean, obviously, they're gonna have to do it then.

McNamara: You have to put a blockade in following any limited action.

Robert Kennedy: Then we're gonna have to sink Russian ships. Then we're gonna have to sink Russian submarines.

Now, [think] whether it wouldn't be the argument, if you're going to get into it at all, whether we should just get into it, and get it over with, and take our losses. And if he wants to get into a war over this . . .

Hell, if it's war that's gonna come on this thing, or if he sticks those kinds of missiles after the warning, then he's gonna get into a war 6 months from now, or a year from now. So . . .

McNamara: Mr. President, this is why I think tonight we ought to put on paper the alternative plans and the probable, possible consequences thereof, in a way that State and Defense could agree on. Even if we disagree, then put in both views. Because the consequences of these actions have not been thought through clearly. The one that the Attorney General just mentioned is illustrative of that.

President Kennedy: If it doesn't increase very much their strategic strength, why is it—can any Russian expert tell us—why they . . . ? After all, Khrushchev demonstrated a sense of caution over Berlin. He's been cautious. I mean, he hasn't been . . .

Ball: Several possibilities, Mr. President. One of them is that he has given us word now that he's coming over in November to the UN. He may be proceeding on the assumption, and this lack of a sense of apparent urgency would seem to support this, that this isn't going to be discovered at the moment and that, when he comes over, this is something he can do, a ploy—that here is Cuba armed against the United States. Or possibly use it to try to trade something in Berlin, saying he'll disarm Cuba if we'll yield some of our interests in Berlin and some arrangement for it. I mean that this is a trading ploy.

Bundy: I would think one thing that I would still cling to is that he's not likely to give Fidel Castro nuclear warheads. I don't believe that has happened or is likely to happen.

DOCUMENT NO. 7

EXCOMM MEETING, OCTOBER 18, 1962[7]

The debate continued in the ExComm. News that intelligence analysts had identified IRBM sites hardened the attitudes of those advisers who favored air strikes when the ExComm met. (IRBMs had twice the range of MRBMs.) To avoid the inevitable casualties in an air strike, some of the ExComm favored blockading Cuba to prevent supplies and equipment from reaching the Soviet forces.

γ　　　　　γ　　　　　γ

President Kennedy: The question is really whether the Soviet reaction, and who knows this, would be measurably different if they were presented with an accomplished fact, the days or the one day [unclear] the invasion—the accomplished fact, whether their reaction would be different than it would be if they were given a chance to pull them out.

If we said to Khrushchev the "we would have to take action against you. But if you begin to pull them out, we'll take ours out of Turkey." Either that, or whether he would then send back: "If you take these out, we're going to take Berlin" or "we're going to do something else." That would be . . .

Thompson: An important factor there is, if you do this first strike, you would kill a lot of Russians, and that has a public reaction. On the other hand, if you give him notice, the thing I would fear the most is a threat to Turkey and Italy to take action [unclear].

Bundy: What is your preference, Tommy?

Thompson: My preference is this blockade plan, this declaration of war and these steps leading up to it. I think it's very highly doubtful that the Russians would resist a blockade against military weapons, particularly offensive ones, if that's the way we pitched it before the world.

President Kennedy: What do we do with the weapons already there?

Thompson: Demand they're dismantled, and say that we're going to maintain constant surveillance, and if they are armed, we would then take them out. And then maybe do it.

[7] Reprinted by permission of the publisher from *The Kennedy Tapes* by Ernest R. May and Philip D. Zelikow, Cambridge, MA: Harvard University Press, Copyright © 1997 by the President and Fellows of Harvard College, pp. 137–138, 142–146, 161–162.

I think we should be under no illusions, this is probably in the end going to lead to the same thing. But we do it in an entirely different posture and background and much less danger of getting up into the big war.

The Russians have a curious faculty of wanting a legal basis despite all of the outrageous things they've done. There are some other points to this. The fact that you have a declaration of war, I think they would be running a military blockade legally established, and [this would] greatly deter them.

President Kennedy: In other words . . . Could you maybe run through [this idea] for [unclear] because he hasn't heard the explanation of the blockade.

Alexis Johnson: There is a paper there on that, course number two there [not referring to strike options], Mr. President. There was a concept for this.

President Kennedy: However, under this plan, we would not take these missiles that they now have out, or the planes they now have out.

Alexis Johnson: Not in the first stage, which is why I think it would be useful to say that if they were made operational we might, or would—

President Kennedy: Of course, then he would say that "if you do that, then we will" . . .

Thompson: As Chip [Bohlen] said, I agree with him, that if they're prepared to say: "All right, if you do this, then this is nuclear world war," then they would do that anyway. I think he would make a lot of threatening language and very big terms in keeping his—

President Kennedy: I think it is more likely he would just grab Berlin.

Thompson: I think if we just made the first strike, then I think his answer would be, very probably, to take out one of our bases in Turkey, and make it quick too and then say: "I want to talk."

I think the whole purpose of this exercise is to build up to a talk with you, in which he tries to negotiate out the bases. There are a lot of things that point to that. One thing that struck me very much is, it's so easy to camouflage these things, or hide them in the woods. Why didn't they do it in the first place? They surely expected us to see them at some stage. The purpose was for preparation of negotiations.

Robert Kennedy: Maybe they have something.

Thompson: They may.

Taylor: May I ask whether military moves in these 5 to 8 days would be acceptable from the point of view of the State Department?

Rusk: I think it would be helpful, certainly be helpful—

[Several sentences unclear.]

Thompson: Now, of course, Mr. President, there are obvious counters to the blockade. The obvious one being Berlin.

President Kennedy: Yes.

Robert Kennedy: Also the argument against the blockade is that it's a very slow death, and it builds up, and goes over a period of months, and during that period of time you've got all these people yelling and screaming about it, you've got the invasion of Russian ships, shooting down the Russian planes that try to land there. You have to do all those things.

Alexis Johnson: On the Soviet reaction, it was Tommy and Chip that predicted the Soviets would not try to run the blockade, then they would have deserted their friends in Cuba. And I think there would be considerable political chaos in Cuba, if the Soviets deserted them . . .

Thompson: Also, I would assume you would be in negotiations with Chairman Khrushchev.

Rusk: [Unclear] in all logic he would have the blockade [unclear]. I guess that all of these military actions are viable for the blockade.

Unidentified: I agree . . .

President Kennedy: The only offer we would make, it seems to me, that would have any sense, the point being to give him some out, would be giving him some of our Turkey missiles.

Bundy: I believe, Mr. President, that is equally valid if we make the sudden strike. Now, I think it may well be important to have a message for Khrushchev's hands at that moment, saying, among other things, wicked things that led to this, but also that we understand this base problem. If they scrub them, then we do expect to dismantle our Turkish base. That has one small advantage, which is that if he strikes back, we will have at least given him a peaceful out.

I don't think we can keep that Turkish base.

Thompson?: But you get to the same point by doing this thing simultaneously, than you do if you don't.

McCone: [Unclear] seems to be a Cuba-Turkey exchange. It's quite serious. Now, it's true that we have talked with the Turks a year ago about getting those, taking the, Jupiters out of there for other reasons . . .

[Unclear brief exchange, in which someone refers to putting "a Polaris or two in those waters."]

Bundy: Which should make everyone feel better. We have [unclear] Soviet submarines are going to be in the Caribbean, and this is a political not a military problem.

Ball: If there is a strike without a preliminary discussion with Khrushchev, how many Soviet citizens will be killed? I don't know.

McNamara: Maybe several hundred, perhaps minimal—

Unidentified: Killed, as in casualties? Killed.

McNamara: Yeah, absolutely. We're using napalm, 750-pound bombs. This is an extensive strike we're talking about.

Unidentified: Well, I hope it is.

Ball: I think we must assume we'll kill several hundred Soviet citizens. Having killed several hundred Soviet citizens, what kind of response does Khrushchev have open to him?

It seems to me that it must just be a strong response, and I think we should expect that. And, therefore, the question really is: Are we willing to pay some kind of a rather substantial price to eliminate these missiles? I think the price is going to be high. It may still be worth paying to eliminate the missiles. But I think we must assume it's going to be high. The very least it will be, will be to remove the missiles in Italy and Turkey. I doubt we could settle for that.

Dillon?: Well, I think they'll take Berlin.

Ball: Mr. President, I think that it's easy, sitting here, to, to underestimate the kind of sense of a funk that you would have in the allied countries within—even perhaps in Latin America, if we act without warning, without giving Khrushchev some way out. Even though it may be illusory, I think we still have to do it, because I think that the impact on the opinion and the reaction would be very much different than a course of action where we strike without warning, that's like Pearl Harbor. It's the kind of conduct the one might expect of the Soviet Union. It is not conduct that one expects of the United States. And I have a feeling that this 24 hours to Khrushchev is really indispensable.

President Kennedy: And then if he says: "If you are going to do that, we're going to grab Berlin." The point is, he's going to grab Berlin anyway. He's going to take Berlin anyway.

Unidentified: We pay that price.

McNamara: I suspect the price we pay to Khrushchev will be about the same, whether we give him the advance warning or don't give him the advance warning. The advance warning has the advantage of possibly giving him an out that would reduce the requirement that we enter with military force. That's a fair possibility; not great. It has the advantage George has mentioned of causing less friction with the rest of the world.

It has some disadvantages, a reduction of military surprise, but the disadvantage of that is not very great. It carries with it, however, I believe, the great disadvantage that once you start down that course he outmaneuvers you.

Dillon: Well, the only advantage I see to it is the one you say, George, and that is that if you decide to do this, and you want to put yourself into the right position with the world, you [do this] as part of a [military] program that never stops. You have 24-hour notice. But you're under no illusion that anything he says is going to stop you [from proceeding with military action].

Sorensen: Well, can I make a suggestion there, Mr. President?

It seems to me that the various military courses have been outlined here as the Secretary says. They need to be developed in more detail, step by step and so on. But there has also been general but not unanimous agreement you are likely to need some kind of representation to Khrushchev ahead of time, maybe very shortly ahead of time. And I think you ought to have, in great detail, drawn up what that representation would consist of. Whether it will be a letter. What will be a satisfactory answer.

President Kennedy: Yes. Well, we certainly have to do the Khrushchev. And decide how much time in advance we'd do it, or whether I would make a public statement that we really had talked about the afternoon before.

The question now is: How do we want to function?

Rusk: Well, I think we ought to draw the group together and set the military . . .

McNamara: I believe the military problem, the military plan, seems like [unclear]. But really what I was thinking of is this give-and-take here, which we haven't gone through. I think the price of any one of these actions is going to be very, very high. I think there are a whole series of actions that of course you can take. And it seems to me we have to narrow those down and then we ought to consider how can we reduce that price.

And I would suggest, therefore, that, under the guidance of State—this is primarily an international political problem. We develop two groups here, and then we have Defense and State people in those two groups and we take 2 or 3 hours this afternoon to let these two groups take these two basic alternatives. They can derive any number of variations they wish to.

But one is a minimum military action, a blockade approach, with a slow buildup to subsequent action. The other is a very forceful military action with a series of variances as to how you enter it. And consider how the Soviets are going to respond. This is what we haven't done.

Thompson: Well, not only the Soviet response, but what the response to the response will be.

McNamara: How we respond to these responses.

McCone: We've done a good deal of work on that already.

McNamara: Well, I think it would be useful to pull it together.

President Kennedy: Well, let's see. Mr. Secretary, I will meet with you at 4:30 with Tommy before the Gromyko [meeting] to see where we are in this conversation. And at the end of the Gromyko conversation, we may want to have . . . I don't think we'll go 3 or 4 hours, but let's say we finish in 2 hours. I don't know how much it is. And then, whether we ought to, some time this evening, have another meeting based on what Gromyko said and see where we are.

DOCUMENT NO. 8

PRESIDENT KENNEDY'S MEETING WITH ANDREI GROMYKO, OCTOBER 18, 1962[8]

After meeting with the Excomm, President Kennedy had a previously scheduled meeting with Soviet Foreign Minister Andrei Gromyko. Kennedy did not reveal the U-2 photographs of the missile sites which were in his possession. Consequently Gromyko did not know that Operation Anadyr was no longer a secret.

γ γ γ

Cable from Soviet Foreign Minister
Gromyko on 18 October 1962 meeting
with President Kennedy, 20 October
1962 (excerpts)

During the meeting with President Kennedy at the White House on 18 October I transmitted to him, his spouse and other members of his family regards from the head of the Soviet Government N.S. Khrushchev and from Nina Petrovna.

Kennedy expressed his gratitude to N.S. Khrushchev for the regards.

Further I said that I would like to give an account of the Soviet Government policy on a number of important issues.

[section deleted—trans.]

Now I would like to expound the Soviet government's position on the Cuban issue and the USSR's assessment of the actions of the USA.

The Soviet government stands for the peaceful coexistence of states with different social systems, against the interference of one state into the internal affairs of others, against the intervention of large states into the affairs of small countries. Literally, that is the core of the Soviet Union's foreign policy.

It is well known to you, Mr. President, the attitude of the Soviet government and personally of N.S. Khrushchev toward the dangerous developments connected with the USA administration position on the is-

[8] *Cold War International History Project Bulletin* No. 8-9 (1996/1997), pp. 279–282.

sue of Cuba. An unrestrained anti-Cuban campaign has been going on in the USA for a long time and apparently there is a definite USA administration policy behind it. Right now the USA are making an attempt to blockade Cuban trade with other states. There is talk about a possibility of actions of organized policy in this region under the USA aegis.

But all of this amounts to a path that can lead to grave consequences, to a misfortune for all mankind, and we are confident that such an outcome is not desired by any people, including the people of the USA.

The USA administration for some reason considers that the Cubans must solve their domestic affairs not at their discretion, but at the discretion of the USA. But on what grounds? Cuba belongs to the Cuban people, not to the USA or any other state. And since it is so, then why are the statements made in the USA calling for an invasion of Cuba? What do the USA need Cuba for?

Who can in earnest believe that Cuba represents a threat to the USA? If we speak about dimensions and resources of the two countries—the USA and Cuba—then it is clear that they are a giant and a baby. The flagrant groundlessness of such charges against Cuba is obvious.

Cuba does not represent, and cannot represent, any threat to the countries of Latin America. It is strange to think as if small Cuba can encroach on the independence of either this or that country of Latin America. Cuban leaders and personally Fidel Castro have declared more than once in front of the whole world and in a most solemn manner that Cuba does not intend to impose their system, that they firmly favor the non-interference of states into the internal affairs of each other. . . .

The Cubans want to make secure their own home, their independence. They appeal for reason, for conscience. They call on the USA to renounce encroachments upon the independence of Cuba, to establish normal relations with the Cuban state.

The question is: Is it worthwhile to whip up a campaign and organize different sorts of hostile activity around Cuba and at the same time inimical actions against those states which maintain good relations with Cuba, respect its independence, and lend Cuba a helping hand at a difficult moment? Is it not a destruction of international law, of the UN principles and purposes?

Is it possible, Mr. President, for the Soviet Union, taking into account all of this, to sit cross-handed and to be a detached onlooker? You say that you like frankness. Giving an account of the Soviet government position frankly as well, I would like to stress that nowadays is not the middle of the XIX century, is not the time of colonial partition and not the times when a victim of aggression could raise its voice only weeks and months after an assault. American statesmen frequently declare that the USA is a great power. This is correct, the USA is a great power, a rich and strong power. And what kind of power is the Soviet Union?

You know that N.S. Khrushchev was positively impressed by your realistic statement during the Vienna meeting about the equality of forces of the two powers—the USSR and USA. But insofar as it is so, inasmuch as the USSR is also a great and strong power it cannot be a mere spectator while there is appearing a threat of unleashing a large war either in connection with the Cuban issue or [with a] situation in whatever other region of the world. . . .

So far as the aid of the Soviet Union to Cuba is concerned, the Soviet government has declared and I have been instructed to reaffirm it once more, our aid pursues exclusively the object of rendering Cuba assistance to its defensive capacity and development of its peaceful economy. Neither industry nor agriculture in Cuba, neither land-improvement works nor training of the Cuban personnel carried out by the Soviet specialists to teach them to use some defensive types of armaments, can represent a threat to anybody. Had it been otherwise, the Soviet government would never be involved in such aid. And such an approach applies to any country. . . .

Regarding the Cuban issue I [Kennedy] must say that really it became grave only this summer. Until then the Cuban question had been pushed by us to the background. True, Americans had a certain opinion about the present Cuban government and refugees from Cuba were exciting public opinion against that government. But the USA administration had no intentions to launch an aggression against Cuba. Suddenly, Mr. Khrushchev, without notifying me, began to increase at a brisk pace supplies of armaments to Cuba, although there was no threat on our side that could cause such a necessity. If Mr. Khrushchev addressed me on this issue, we could give him corresponding assurances on that score. The build-up of the Cuban military might has badly impressed the American people and the USA congress. As President I was trying to calm public opinion and I have declared that, taking into account the kind of aid rendered by the Soviet Union to Cuba, we must keep cool and self-controlled. But I was not able to find a satisfactory explanation for those actions of the Soviet Union.

Kennedy said later, that the Soviet Union is aware of the American opinion regarding the present regime in Cuba. We consider that it would be better if there were another government. But we do not have any intentions to attack Cuba.

You are saying that we have established a blockade around Cuba, but that is not the case. We have only taken the decision that the ships, after bringing cargo to Cuba, will be barred entry to the American ports to pick up freight.

The actions of the Soviet Union create a very complicated situation and I don't know where the whole thing can bring us. The present situation is, perhaps, the most dangerous since the end of the Second World War. We, certainly, take on trust statements of the Soviet Union about the sort of armaments supplied by you to Cuba. As President I am trying to restrain those people in the USA who are favoring an invasion of Cuba. For example, last Sunday in one of my speeches I declared against one of the American senators, who had previously supported such an invasion.

I repeat, a very dangerous situation has nevertheless arisen regarding this issue and I don't know what can be the outcome.

I answered Kennedy that once there was an attempt to organize an invasion of Cuba and it is known what was the end of the affair. From different official statements and your own statements, Mr. President, everybody know[s] what were the circumstances and how that invasion was arranged. Everybody knows also that the USA administration needs only to move a finger and no Cuban exiles, nor those who support them in the USA and some countries of the Caribbean, would dare launch any adventure against Cuba.

At this moment Kennedy put in a remark that he had already had an exchange of opinions with N.S. Khrushchev on the issue of the invasion of Cuba in 1961 and had said that it was a mistake.

I should be glad, Kennedy stressed, to give assurances that an invasion would not be repeated neither on the part of Cuban refugees, nor on the part of the USA armed forces.

But the issue is, Kennedy said, that as a result of the USSR government's action in July of the current year the situation suddenly has changed for the worse.

Proceeding with the previous idea, I said that for the Cuban government the vital issue is the question what is to be done next. The question comes to the following: either they will stay unprepared to repulse new attempts at invasion or they must undertake steps to ensure their country from attack, take care of their defense. We have already said that the Soviet government has responded to the call of Cuba for help only because that appeal had the aim of providing Cubans with bread and removing the threat hanging over Cuba by strengthening its defensive capacity. Regarding help, rendered by the Soviet Union, in the use of some exclusively defensive armaments, by no means can it be seen as a threat to the USA. If, I repeat, the situation were different the Soviet government never would have gone along with such an aid.

Kennedy said that, to make things completely clear on this issue, he would like to announce once more that the USA do not have any intentions to invade Cuba. Nevertheless, intensified armaments supplies to Cuba on the part of the Soviet Union, which began in July of the current year, have complicated the situation greatly and made it more dangerous. . . .

In conclusion I would like to say the following:

The Head of the Soviet government N.S. Khrushchev has entrusted me to convey to you that his opinion is that it would apparently be useful to have a meeting between the Head of the Soviet government and the USA President in order to discuss the issues that separate us and first of all the questions of the German peace treaty and West Berlin.

If N.S. Khrushchev has the opportunity, he will arrive in New York in the second half of November in order to attend the session of the UN General Assembly. Thus, we are speaking about a possibility of his arrival in the USA after the elections to Congress. Kennedy said that in the case of N.S. Khrushchev coming to the USA he would be glad to meet him once more. . . .

I thanked the President for the conversation during which we have discussed questions that represent interests for both countries, concerning important aspects of the foreign policies of the USSR and the USA. I also underlined the view of the Soviet government that it would be a great historic achievement if the USSR and the USA come to terms over those questions that divide us. . . .

For my part I assured the President once more that the policy of the Soviet Union always has been and remains directed at strengthening peace and the elimination of differences in the relations among all countries, above all in relations between the USSR and the USA, with whom the Soviet Union wants to live in peace and friendship.

[This policy] also applies to the Cuban issue, which was not invented by the Soviet Union, it applies to the question of signing the German peace treaty and normalization on its basis of the situation in West Berlin and it applies to all the other issues that separate our two countries. Our policy is the policy of peace, friendship, the policy of removing differences by peaceful means.

DOCUMENT NO. 9

ANDREI GROMYKO'S TELEGRAM TO THE CENTRAL COMMITTEE OF THE COMMUNIST PARTY OF THE SOVIET UNION, OCTOBER 19, 1962[9]

Following his meeting with President Kennedy, Gromyko sent a report to the Central Committee of the Communist Party on the attitude of the United States government regarding the Cuban question. His report indicated that he had no idea that the Kennedy administration had knowledge of the MRBMs in Cuba.

γ   γ   γ

To the CCCPSU

Everything which we know about the position of the USA government on the Cuban question allows us to conclude that the overall situation is completely satisfactory. This is confirmed by official announcements of American officials, including Kennedy, in his discussion with us on October 18, and all information which reaches us via unofficial channels and from representatives of other countries.

There is reason to believe that the USA is not preparing an intervention in Cuba and has put its money on obstructing Cuba's economic relations with the USSR and other countries, so as to destroy its economy and to cause hunger in the country, and in this way creating dissatisfaction among the population and prompting an uprising against the regime. This is based on a belief that the Soviet Union will not over a long period be able to provide Cuba with everything it needs.

The main reason for this American position is that the Administration and the overall American ruling circles are amazed by the Soviet Union's courage in assisting Cuba. Their reasoning is thus: The Soviet government recognizes the great importance which the Americans place on Cuba and its situation, and how painful that issue is to knowing all that, still provides such aid to Cuba, means that it is fully committed to repulsing any American intervention in Cuba. There is no single opin-

[9] *Cold War International History Project Bulletin* No. 5 (1995), pp. 66–67.

ion as to how and where that rebuff will be given, but that it will be given they do not doubt.

In these last days the sharpness of the anti-Cuban campaign in the USA has subsided somewhat, while the sharpness of the West Berlin question has stood out all the more. Newspapers bleat about the approaching crisis vis a vis West Berlin, the impending in the very near future signing of the agreement with the GDR, and so on. The goal of such a change in the work of the propaganda machine is to divert somewhat public attention from the Cuba issue. All this is not without the participation of the White House.

Even the rumor to the effect that the Soviet Union has made it known that it can soften its position on the Cuban issue if the West will soften its own position in West Berlin was basically intended to mollify the public vis a vis Cuba.

The wide publication of the results of an election survey conducted here by the Gallup (sic) Institute showing that the vast majority of Americans are against an American intervention in Cuba serves this same goal. In this regard, we have to note that the leadership of the institute in the past traditionally were more sympathetic to Republicans. Therefore, its publication in this case deserves special attention. This was not done without the encouragement of the White House either: in this way a nudge was given to the extremist groups in Congress which support extreme measures.

Also deserving of attention is the fact that Congress has now "gone on recess." This suggests that the pressure on Kennedy from the extreme groups in Congress will be less during the recess.

The position of the USA allies, particularly the British, also played a role. They did not support calls for the unleashing of aggression against Cuba, although they equally approved of other anti-Cuban steps of the USA.

It is not possible, of course, to be completely insured against USA surprises and adventures, even in the Cuba issue: all the same, taking into account the undeniable objective facts and the corresponding official public statements, and also the assurances given to us that the USA has no plans for intervention in Cuba (which undeniably commits them in many respects), it is possible to say that in these conditions a USA military adventure against Cuba is almost impossible to imagine.

19/X-62   A. GROMYKO

DOCUMENT NO. 10

PRESIDENT KENNEDY AND
THE JOINT CHIEFS OF STAFF,
OCTOBER 19, 1962[10]

President Kennedy had only one meeting with the Joint Chiefs of Staff during the Cuban missile crisis. He had excluded them from the meetings of the ExComm. At the urging of General Maxwell Taylor, he invited the Joint Chiefs to a meeting to allay their unhappiness over not being consulted. They had been urging a powerful air strike, followed by a blockade and invasion of the island to wipe out the threat of missiles and to overthrow Castro.

γ   γ   γ

Taylor: Mr. President, as you know, we've been meeting on this subject ever since we discovered the presence of missiles in Cuba. And I would say the debates in our own midst have followed very closely in parallel with those that you've heard from your other advisers.

From the outset I would say that we found we were united on the military requirement: we could not accept Cuba as a missile base; that we should either eliminate or neutralize the missiles there and prevent any others coming in. From a military point of view that meant three things.

First, attack with the benefit of surprise those known missiles and offensive weapons that we knew about. Second, we continue surveillance then to see what the effect would be. And third, a blockade to prevent the others from coming in.

I would say, again, from a military point of view, that seemed clear. We were united on that.

There has been one point, the importance of which we recognize, where we have never really firmed up our own position. Namely, the political requirements and the measures to offset the obvious political disabilities of this course of action. We know it's not an easy course of action, and it has at least two serious weaknesses.

[10] Reprinted by permission of the publisher from *The Kennedy Tapes* by Ernest R. May and Philip D. Zelikow, Cambridge, MA: Harvard University Press, Copyright © 1997 by the President and Fellows of Harvard College, pp. 174–185.

The first is we're never sure of getting all the missiles and the offensive weapons if we fire a strike. Secondly, we see—all of us, all of your advisers—a very damaging effect of this on our alliances.

To offset that, I have reported back some of the political measures considered. I think most of us would say we recognize that some of those things must be done, although they would be at some loss to military effectiveness by strike. I reported the trend last night, that I've detected for a couple of days, to move away from what I would call a straight military solution toward one based on military measures plus blockade. And that has been reported to the Chiefs this morning. I've taken the task Mr. McNamara assigned last night and we're working on that at this time.

I think the benefit this morning, Mr. President, would be for you to hear the other Chiefs' comments, either on our basic, what I call the military, plan, or how they would see the blockade plan.

President Kennedy: Let me just say a little, first, about what the problem is, from my point of view.

First, in general, I think we ought to think of why the Russians did this. Well, actually, it was a rather dangerous but rather useful play of theirs. We do nothing; they have a missile base there with all the pressure that brings to bear on the United States and damage to our prestige.

If we attack Cuban missiles, or Cuba, in any way, it gives them a clear line to go ahead and take Berlin, as they were able to do in Hungary under the Anglo war in Egypt. We will have been regarded as [unclear]. We would be regarded as the trigger-happy Americans who lost Berlin. We would have no support among our allies. We would affect the West Germans' attitude toward us. And [people would believe] that we let Berlin go because we didn't have the guts to endure a situation in Cuba. After all, Cuba is 5 or 6,000 miles from them. They don't give a damn about Cuba. But they do care about Berlin and about their own security. So they would say that we endangered their interests and security. And the implication [would be] that all the rest [happened] because of the end reaction that we took in Cuba.

So I think they've got . . . I must say I think it's a very satisfactory position from their point of view. If you take the view that what really . . . And clearly, if we do nothing then they'll have these missiles and they'll be able to say any time we ever try to do anything about Cuba, they'll fire these missiles. So that I think it's dangerous, but rather satisfactory, from their point of view.

If you take the view, really, that what's basic to them is Berlin and . . . There isn't any doubt. In every conversation we've had with the Russians, that's what . . . Even last night we [Gromyko and I] talked about Cuba for a while, but Berlin—that's what Khrushchev's committed himself to personally. So, actually, it's a quite bizarre situation [in Berlin] from their point of view.

Now, that's what makes our problem so difficult. If we go in and take them out on a quick air strike, we neutralize the chance of danger to the United States of these missiles being used, and we prevent a situation from arising, at least within Cuba, where the Cubans themselves have the means of exercising some degree of authority in this hemisphere.

On the other hand, we increase the chance greatly, as I think—there's bound to be a reprisal from the Soviet Union, there always is—[of] their just going in and taking Berlin by force. Which leaves me only one alternative, which is to fire nuclear weapons—which is a hell of an alternative—and begin a nuclear exchange, with all this happening.

On the other hand, if we begin the blockade that we're talking about, the chances are they will begin a blockade and say that we started it. And there'll be some question about the attitude of the Europeans. So that once again they will say that there will be this feeling in Europe that the Berlin blockade has been commenced by our blockade.

So I don't think we've got any satisfactory alternatives. Whether we balance off that, our problem is not merely Cuba but it is also Berlin. And when we recognize the importance of Berlin to Europe, and recognize the importance of our allies to us, that's what has made this thing be a dilemma for 3 days. Otherwise, our answer would be quite easy.

On the other hand, we've got to do something. Because if we do nothing, we're going to have the problem of Berlin anyway. That was made clear last night [in the meeting with Gromyko]. We're going to have this knife stuck right in our guts, in about 2 months [when the IRBMs are operational]. And so we've got to do something. Now, the question really is, what are we going to [unclear]?

It's safe to say 2 of these missiles [sites] are operational now; [they] can be launched 18 hours after the decision to fire has been reached. We've seen [unclear]. These missiles could be launched within 18 hours after the decision to fire. [Unclear recapitulation of the morning's intelligence briefings on the missile status.] They'd [the IRBMs] be ready in December of '62. It depends on [references to delivery systems and nuclear warheads] intermediate range. Communication, targeting, and an integrated air-defense system are now gaining operational status.

McCone?: That means that we're hearing electronic emissions now, suggesting that they have sectors for the air defense of Cuba. I believe this is the latest intelligence file.

President Kennedy: I just wanted to say that these were some of the problems that we have been clearing up. Let's hear from . . .

Taylor: Well, I would just say one thing and then turn it over to General LeMay. We recognize all these things, Mr. President. But I think we'd all be unanimous in saying that really our strength in Berlin, our strength anyplace in the world, is the credibility of our response under certain conditions. And if we don't respond here in Cuba, we think the credibility is sacrificed.

President Kennedy: That's right. That's right. So that's why we've got to respond. Now the question is: What is our response?

LeMay: Well, I certainly agree with everything General Taylor has said. I'd emphasize, a little strongly perhaps, that we don't have any choice except direct military action. If we do this blockade that's proposed, a political action, the first thing that's going to happen is your missiles are going to disappear into the woods, particularly your mobile ones. Now, we can't find them, regardless of what we do, and then we're going to take some damage if we try to do anything later on.

President Kennedy: Well, can't they [put] some of these undercover now [unclear], now that they've been alerted?

LeMay: There is a possibility of that. But the way they line these others up—I'll have to say it's a small possibility. If they were going to hide any of them, I would think they would have hid them all. I don't think there are any hid. So the only danger is that we haven't picked up some position in plain sight. This is possible. If we do low-altitude photography over them, this is going to be a tip-off, too.

Now, as for the Berlin situation, I don't share your view that if we knock off Cuba, they're going to knock off Berlin. We've got the Berlin problem staring us in the face anyway. If we don't do anything to Cuba, then they're going to push on Berlin and push *real hard* because they've got us *on the run*. If we take military action against Cuba, then I think that the—

President Kennedy: What do you think their reply would be?

LeMay: I don't think they're going to make any reply if we tell them that the Berlin situation is just like it's always been. If they make a move, we're going to fight. I don't think it changes the Berlin situation at all, except you've got to make one more statement on it.

So I see no other solution. This blockade and political action, I see leading into war. I don't see any other solution. It will lead right into war. This is almost as bad as the appeasement at Munich.

[Pause.]

Because if this whole blockade comes along, MiGs are going to fly. The IL-28s are going to fly against them [U.S. ships]. And we're just going to gradually slip into a war under conditions that are at great disadvantage to us, with missiles staring us in the face, that can knock out our airfields in the southeastern portions [of the United States]. And if they use nuclear weapons, it's the population down there. We just slipped into a war under conditions that we don't like. I just don't see any other solution except direct military intervention *right now*.

Anderson: Well, Mr. President, I feel that the course of action recommended to you by the Chiefs from the military point of view is the right one. I think it's the best one from the political point of view.

I'll address myself to the alternative of the blockade. If we institute a blockade, from a military point of view, we can carry it out. It is easier for us and requires less forces if we institute a complete blockade rather than a partial blockade, because instituting a partial blockade involves visit and search of all of these neutral ships, and taking them in, perhaps, to ports, which will certainly cause a great deal of [unclear], than if we go ahead and institute a complete blockade.

If we institute a complete blockade, we are immediately having a confrontation with the Soviet Union, because it's the Soviet-bloc ships which are taking the material to Cuba.

The blockade will not affect the equipment that is already in Cuba, and will provide the Russians in Cuba time to assemble all of these missiles, to assemble the IL-28s, to get the MiGs in a contract-manner control system ready to go. And I feel that, as this goes on, I agree with General LeMay that this will escalate and then we will be required to take other military action at greater disadvantage to the United States, to our military forces, and probably would suffer far greater casualties within the United States if these fanatics do indeed intend to fire any missiles.

We certainly cannot guarantee under those circumstances that we could prevent damage and loss of life in the United States itself. I think we have a good chance of greatly minimizing any loss of life within the United States under the present conditions, if we act fairly soon, although we do recognize that will be very fast. I do not see that, as long as the Soviet Union is supporting Cuba, that there is any solution to the Cuban problem except a military solution.

On the other hand, we recognize fully the relationship to the Berlin situation. The Communists have got in this case a master situation, from their point of view, where every course of action posed to us is characterized by unpleasantries and disadvantages. It's the same thing as Korea all over again, only on a grander scale.

We recognize the great difficulty of a military solution in Berlin. I think, on balance, the taking of positive, prompt, affirmative action in Berlin demonstrated the competence, the ability, the resolution of the United States. Our balance, I would judge it, would be to deter the Russians from more aggressive acts in Berlin, and if we didn't take any action, they'd feel that we were weak. So I subscribe fully to the concept that [unclear].

President Kennedy: Is seems to me that we have to assume that just in order to—military . . . When we grabbed their 2 UN people [as spies] and they threw 2 of ours out [of the Moscow embassy], we've got to assume that's going to be an [unclear]. They may not do it, any more than we can let these go on without doing something. They can't let us just take out, after all their statements, take out their missiles, kill a lot of Russians and not do anything.

It's quite obvious that what they think they can do is try to get Berlin. That may be a risk we have to take, but—

LeMay: Well, history has been, I think, the other way, Mr. President. Where we have taken a strong stand they have backed off. . . .

Taylor: I would agree, Mr. President. I think from the point of view of face that they'll do something. But I think it will be considerably less, depending on the posture we show here. I can't really see them putting the screws in. The dangers of hitting Berlin are just as great or greater after our action down here, because we have our [unclear].

President Kennedy: They've got to wait for 3 months until they get these things all ready, and then squeeze us in Berlin. But I think at that point, for what it is worth—it may not be worth much—but a least we have the support of Europe.

Taylor: That is true. . . .

Wheeler: Mr. President, in my judgment, from a military point of view, the lowest-risk course of action it would take in protecting the people of the United States against a possible strike on us is to go ahead with a surprise air strike, the blockade, and an invasion, because these series of actions progressively will give us increasing assurance that we really have gone after the offensive capability of the Cuban/Soviets corner. Now, admittedly, we can never be absolutely sure until and unless we actually occupy the island.

Now, I've also taken into consideration a couple of other things at the present time. To date, Khrushchev has not really confronted us with Soviet power. In other words, he has not declared Cuba a part of the Warsaw Pact. Nor has he made an announcement that this is a Soviet base, although I think that there is a chance that he may do that any time, particularly later in November, when he comes to the United States. And this course of action would then immediately have us confronting the Soviets and not Cubans. And at that time Soviet prestige, world prestige, would be at stake, which it is not at the present time.

The effect of this base in Cuba, it seems to me, has at least two sizable advantages from his point of view and two sizable disadvantages from our point of view.

First, the announcement of a Soviet base in Cuba would immediately have a profound effect in all of Latin America at least and probably worldwide because the question would arise: Is the United States incapable of doing something about it or unwilling to do something about it? In other words, it would attack our prestige.

Not only that. Increasingly, they can achieve a sizable increase in offensive Soviet strike capabilities against the United States, which they do not now have. They do have ICBMs that are targeted at us, but they are in limited numbers. Their air force is not by any manner of means of the magnitude and capability that they probably would desire. And this short-range missile course gives them a sort of a quantum jump in their capability to inflict damage on the United States. And so as I say, from a military point of view, I feel that the lowest-risk course of action is the full gamut of military action by us. That's it.

President Kennedy: Thank you, General.

Shoup: Mr. President, there's a question in my mind. Under what circumstance would Cuba want to inflict damage on the United States? The placing of the kind of weapons and the bombers that can do that certainly demand a hell of a lot of attention. There's one feature of this that I've been unable to reconcile. And I wonder whether the American people and the other nations of the world can reconcile it, and that is that we are now so anxious or we're discussing the anxiety of eliminating the possibility of damage to America from the Cuban air raid, whereas for a good many months the world has known, and we've known, that we have tremendously greater potential already aimed in on us from Russia and it has been for many months. We didn't attack Russia. I think that's a hard thing to reconcile, at least it is in my mind, and I would think it would be in the American public and other nations of the world. If it's a matter of distance, that it's closer now, well, missiles land pretty . . . If they have nuclear warheads down there, we know they have them in Russia. So if they want to inflict damage, it's a question of whether Khrushchev wants to have them do it, and him keep out of it. . . .

So, in my opinion, if we want to eliminate this threat that is now closer, but it's not nearly the threat that we've experienced all these months and months, if we want to eliminate it, then we're going to have to go in there and do it as a full-time job to eliminate the threat against us. Then if you want to take over the place and really put in a new government that is non-Communist, then you'll have to invade the place. And if that decision is made, we must go in with plenty of insurance of a decisive success in as quick [a time] as possible.

President Kennedy: Well, it is a fact that the number of missiles there, I would say that no matter what they put in there, we could live today under. If they don't have enough ICBMs today, they're going to have them in a year. They obviously are putting in [unclear] missiles. . . .

Taylor: We've begun the blockade plan study, and now it's the only implication that we'd really have to go into deeply.

There are a few things that strike us from the outset. One is the difficulty of maintaining surveillance. We just don't see how they can do that without taking losses and getting into some form of air warfare [unclear].

Second, they're targeting Guantanamo, which is curious. [Unclear] obstacle to some degree. I might ask Admiral Anderson to comment on how we can protect our position in Guantanamo during a state of blockade.

Anderson: Well, our position in Guantanamo becomes increasingly vulnerable, because strictly the imposition of the blockade is going to infuriate the Cubans, and they have got a mass of militia, and they can come on around Guantanamo. And I don't know whether they would actually attack Guantanamo or not. But we would certainly have to provide increased forces around there to defend Guantanamo, which we're in the process of reinforcing right now. Also, they have these short-range cruise missiles. They have 3 groups of those [unclear] coastal defense. Their navy, their aircraft all pose a threat to Guantanamo. So the threat is greatly increased and intensified during the course of a blockade.

Taylor: I think Guantanamo is going to cease to be a useful naval base, become more a fortress that's more or less in a permanent state of siege.

President Kennedy: If we were going to do the . . . You see, there's a good deal of difference between taking a strike which strikes just the missiles that are involved—one action, which has a certain effect of escalating attack. And the other is to do a strike which takes out all the planes necessary [unclear] to the period of an invasion, which takes a period of 14 days or something like that to get mounted. Maybe 18 days. What we have to assume is—I don't know what the Soviet response to each of these would have to be. If one were slowly building up to an invasion and fighting our way across the island . . . It's a different situation from taking out these offensive weapons. . . .

President Kennedy: Well, I think that what we have—they're going to be here for some time. And what we've talked about is having ground-to-ground missiles.

You know, as I say, the problem is not really so much war against Cuba. But the problem is part of this worldwide struggle with the Soviet Communists, particularly, as I say, over Berlin. And with the loss of Berlin, the effect of that and the responsibility we would bear. As I say, I think the Egyptian and the Hungary thing and the obvious parallels are what I'm concerned about.

LeMay: If you lose in Cuba, you're going to get more and more pressure right on Berlin.

Taylor: [Unclear] worldwide problem that shouldn't have been avoided, Mr. President. We haven't ignored it. We have been deterred, to my view, from getting ready to invade Cuba, as I think you know.

On the other hand, now that we see that it's not much going to be a place where they need a little supply of mobile missiles, as I thought perhaps earlier in the week, but really an organized base where the numbers of missile complexes are—

President Kennedy: Of course General Shoup's point, which he's held for many years, is as soon as they got it, if it isn't today, within a year they're going to have enough [unclear] stocked [unclear] the number of ICBMs they have. They may not be quite as accurate. But you get to put them on a city [unclear]. A hundred, you're talking about the destruction of a country, so that our problem is that we begin to duplicate that here. And we're losing all our cities.

Taylor: And we can never talk about invading again, after they get these missiles, because they got the gun pointed at our head.

President Kennedy: Well, the logical argument is that we don't really have to invade Cuba. That it's just one of the difficulties that we live with in life, like you live with the Soviet Union and China.

That problem, however, is for us not to do anything, then wait until we finish up Berlin, and then we can't do anything about Cuba. But I do think we ought to be aware of the fact that the existence of these missiles does not add to the danger but does create a danger right there now. Right there [in the Soviet Union] now they've got enough to keep us, between submarines and ICBMs, whatever planes they do have, and now they discovered the [unclear] country [unclear], they pretty well got us here anyway.

Taylor: By logic we ought to be able to say we can deter these missiles as well as the Soviet missiles, the ones from the Soviet Union. I think the thing that worries us, however, is these being potentially under the control of Castro. Castro would be quite a different fellow [unclear] missiles than Khrushchev. I don't think that's the case now, [but] then perhaps Khrushchev was never willing to do so. But there's always the risk of their falling into Cuban hands.

Shoup: Mr. President, one other item about the Guantanamo thing. Any initiative on our part immediately gives them the, I don't know, not the authority but the right probably to let fly at Guantanamo Bay. And first, the weapons that they have, including now another SAM site to work on the place, plus surface-to-surface missiles . . . They have a considerable number of gun emplacements within range of Guantanamo. So unless something is done to also at the same time neutralize this ability to take on Guantanamo, well, Guantanamo is in one hell of a fix.

President Kennedy: [Unclear] General, what can we do about Guantanamo if we do this air strike and they retaliate?

Anderson: Mr. President, all our thinking on Guantanamo is this. We're reinforcing it right now, building up the strength for the defense of Guantanamo. We have air all earmarked to suppress the weapons which would be brought to bear immediately on Guantanamo. We would evacuate the dependents from Guantanamo immediately prior to the air strike; get them clear. I think that with the forces that we've put in there and the air that is available, we can handle the situation in Guantanamo.

LeMay: Most of the naval air is available to defend Guantanamo.

Taylor: This can go on indefinitely. This could become a sort of Cuban Quemoy, where the shelling goes on, really, [unclear].

Shoup: It eliminates the airfield there, in a sense so we can operate. They do bombs; we can't operate. But it certainly terrifically reduces the potential value of the airfield there, the potential value of the shipping area, and what you then have is just a hunk of dirt that you're hanging on to for pride, prestige, political reasons, or what have you.

Taylor: It's a liability, actually.

Shoup: It becomes of no value unless [we destroy] the weapons, and that, of course, includes the doggone airplanes that can bomb it. Unless the weapons that can cause trouble there are eliminated, all you have is a hunk of dirt that's taken a hell of a lot of people to hang on to.

President Kennedy: Well, let me ask you this. If we go ahead with this air strike, either on the missiles or the missiles and the planes, I understand your recommendations are to do both. When will that be ready?

LeMay: We can be ready for attack at dawn on the 21st [Sunday], I think it's the earliest possible date. The optimal date is maybe Tuesday morning [October 23].

President Kennedy: Tuesday is the optimal.

DOCUMENT NO. 11

PRESIDENT KENNEDY BRIEFS SENATORS AND CONGRESSMEN, OCTOBER 22, 1962[11]

Before delivering his televised address to the nation, it was necessary for President Kennedy to brief Democratic and Republican leaders of Congress on the Cuban missile crisis. Because Congress was not in session, it was often necessary to dispatch military officers with messages and when necessary transportation to bring senators and congressmen back to Washington. Among the more important were Senators Richard Russell (Democrat, Georgia) and J. William Fulbright (Democrat, Arkansas). Fulbright had been a severe critic of the Bay of Pigs fiasco.

γ   γ   γ

President Kennedy: Perhaps a word from Ambassador Thompson. He has had a lot of conversations with Khrushchev. Perhaps you might wish to say something about evaluation of his purposes.

Thompson: Mr. President, I had a talk with Khrushchev at the end of July. He made very clear that he was . . . He gave an indication that time was running out on his going any further on the Berlin issue. And that at the same time he felt that he had gone too far in to go back, and he was concerned that if he went forward, he would either lose or start a war.

It also seems subsequently that his timing—his indication was that he didn't want to talk until the end of November—was related to this buildup. Of course, the concern is then that—what would you do about it is to . . . The effect on our lives is that if, in fact, one of his purposes, or a main one, was the showdown on Berlin. In my view that's the main thing that he had in mind.

Russell: I'm sorry, I didn't get that last.

Thompson: That that was the main thing he had in mind. The purpose was to have a showdown on Berlin and he thought this would help him in that.

[11] Reprinted by permission of the publisher from *The Kennedy Tapes* by Ernest R. May and Philip D. Zelikow, Cambridge, MA: Harvard University Press, Copyright © 1997 by the President and Fellows of Harvard College, pp. 254–261, 264–266, 270–273.

Russell: You mean the buildup in Cuba?

Thompson: Mm-hmm [agreeing].

Unidentified: Mr. President, Mr. Thompson, then you tie this, what we've just heard, into Berlin?

Thompson: That's correct.

Rusk: Mr. President, I would like to make one or two comments, if I may, because I think that this does mean a major and radical move in Soviet policy and Soviet action. This is the first time that these missiles are known to be outside of the Soviet Union. They are not even in the satellite countries of Eastern Europe.

We have had some impression over the past few months that they had been going through a reappraisal of policy. And we've had an impression coming out of it, of a toughness which was not visible, say, a year ago. Indications from Peiping [Beijing], for example, is they are somewhat more satisfied with Soviet policy than they were, things of that sort.

I want to emphasize that this is the most major development from the Soviet point of view since the Berlin blockade of 1947 and '48 [actually 1948–49]. Why they choose to pursue such a reckless and hazardous approach to this client is just speculation. This has both military and, of course, political ramifications.

But I think we ought not, in any sense, to underestimate the gravity of this development in terms of what it means to the Soviet point of view. They are taking risks here which are very heavy indeed and—

Russell: Very heavy what?

Rusk: Risks which are very heavy indeed.

I think, I think, there is real reason to think there has been quite a debate going on in the Soviet Union about the course of action. The peaceful-coexistence theme was not getting them very far, and I think the theme's clear now that the hard-line boys have moved into the ascendancy. So one of the things that we have to be concerned about is not just the missiles, but the entire development of Soviet policy as it affects our situation around the globe.

Russell: Secretary, do you see any off chance that it'll get any better? That they'll keep on establishing new bases and dividing our space. How can we gain by waiting?

Rusk: I'm not suggesting that it'll get any better.

President Kennedy: As I say, this information became available Tuesday morning. Mobile bases can be moved very quickly, so we don't know, [but] we assume we have all the ones that are there now. But the

CIA thinks there may be a number of others that are there on the island and have not been set up which can be set up quite quickly because of the mobility.

Intermediate-range ballistic missiles, of course, because of its nature, can take a longer time. We'll be able to spot those. The others might be set up in the space of a very few days.

Beginning Tuesday morning after we saw these first ones, we ordered intensive surveillance of the island, a number of U-2 flights until Wednesday and Thursday. I talked with—asked Mr. McCone to go up and brief General Eisenhower on Wednesday [October 17].

We decided, the Vice President and I, to continue our travels around the country in order not to alert this—until we had gotten all the available information we could. A lot of information came in on Sunday morning giving us this last site [Remedios IRBM site] which we mentioned.

We are presented with a very, very difficult problem because of Berlin as well as other reasons, but mostly because of Berlin, which is rather . . . The advantage is, from Khrushchev's point of view, he takes a great chance but there are quite some rewards to it. If we move into Cuba, he sees the difficulty I think we face. If we invade Cuba, we have a chance that these missiles will be fired on us.

In addition, Khrushchev will seize Berlin and that Europe will regard Berlin's loss, which attaches such symbolic importance to Berlin, as having been the fault of the United States by acting in a precipitous way. After all, they are 5 or 6,000 miles from Cuba and much closer to the Soviet Union. So these missiles don't bother them, and maybe they should think they should not bother us.

So that whatever we do in regard to Cuba, it gives him the chance to do the same with regard to Berlin. On the other hand, to not do anything but argue that these missile bases really extend only what we had to live under for a number of years—from submarines which are getting more and more intense, from the Soviet intercontinental ballistic missile system, which is in a rapid buildup [and] has a good deal of destruction which it could bring on us, as well as their bombers—that this adds to our hazards but does not create a new military hazard. And that we should keep our eye on the main site, which would be Berlin.

Our feeling, however, is that that would be a mistake. So that, beginning tonight, we're going to blockade Cuba, carrying out the [action] under the Rio Treaty. We called for a meeting of the Rio Pact countries and hope to get a two-thirds vote from them to give the blockade legality. If we don't get it, then we'll have to carry it out illegally or under declaration of war, which is not as advantageous to us.

Unidentified: Now, we don't know if Khrushchev would respond to a complete blockade?

President Kennedy: A blockade as it will be announced will be for the movement of weapons into Cuba. But we don't know what the [Soviet-] bloc ships will do. In order not to give Khrushchev the justification for imposing a complete blockade on Berlin, we are going to start with a blockade on the shipment of offensive weapons into Cuba that will stop all ships.

Now, we don't know what the bloc ships will do. We assume that they will probably . . . We don't know what they'll do, whether they'll try to send one through, make us fire on it, and use that as a justification on Berlin or whether he'll have them all turn back. In any case we're going to start on offensive weapons.

We will then consider extending it as the days go on to other—petroleum, oil, lubricants and other matters, except food and medicine. These are matters we will reach a judgment on as the days go on.

Now, in the meanwhile, we are making the military preparations with regard to Cuba so that if the situation deteriorates further, we will have the flexibility. Though the invasion is—the only way to get rid of these weapons is—the only other way to get rid of them is if they're fired, so that we're going to have to, it seems to me, watch with great care.

Let's say if we invade Cuba, there's a chance that these weapons will be fired at the United States. If we attempt to strike them from the air, then we will try to get them all, because they're mobile. And we know where the sites are, inasmuch as we can destroy the sites. But they can move them and set them up in another 3 days someplace else, so that we have not got a very easy situation.

There's a choice between doing nothing if we felt that that would compel Berlin rather than help [unclear] compel Latin America. So after a good deal of searching we decided this was the place to start. I don't know what their response would be. We've got two, three, four problems. One will be if we continue to surveil them and they shoot down one of our planes. We then have the problem of taking action against part of Cuba.

So I think that—I'm going to ask Secretary McNamara to detail what we're doing militarily—if there's any strong disagreement in what at least we set out to do, I want to hear it. Otherwise, I think what we ought to do is try to keep in very close contact before anything gets done of a major kind differently. Then it may have to be done in the next 24 to 48 hours, because I assume the Soviet response will be very strong and we'll all meet again. Needless to say, the Vice President and I have concluded our campaigning.

Fulbright?: Mr. President, do I understand that you have decided, and will announce tonight, the blockade?

President Kennedy: That's right. The quarantine.

Rusk: Mr. President, may I add one point to what you just said on these matters?

We do think this first step provides a brief pause for the people on the other side to have another thought before we get into an utterly crashing crisis, because the prospects ahead of us at this moment are very serious. Now, if the Soviets have underestimated what the United States is likely to do here, then they've got to consider whether they revise their judgment quick and fast.

The same thing with respect to the Cubans. Quite apart from the OAS and the UN aspects of it, a brief pause here is very important in order to give the Soviets a chance to pull back from the frontier. I do want to say, Mr. President, I think the prospects here for a rapid development of the situation can be a very grave matter indeed.

Russell: Mr. President, I could not space out under these circumstances and live with myself. I think that our responsibilities are quite immense, and stronger steps than that in view of this buildup there, and I must say that in all honesty to myself.

I don't see how we are going to get any stronger or get in any better position to meet this threat. It seems to me that we are at a crossroads. We're either a first-class power or we're not. You have warned these people time and again, in the most eloquent speeches I have read since Woodrow Wilson, that's what would happen if there was an offensive capability created in Cuba. They can't say they're not on notice.

The Secretary of State says: "Give them time to pause and think." They'll use that time to pause and think, to get better prepared. And if we temporize with this situation, I don't see how we can ever hope to find a place where . . .

Why, we have a complete justification by law for carrying out the announced foreign policy of the United States that you have announced time—that if there was an offensive capability there, that we would take any steps necessary to see that certain things should stop transit. They can stop transit, for example, though, in the Windward Passage and the Leeward Passage, easily with the nuclear missiles and with these ships. They could blow Guantanamo off the map. And you have told them not to do this thing. They've done it. And I think that we should assemble as speedily as possible an adequate force and clean out that situation.

The time is going to come, Mr. President, when we're going to have to take this step in Berlin and Korea and Washington, D.C., and Winder, Georgia, for the nuclear war. I don't know whether Khrushchev will launch a nuclear war over Cuba or not. I don't believe he will. But I think that the more that we temporize, the more surely he is to convince himself that we are afraid to make any real movement and to really fight.

President Kennedy: Perhaps, Mr. Senator, if you could just hear Secretary McNamara's words, then we could . . .

Russell: Pardon me. You just said, if anybody disagrees, and I couldn't sit here, feeling as I do . . .

President Kennedy: I understand. Let me just say—and then we can have a roundtable.

McNamara: The President has asked that we initiate a quarantine. We are redeploying our vessels into position to start those operations. They'll become effective as promptly as the initial political moves are completed. Sometime tomorrow or the next day.

Our orders are to hail the incoming vessels, both Soviet and non-Soviet, surface and submerged, to stop them, to search them, to divert those carrying designated goods, offensive weapons initially, to ports of their choosing. If they refuse to stop, to disable them and then to take them in as prizes.

This operation, obviously, is going to lead to the application of military force. It is entirely probable that the first ship, first Soviet ship hailed, will attempt to penetrate the quarantine, in which case Admiral Dennison has orders to disable the ship, reducing the damage to the minimum for that purpose, but sinking it if necessary.

Vinson?: Mr. Secretary, may I just interrupt to ask if taking a ship into custody, would that include the seizure or the destruction of offensive weapons found on board the ship? Or would the weapons on board the ship accompany the ship into quarantine?

McNamara: It depends on the character of the weapon. If there is any danger associated with moving the weapon in a prize to port, it would be destroyed at sea. . . .

Russell: Mr. President, I don't want to make a nuisance of myself, but I would like to complete my statement.

My position is that these people have been warned. They've had all the warning they could expect, and our Secretary of State speaks about the cause. When you enforce this blockade, Khrushchev's never said up until now that he would fight over Cuba. He even goes as far as rattling his missiles, and making firmer and firmer and firmer statements about what he's going to do about Cuba. And you are only making sure that when that day comes, when if they do use these MiGs to attack our shipping or drop a few bombs around Miami or some other place, and we do go in there, that we'll lose a great many more men than we would right now and—

President Kennedy: But, Senator, we can't invade Cuba versus . . . The case was somehow to assemble our force to invade Cuba. That's one of the problems we've got, we have, in order to surface the movement of troops beyond what has been surfaced in the last 48 hours. But we have to bring some troops from the West Coast, and to assemble the force which would give us the 90,000-odd men who might participate in an invasion will take some days. That's why I wanted Secretary McNamara . . . We are now assembling that force, but it is not in a position to invade Cuba in the next 24 to 48 hours.

Now, I think it may very well come to that before the end of the week. But we are moving all of the forces that we have, that will be necessary for an invasion, to the area around Cuba as quickly as we possibly can.

Russell: I think if it were a *fait accompli* we—

President Kennedy: Exactly. I agree.

Russell: —we'd be much better—we'd much narrowerly escape an all-out war with Russia.

President Kennedy: We don't have the forces to seize Cuba.

Russell: Well, we can assemble them.

President Kennedy: Well, that's what we're doing now.

Russell: Oh, all right.

President Kennedy: But Secretary McNamara can say we just don't have forces ready.

Russell: This blockade is going to put them on the alert. It's going to give the Russians . . . Khrushchev will be making various statements, and he'll get worse everywhere he goes and making more and more sure that, when we are forced to take action in Cuba, that we will still have to further divide our forces and be weaker at every border around the whole periphery of the free world. . . .

Russell: Excuse me again, but do you see a time ever in the future when Berlin will not be hostage to this?

President Kennedy: No, I think Berlin is—

Russell: Depending on what they do down there, whether they fire on us or not. Berlin will be hostage to these same circumstances.

President Kennedy: No doubt. There is no doubt.

Russell: And if we're going to back up on that, we might as well pull our armies in from Europe and save 15 to 25 billion dollars a year and just defend this continent. We've got to take a chance somewhere, sometime, if we're going to retain our position as a great world power and . . .

You know, General LeMay sat right here the last time we met here—I notice he's not here today, I don't believe he is—and said that he could get in under this radar and knock out all these installations. I didn't hardly think that he could at that time, but he said it unequivocally. I talked to him about it later. Of course, now I think that the Navy and the Marine Corps could do a much better job on knocking them out with conventional weapons, that I assume that we want to use, than the Air Force would.

President Kennedy: Now let me just answer that, Mr. Senator. That has been one of the matters which we've been concerned about this week, whether a strike of the kind that you're talking about, unannounced, would be able to knock these out. That was one of the reasons why this matter has been held up.

The difficulty with that is, we're not sure of getting them all. We don't know what the orders are. If there was a second strike on Turkey or Italy, where we've got missile bases, the commanders might fire. They might think that it was part of a general attack. We're not sure of getting them all.

In addition, there are at least as many which are still probably in trailers, we figure, and not at the site. So that you would do the Pearl Harbor attack and you'd only get half . . . [tape interrupted] . . . hasn't had at all, the chance somebody's going to blow that button.

Russell: You said after the Cuban on October—I recall it very well because I heard it over the radio—that you hoped that the Organization of American States would stand up with us to meet this finish but that, if it didn't, that we would undertake it alone. Now I understand that we [are] still waiting on the Secretary of State to try and to get them to agree to it.

President Kennedy: I'm not waiting.

Russell: I think we can [unclear] from here. I'm through. Excuse me. I would have been arguing with myself . . . So I hope you forgive me, but you asked for opinion—

President Kennedy: No, I did ask for opinions. But it's a very difficult problem that we're faced with. I'll just tell you that. It's a very difficult choice that we're faced with together. Now, the—

Russell: Oh, my God, I know that. A war, our destiny, will hinge on it. But it's coming someday, Mr. President. Will it ever be under more auspicious circumstances? We've got this little war over here now between China and India that they may clean up tomorrow except . . . Now, that will make a great deal of difference if we moved in down there to clean up Cuba, that war there as far as India and China concerns me, all over the world. I mean, what Russia would do because they are occupied with fighting each other there.

Now, I don't see how we are going to be better off next year, including with the Organization of American States. I assume this blockade will be effective for a while till they make up their minds to try to force their way through.

President Kennedy: Well now, the Organization of American States, quite obviously we'd do better if we'd gotten the other Latin American countries tied in. It's foolish to kick the whole Rio Treaty out the window.

Russell: Well, I don't want to do that.

President Kennedy: We're going to do the blockade in any case, Senator. The legality of the blockade depends—it's a peacetime blockade—upon the endorsement, under the Rio Treaty, of the OAS, which meets tomorrow morning. If they don't give us the 14 votes, the two-thirds vote, then we're going to do it anyway. But in that case we are going to have to have what's legally an illegal blockade or a declaration of war.

Now, we will carry a blockade on in any case. We hope with the endorsement—this will make it in a much more satisfactory position if we had that endorsement. But we're going to do it anyway.

In the meanwhile, we've prepared these troops, and then we'll have to just make the judgment later in the week about what we're going to do about it. I understand the force of your arguments. The only point we all have to consider is, if we invade, we take the risk, which we have to contemplate, that their weapons will be fired. . . .

Russell: Mr. President, but I think if Khrushchev ever starts talking around like before he moved in Hungary, that that would start World War III. And I think if we delay here and let him make a great many statements about what he's going to do, and get up a tremendous row in this hemisphere between the nations here, that we'd be much more likely to have to abandon the venture completely, which I greatly feel we will before we're through. Or else we will start a much greater war over the world than we would—

President Kennedy: I understand.

Russell: You know, the right of self-defense is pretty elemental, and you relied on that in that very telling statement you made. You relied on that, the right of self-defense, and that's what we'd be doing.

Unidentified: Senator, if it becomes necessary, in my judgment, to have an invasion, and you have a superior force, then you should apprise the Cuban people, because then they would be anxious to be on the winning side. If they are convinced that you are going to have a speedy victory then they'll lend their support. If they think it's going to be a long-drawn-out fight, you are liable to have many of the people supporting Castro.

Fulbright: Mr. President, one thing about this blockade that does not appeal to me is you really do have to confront the Russians directly on the ships, whereas if you invade without the blockade, they are not confronted and illegally. I mean it's just between us and Cuba. I think a blockade is the worst of the alternatives, because if you're confronted with a Russian ship, you are actually confronting Russia. This way, if you have the invasion against Cuba, this is not actually an affront to Russia. They don't pretend that they're not—

President Kennedy: I don't think after statements they've made . . . I think you have to assume they would not let us build up over a 6-, 7-, or 8-day period an invasion force without making these statements.

In addition, I think the inevitable result would be the immediate seizure of Berlin. It may be anyway.

Fulbright: I don't see a blockade as being . . . It seems to me the alternative is either just to go to the UN and solve without this, or an invasion. A blockade seems to me the worst alternative. . . .

President Kennedy: Let's say we get it legal under the Rio Treaty, and

I think we've got a legal right to take the action we have in regard to the shipment of offensive weapons in there.

Now, when you talk about the invasion, the first [point], excluding the risk that these missiles will be fired, we do have the 7 or 8,000 Russians there. We are going to have to shoot them up. And I think that it would be foolish to expect that the Russians would not regard that as a far more direct thrust than they're going to regard on the ships. And I think that the inevitable end result will be the seizure of Berlin.

Now, as I say, we may have to come up with all that and . . . But, I think, if we're talking about nuclear war, the escalation ought to be at least with some degree of control. In addition, we've got this 7-day period. But you can't . . . I don't think in stopping Russian ships—I know that's offensive to the Russians. When you start talking about the invasion it's infinitely more offensive.

Fulbright: But not to the Russians, it seems to me. They have no right to say that. We're [not] going to attack on Russia. I don't think that they have.

Dirksen: I can't quite agree, Bill.

Mr. President, as this thing moves on, and it will take on acceleration, do you contemplate calling the leadership again?

President Kennedy: Yes, I will.

Unidentified: Very soon?

President Kennedy: That's right.

Unidentified: You see, your people are making arrangements for sending them back home. Have you views on it?

President Kennedy: Well, it really will depend a little on what happens, but it may be very quickly. But I think that we ought to go on the assumption that we might meet definitely Thursday, but maybe before if events require it. It's going to take some time to carry out this invasion before the next meeting, and at that time we may want to reach a judgment on that. In the meanwhile, we ought to be assembling all our forces. . . .

DOCUMENT NO. 12

PRESIDENT KENNEDY'S RADIO AND
TELEVISION ADDRESS TO THE NATION,
OCTOBER 22, 1962[12]

About noon on October 22, Pierre Salinger, President Kennedy's press secretary, informed the television networks that the president would speak at 7:00 PM on "a matter of highest national urgency." At 7 PM that evening, Kennedy sat down before the television cameras in the Oval Office and began to read the most significant address of the Cold War as he told the American people and the Soviet government about the Cuban missile crisis and the measures he had ordered to deal with the crisis.

γ   γ   γ

Good evening, my fellow citizens:

This Government, as promised, has maintained the closest surveillance of the Soviet military buildup on the island of Cuba. Within the past week, unmistakable evidence has established the fact that a series of offensive missile sites is now in preparation on that imprisoned island. The purpose of these bases can be none other than to provide a nuclear strike capability against the Western Hemisphere.

Upon receiving the first preliminary hard information of this nature last Tuesday morning at 9 a.m., I directed that our surveillance be stepped up. And having now confirmed and completed our evaluation of the evidence and our decision on a course of action, this Government feels obliged to report this new crisis to you in fullest detail.

The characteristics of these new missile sites indicate two distinct types of installations. Several of them include medium range ballistic missiles, capable of carrying a nuclear warhead for a distance of more than 1,000 nautical miles. Each of these missiles, in short, is capable of striking Washington, D.C., the Panama Canal, Cape Canaveral, Mexico City, or any other city in the southeastern part of the United States, in Central America, or in the Caribbean area.

Additional sites not yet completed appear to be designed for intermediate range ballistic missiles—capable of traveling more than twice as

[12] *Public Papers of the Presidents of the United States. John F. Kennedy. January 1 to December 31, 1962* (Washington, D.C., 1963), pp. 806–809.

far—and thus capable of striking most of the major cities in the Western Hemisphere, ranging as far north as Hudson Bay, Canada, and as far south as Lima, Peru. In addition, jet bombers, capable of carrying nuclear weapons, are now being uncrated and assembled in Cuba, while the necessary air bases are being prepared.

This urgent transformation of Cuba into an important strategic base—by the presence of these large, long-range, and clearly offensive weapons of sudden mass destruction—constitutes an explicit threat to the peace and security of all the Americas, in flagrant and deliberate defiance of the Rio Pact of 1947, the traditions of this Nation and hemisphere, the joint resolution of the 87th Congress, the Charter of the United Nations, and my own public warnings to the Soviets on September 4 and 13. This action also contradicts the repeated assurances of Soviet spokesmen, both publicly and privately delivered, that the arms buildup in Cuba would retain its original defensive character, and that the Soviet Union had no need or desire to station strategic missiles on the territory of any other nation.

The size of this undertaking makes clear that it has been planned for some months. Yet only last month, after I had made clear the distinction between any introduction of ground-to-ground missiles and the existence of defensive antiaircraft missiles, the Soviet Government publicly stated on September 11 that, and I quote, "the armaments and military equipment sent to Cuba are designed exclusively for defensive purposes," that, and I quote the Soviet Government, "there is no need for the Soviet Government to shift its weapons . . . for a retaliatory blow to any other country, for instance Cuba," and that, and I quote their government, "the Soviet Union has so powerful rockets to carry these nuclear warheads that there is no need to search for sites for them beyond the boundaries of the Soviet Union." That statement was false.

Only last Thursday, as evidence of this rapid offensive buildup was already in my hand, Soviet Foreign Minister Gromyko told me in my office that he was instructed to make it clear once again, as he said his government had already done, that Soviet assistance to Cuba, and I quote, "pursued solely the purpose of contributing to the defense capabilities of Cuba," that, and I quote him, "training by Soviet specialists of Cuban nationals in handling defensive armaments was by no means offensive, and if it were otherwise," Mr. Gromyko went on, "the Soviet Government would never become involved in rendering such assistance." That statement also was false. . . .

For many years, both the Soviet Union and the United States, recognizing this fact, have deployed strategic nuclear weapons with great care, never upsetting the precarious status quo which insured that these weapons would not be used in the absence of some vital challenge. Our own strategic missiles have never been transferred to the territory of any other nation under a cloak of secrecy and deception; and our history—unlike that of the Soviets since the end of World War II—demonstrates that we have no desire to dominate or conquer any other nation or impose our system upon its people. Nevertheless, American citizens have become adjusted to living daily on the bull's-eye of Soviet missiles located inside the U.S.S.R. or in submarines.

In that sense, missiles in Cuba add to an already clear and present danger—although it should be noted the nations of Latin America have never previously been subjected to a potential nuclear threat.

But this secret, swift, and extraordinary buildup of Communist missiles—in an area well known to have a special and historical relationship to the United States and the nations of the Western Hemisphere, in violation of Soviet assurances, and in defiance of American and hemispheric policy—this sudden, clandestine decision to station strategic weapons for the first time outside of Soviet soil—is a deliberately provocative and unjustified change in the status quo which cannot be accepted by this country, if our courage and our commitments are ever to be trusted again by either friend or foe.

The 1930's taught us a clear lesson: aggressive conduct, if allowed to go unchecked and unchallenged, ultimately leads to war. This nation is opposed to war. We are also true to our word. Our unswerving objective, therefore, must be to prevent the use of these missiles against this or any other country, and to secure their withdrawal or elimination from the Western Hemisphere.

Our policy has been one of patience and restraint, as befits a peaceful and powerful nation, which leads a worldwide alliance. We have been determined not to be diverted from our central concerns by mere irritants and fanatics. But now further action is required—and it is under way; and these actions may only be the beginning. We will not prematurely or unnecessarily risk the costs of worldwide nuclear war in which even the fruits of victory would be ashes in our mouth—but neither will we shrink from that risk at any time it must be faced.

Acting, therefore, in the defense of our own security and of the entire Western Hemisphere, and under the authority entrusted to me by the

Constitution as endorsed by the resolution of the Congress, I have directed that the following *initial* steps be taken immediately:

First: To halt this offensive buildup, a strict quarantine on all offensive military equipment under shipment to Cuba is being initiated. All ships of any kind bound for Cuba from whatever nation or port will, if found to contain cargoes of offensive weapons, be turned back. This quarantine will be extended, if needed, to other types of cargo and carriers. We are not at this time, however, denying the necessities of life as the Soviets attempted to do in their Berlin blockade of 1948.

Second: I have directed the continued and increased close surveillance of Cuba and its military buildup. The foreign ministers of the OAS, in their communique of October 6, rejected secrecy on such matters in this hemisphere. Should these offensive military preparations continue, thus increasing the threat to the hemisphere, further action will be justified. I have directed the Armed Forces to prepare for any eventualities; and I trust that in the interest of both the Cuban people and the Soviet technicians at the sites, the hazards to all concerned of continuing this threat will be recognized.

Third: It shall be the policy of this Nation to regard any nuclear missile launched from Cuba against any nation in the Western Hemisphere as an attack by the Soviet Union on the United States, requiring a full retaliatory response upon the Soviet Union.

Fourth: As a necessary military precaution, I have reinforced our base at Guantanamo, evacuated today the dependents of our personnel there, and ordered additional military units to be on a standby alert basis.

Fifth: We are calling tonight for an immediate meeting of the Organ of Consultation under the Organization of American States, to consider this threat to hemispheric security and to invoke articles 6 and 8 of the Rio Treaty in support of all necessary action. The United Nations Charter allows for regional security arrangements—and the nations of this hemisphere decided long ago against the military presence of outside powers. Our other allies around the world have also been alerted.

Sixth: Under the Charter of the United Nations, we are asking tonight that an emergency meeting of the Security Council be convoked without delay to take action against this latest Soviet threat to world peace. Our resolution will call for the prompt dismantling and withdrawal of all offensive weapons in Cuba, under the supervision of U.N. observers, before the quarantine can be lifted.

Seventh and finally: I call upon Chairman Khrushchev to halt and eliminate this clandestine, reckless, and provocative threat to world peace and to stable relations between our two nations. I call upon him further to abandon this course of world domination, and to join in an historic effort to end the perilous arms race and to transform the history of man. He has an opportunity now to move the world back from the abyss of destruction—by returning to his government's own words that it had no need to station missiles outside its own territory, and withdrawing these weapons from Cuba—by refraining from any action which will widen or deepen the present crisis—and then by participating in a search for peaceful and permanent solutions.

This Nation is prepared to present its case against the Soviet threat to peace, and our own proposals for a peaceful world, at any time and in any forum—in the OAS, in the United Nations, or in any other meeting that could be useful—without limiting our freedom of action. We have in the past made strenuous efforts to limit the spread of nuclear weapons. We have proposed the elimination of all arms and military bases in a fair and effective disarmament treaty. We are prepared to discuss new proposals for the removal of tensions on both sides—including the possibilities of a genuinely independent Cuba, free to determine its own destiny. We have no wish to war with the Soviet Union—for we are a peaceful people who desire to live in peace with all other peoples.

But it is difficult to settle or even discuss these problems in an atmosphere of intimidation. That is why this latest Soviet threat—or any other threat which is made either independently or in response to our actions this week—must and will be met with determination. Any hostile move anywhere in the world against the safety and freedom of peoples to whom we are committed—including in particular the brave people of West Berlin—will be met by whatever action is needed.

Finally, I want to say a few words to the captive people of Cuba, to whom this speech is being directly carried by special radio facilities. I speak to you as a friend, as one who knows of your deep attachment to your fatherland, as one who shares your aspirations for liberty and justice for all. And I have watched and the American people have watched with deep sorrow how your nationalist revolution was betrayed—and how your fatherland fell under foreign domination. Now your leaders are no longer Cuban leaders inspired by Cuban ideals. They are puppets and agents of an international conspiracy which has turned Cuba against your friends and neighbors in the Americas—and turned it into the first Latin American country to become a target for nuclear war—the first Latin American country to have these weapons on its soil.

These new weapons are not in your interest. They contribute nothing to your peace and well-being. They can only undermine it. But this country has no wish to cause you to suffer or to impose any system upon you. We know that your lives and land are being used as pawns by those who deny your freedom.

Many times in the past, the Cuban people have risen to throw out tyrants who destroyed their liberty. And I have no doubt that most Cubans today look forward to the time when they will be truly free—free from foreign domination, free to choose their own leaders, free to select their own system, free to own their own land, free to speak and write and worship without fear or degradation. And then shall Cuba be welcomed back to the society of free nations and to the associations of this hemisphere.

My fellow citizens: let no one doubt that this is a difficult and dangerous effort on which we have set out. No one can foresee precisely what course it will take or what costs or casualties will be incurred. Many months of sacrifice and self-discipline lie ahead—months in which both our patience and our will will be tested—months in which many threats and denunciations will keep us aware of our dangers. But the greatest danger of all would be to do nothing.

The path we have chosen for the present is full of hazards, as all paths are—but it is the one most consistent with our character and courage as a nation and our commitments around the world. The cost of freedom is always high—but Americans have always paid it. And one path we shall never choose, and that is the path of surrender or submission.

Our goal is not the victory of might, but the vindication of right—not peace at the expense of freedom, but both peace *and* freedom, here in this hemisphere, and, we hope, around the world. God willing, that goal will be achieved.

Thank you and good night.

DOCUMENT NO. 13

THE EXCOMM MEETING, OCTOBER 23, 1962[13]

As the quarantine was being put into effect, the president met with his advisors, now officially the Executive Committee of the National Security Council, to consider the problems related to the quarantine. None of them had any experience in managing such an operation.

γ   γ   γ

Rusk: The mobs [of protesters] that we simulated turned up in London instead of Havana. 2,000 people.

President Kennedy: Surrounding the American embassy?

Rusk: Bertrand Russell's [British peace movement] people stormed the embassy there. We haven't had any reports of them disarming Cuba.

Unidentified: South America? [Unclear] Chile. The Communist-dominated unit was beginning a nationwide strike. It's much the most serious.

President Kennedy: Okay.

Now, what do we do tomorrow morning when these 8 [Soviet] vessels continue to sail on? We're all clear about how we enter?

McNamara: Well, this is the problem. We want to be very careful. I think we should wait until early in the morning to say exactly what instructions we'll give to Dennison. We ought to try to avoid shooting a ship, a Soviet ship carrying wheat to Cuba or medicine or something of that kind of item. And therefore, I would propose to try to pick a ship which almost certainly carries offensive weapons as the first ship. And not allow any other Soviet ship to be hailed until that particular ship has been hailed. Now, this is going to be difficult because it means we have to try to see in advance what the ships . . .

President Kennedy: Does it mean, though, that by the end of the day, Thursday [October 25], there will be ships arriving in Cuba which will make it, clear, from before the blockade?

McNamara: Oh yes.

President Kennedy: The only problem I see, Bob, I would think that

[13] Reprinted by permission of the publisher from *The Kennedy Tapes* by Ernest R. May and Philip D. Zelikow, Cambridge, MA: Harvard University Press, Copyright © 1997 by the President and Fellows of Harvard College, pp. 333–337.

the Soviets, if there is a vessel among them [carrying offensive weapons], that's the one vessel I would think they would turn around.

[22 seconds excised as classified information.]

McNamara: . . . There's been no change in course that we have as yet detected.

Rusk: Well, that could well be the biggest of the ships.

Bundy: They're all going on course, aren't they?

McNamara: They're all going on course. That's right. As best we can tell.

[8 seconds excised as classified information.]

Rusk: I would think that there would be some advantage in testing out on any other kind of ship.

McNamara: You mean a British ship and so on?

Rusk: No. I mean a Soviet ship that didn't have [unclear] at sea.

McNamara: But the instruction from Khrushchev is very likely to be: "Don't stop under any circumstances." So the baby-food ship comes out and we hail it. I think we shoot it. We shoot . . .

President Kennedy: That's what could happen. They're gonna keep going. And we're gonna try to shoot the rudder off or the boiler. And then we're going to try to board it. And they're going to fire guns, machine guns. And we're going to have one hell of a time trying to get aboard that thing and getting control of it, because they're pretty tough, and I suppose they may have soldiers or marines aboard their ships. They have technicians who are in the military. So I would think that the taking of those ships [is] going to be a major operation. We may have to sink it rather than just take it.

Bundy: Or to get aboard it, and blow it up?

President Kennedy: I think that's less likely than having a real fight in trying to board it, because they may have 5, 6, or 700 people aboard there with guns. A destroyer . . .

McNamara: Most of these [Soviet] ships, Mr. President, are not likely to have that kind of a crew on board. The crews are relatively small in the type of ships that we wish to stop.

Rusk: What would we do now about a ship that has been disabled, and it's not going to sink? It just can't go anywhere?

McNamara: We have tows.

Rusk: Dakar?

McNamara: We tow it to a prize port.

Ball: I see, which means a United States port.

McNamara: Yes. Charleston. Jacksonville.

President Kennedy: Well, then we take it back to port and we find out it's got baby food on it.

McNamara: Well, we inspect it before we take it into port to try to— if it's baby food being shipped, we're in . . .

[Unclear brief exchange, culminating in laughter].

President Kennedy: Well, that's what we're going to have to do.

Now, the only thing is, these fellows need as detailed instructions as possible, from those who are knowledgeable about the sea and know just how to proceed on this.

Let's say they shoot, and the boat stops. Then they try a signal for a boarding party, and they say they're not going to permit a boarding party aboard. The ship is drifting. Then I don't think we can probably get aboard, unless we want to go through a machine-gun operation. The destroyers aren't equipped. Now, the ship may be tough to get aboard. You have a real fight aboard there.

Unidentified: Well, the cruisers have helicopters.

McNamara: Unless these freighters are carrying substantial security guards—I don't believe we have evidence they are—it shouldn't be too difficult. In a search there may be a firefight, but it ought to be a small one. The normal—

[Unclear interjections.]

Unidentified: It won't be easy.

Rusk: [Unclear] Khrushchev to turn them around.

Robert Kennedy: We have got the answer on the use of these foreign-built vessels? If you want to get [the order] on the [news] ticker?

President Kennedy: All right. Well, we're sending instructions to how to proceed with all this [the quarantine]. It might be an actuality that they may . . . They may not all realize . . .

First, we want to be sure that nobody on our boats have cameras.

And the second thing is, that they are to understand what's allowed to be the response, first to stop, or not to stop. Secondly, when they do the action as they do, they're liable not to permit you to board.

Now, what do we say if there is machine-gun fire, et cetera—our vessel trying to board. Now, what do we say to them then? Do we let them drift around?

McNamara: I think at that point, Mr. President, we have to leave it to the local commander. Depending on the seas, and whether there is a submarine in the area, there are just a host of circumstances we've thought of. We don't believe we should try to give orders from here in relation to—

President Kennedy: We don't want to tell them necessarily to go aboard there. If we disable it and they should refuse to let us aboard, I think you stay with it, certainly for a day or so, and not boarding. Just let it drift.

Taylor: I think we just have to say, Mr. President, to use a mission type of order: To use the minimum force required to—

President Kennedy: That doesn't give them quite . . . I think it misses the point. If we disabled the ship and they're 800 miles out and they refuse to let us aboard, I don't think that we ought, he ought, to feel that he has to board that thing in order to carry out our orders.

Taylor: Well, he . . . To keep ships from going to Cuba, that's his basic mission now.

President Kennedy: I think in the beginning it would be better, if this situation happened, to let that boat lie there disabled for a day or so, not to try to board it and have them reopen machine guns and have 30–40 people killed on each side. That would be . . .

McNamara: I think there's some problem, Mr. President. If for some reason they are moving in the area, we ought to board it, and inspect it, and get out of there if necessary, towing the ship or leaving the ship there. This [Soviet] sub, moving in, we have some serious problems. This is one of the difficulties we face. Admiral Anderson is somewhat concerned about the possibility that they'll try to sink one of our major vessels, such as a [aircraft] carrier.

Bundy: The submarine just fueled yesterday [unclear], and is moving west.

McNamara: They sent a ship under high speed to fuel a submarine yesterday, which did fuel and was observed fueling. And the sub was obviously going to move into a Cuban area. There may well be others that we're not aware of. I think we have to allow the commander on the scene a certain amount of latitude to—

Bundy: Do you have the [aircraft carrier U.S.S.] *Enterprise* in the area?

McNamara: We have the *Enterprise* in the area, yes. And [the aircraft carrier U.S.S.] *Independence*.

President Kennedy: Do we want to keep the *Enterprise* there?

McNamara: Well, the *Enterprise* is not at this moment anywhere close to the area of the *Kimovsk*.

Bundy: We need aircraft surveillance of the area.

President Kennedy: A submarine could really do these aircraft carriers—could do a lot of damage.

Bundy: Well, we expect to know reasonably well where the submarines are. [Others agree.]

President Kennedy: All right. Mr. Secretary, well, I think I'd make sure that you have reviewed these instructions that go out to him.

McNamara: I have, and I will do so by the end of the night, sir.

Bundy: Well, we have some decisions coming out of this morning['s meeting]. The Attorney General has one, which is the problem of foreign bottoms on coastwise shipping.

Gilpatric: May I first say that we found this is not the problem that we thought. There are only 18 American-flag ships now engaged in coastal trade or any coastal trade on the Atlantic, and they're all specialized types of design, John, and they would not be the type that we would take. The ships that we would requisition or charter are all engaged in the export/import, foreign trade. They represent about 10 percent of the total foreign trade operating out of the Atlantic. Our take would be about 30 percent of the 10 percent, so that we will not have much of an effect on foreign trade. We will be shifting some cargo, some U.S. bottoms to foreign bottoms. It will affect our gold [reserves] probably, but we're talking about 80 to 90 ships, and we're trying to cut down these requirements.

The big impact will be on passenger ships, take the *Independence*, the *Constitution*, and so forth. I don't think we have any problem, John, with coastal trade.

McCone: Intercoastal too? I'm sure offshore ships are coming back— Japan, Honolulu. And lumber and all that.

Gilpatric: We're not going to take those.

Rusk: Maybe we should pick up some ships under charter with the Soviet Union.

Gilpatric: Well, we want [American-] flag ships.

President Kennedy: They may attempt to stop one of our ships. Might not sink 'em.

McNamara: I think it's particularly possible that the Cubans will try to stop or sink some of our ships in the Passages [unclear].

President Kennedy: Are we sending out some warning to our merchant ships?

McNamara: We are sending warnings out to them, and we are also providing air cover of a sort. We can't provide constant cover over every merchant in that area, but we do have air cover over the area, and we will be prepared to attack their attackers. So I think this is a real possibility. We could lose a merchant ship in and around Cuba, quickly.

President Kennedy: Okay.

DOCUMENT NO. 14

LETTER FROM CHAIRMAN KHRUSHCHEV
TO PRESIDENT KENNEDY,
OCTOBER 24, 1962[14]

On October 23, Khrushchev had denounced Kennedy's actions as naked interference in the domestic affairs of Cuba, the Soviet Union and other states, but Kennedy requested that Khrushchev issue instructions to Soviet ships to observe the quarantine. In his reply on October 24, Khrushchev resorted to his favorite ploy: brinkmanship. His words "ultimatum . . . act of aggression . . . nuclear missile war" were intended to frighten Kennedy into some type of concession.

γ   γ   γ

Moscow, October 24, 1962

DEAR MR. PRESIDENT: I have received your letter of October 23, have studied it, and am answering you.

Just imagine, Mr. President, that we had presented you with the conditions of an ultimatum which you have presented us by your action. How would you have reacted to this? I think that you would have been indignant at such a step on our part. And this would have been understandable to us.

In presenting us with these conditions, you, Mr. President, have flung a challenge at us. Who asked you to do this? By what right did you do this? Our ties with the Republic of Cuba, like our relations with other states, regardless of what kind of states they may be, concern only the two countries between which these relations exist. And if we now speak of the quarantine to which your letter refers, a quarantine may be established, according to accepted international practice, only by agreement of states between themselves, and not by some third party. Quarantines exist, for example, on agricultural goods and products. But in this case the question is in no way one of quarantine, but rather of far more serious things, and you yourself understand this.

You, Mr. President, are not declaring a quarantine, but rather are set-

[14] Department of State, *Foreign Relations of the United States. 1961–1963* Volume XI *Cuban Missile Crisis and Aftermath* (Washington, D.C.), 1996, pp. 185–187.

ting forth an ultimatum and threatening that if we do not give in to your demands you will use force. Consider what you are saying! And you want to persuade me to agree to this! What would it mean to agree to these demands? It would mean guiding oneself in one's relations with other countries not by reason, but by submitting to arbitrariness. You are no longer appealing to reason, but wish to intimidate us.

No, Mr. President, I cannot agree to this, and I think that in your own heart you recognize that I am correct. I am convinced that in my place you would act the same way.

Reference to the decision of the Organization of American States cannot in any way substantiate the demands now advanced by the United States. This Organization has absolutely no authority or basis for adopting decisions such as the one you speak of in your letter. Therefore, we do not recognize these decisions. International law exists and universally recognized norms of conduct exist. We firmly adhere to the principles of international law and observe strictly the norms which regulate navigation on the high seas, in international waters. We observe these norms and enjoy the rights recognized by all states.

You wish to compel us to renounce the rights that every sovereign state enjoys, you are trying to legislate in questions of international law, and you are violating the universally accepted norms of that law. And you are doing all this not only out of hatred for the Cuban people and its government, but also because of considerations of the election campaign in the United States. What morality, what law can justify such an approach by the American Government to international affairs? No such morality or law can be found, because the actions of the United States with regard to Cuba constitute outright banditry or, if you like, the folly of degenerate imperialism. Unfortunately, such folly can bring grave suffering to the peoples of all countries, and to no lesser degree to the American people themselves, since the United States has completely lost its former isolation with the advent of modern types of armament.

Therefore, Mr. President, if you coolly weigh the situation which has developed, not giving way to passions, you will understand that the Soviet Union cannot fail to reject the arbitrary demands of the United States. When you confront us with such conditions, try to put yourself in our place and consider how the United States would react to these conditions. I do not doubt that if someone attempted to dictate similar conditions to you—the United States—you would reject such an attempt. And we also say—no.

The Soviet Government considers that the violation of the freedom to use international waters and international air space is an act of aggression which pushes mankind toward the abyss of a world nuclear-missile war. Therefore, the Soviet Government cannot instruct the captains of Soviet vessels bound for Cuba to observe the orders of American naval forces blockading that Island. Our instructions to Soviet mariners are to observe strictly the universally accepted norms of navigation in international waters and not to retreat one step from them. And if the American side violates these rules, it must realize what responsibility will rest upon it in that case. Naturally we will not simply be bystanders with regard to piratical acts by American ships on the high seas. We will then be forced on our part to take the measures we consider necessary and adequate in order to protect our rights. We have everything necessary to do so.

Respectfully,

N. Khrushchev

DOCUMENT NO. 15

KHRUSHCHEV'S LETTER TO KENNEDY
OCTOBER 26, 1962[15]

*President Kennedy had neither retreated nor asked for a summit meeting
on October 25. Nor did he make any offer to compromise. Khrushchev had
tried brinkmanship in vain. Meanwhile, the Kremlin had learned that SAC
was on nuclear alert and the DEFCON status of American forces had
changed. It was time for Khrushchev to concede, to seek an end to the crisis
and ask Kennedy to pledge that United States forces would not invade Cuba
if the missiles were withdrawn from the island.*

γ   γ   γ

Moscow, October 26, 1962, 7 p.m.

1101. Policy. Embassy translation follows of letter from Khrushchev
to President delivered to Embassy by messenger 4:43 p.m. Moscow time
October 26, under cover of letter from Gromyko to me.

Begin text.

Dear Mr. President:

I have received your letter of October 25. From your letter, I got the
feeling that you have some understanding of the situation which has developed and a sense of responsibility. I value this.

Now we have already publicly exchanged our evaluations of the events
around Cuba and each of us has set forth his explanation and his understanding of these events. Consequently, I would think that, apparently,
a continuation of an exchange of opinions at such a distance, even in
the form of secret letters, will hardly add anything to that which one
side has already said to the other.

I think you will understand me correctly if you are really concerned
about the welfare of the world. Everyone needs peace: both capitalists,
if they have not lost their reason, and, still more, Communists, people
who know how to value not only their own lives but, more than anything, the lives of the peoples. We, Communists, are against all wars
between states in general and have been defending the cause of peace

[15] Department of State, *Foreign Relations of the United States 1961–1963*. Volume XI
Cuban Missile Crisis and Aftermath (Washington, D.C., 1996), pp. 235–241.

since we came into the world. We have always regarded war as a calamity, and not as a game nor as a means for the attainment of definite goals, nor, all the more, as a goal in itself. Our goals are clear, and the means to attain them is labor. War is our enemy and a calamity for all the peoples.

It is thus that we, Soviet people, and, together with US, other peoples as well, understand the questions of war and peace. I can, in any case, firmly say this for the peoples of the socialist countries, as well as for all progressive people who want peace, happiness, and friendship among peoples.

I see, Mr. President, that you too are not devoid of a sense of anxiety for the fate of the world—understanding, and of what war entails. What would a war give you? You are threatening us with war. But you well know that the very least which you would receive in reply would be that you would experience the same consequences as those which you sent us. And that must be clear to us, people invested with authority, trust, and responsibility. We must not succumb to intoxication and petty passions, regardless of whether elections are impending in this or that country, or not impending. These are all transient things, but if indeed war should break out, then it would not be in our power to contain or stop it, for such is the logic of war. I have participated in two wars and know that war ends when it has rolled through cities and villages, everywhere sowing death and destruction.

In the name of the Soviet Government and the Soviet people, I assure you that your arguments regarding offensive weapons on Cuba are groundless. It is apparent from what you have written me that our conceptions are different on this score, or rather, we have different definitions for these or those military means, indeed, in reality, the same forms of weapons can have different interpretations.

You are a military man and, I hope, will understand me. Let us take for example a simple cannon. What sort of means is this: offensive or defensive? A cannon is a defensive means if it is set up to defend boundaries or a fortified area. But if one concentrates artillery, and adds to it the necessary number of troops, then the same cannons do become an offensive means, because they prepare and clear the way for infantry to advance. The same happens with missile-nuclear weapons as well, with any type of this weapon.

You are mistaken if you think that any of our means on Cuba are offensive. However, let us not argue now, it is apparent that I will not be able to convince you of this, but I say to you: You, Mr. President, are a military man and should understand: can one advance, if one has on one's territory even an enormous quantity of missiles of various effective radiuses and various power, but using only these means. These missiles are a means of extermination and destruction, but one cannot advance with these missiles, even nuclear missiles of a power of 100 megatons because only people, troops, can advance, without people, any means however powerful cannot be offensive.

How can one, consequently, give such a completely incorrect interpretation as you are now giving, to the effect that some sort of means on Cuba are offensive. All the means located there, and I assure you of this, have a defensive character, are on Cuba solely for the purposes of defense, and we have sent them to Cuba at the request of the Cuban Government. You, however, say that these are offensive means.

But, Mr. President, do you really seriously think that Cuba can attack the United States and that even we together with Cuba can advance upon you from the territory of Cuba? Can you really think that way? How is it possible? We do not understand this. Has something so new appeared in military strategy that one can think that it is possible to advance thus. I say precisely advance, and not destroy, since barbarians, people who have lost their sense, destroy.

I believe that you have no basis to think this way. You can regard us with distrust, but, in any case, you can be calm in this regard, that we are of sound mind and understand perfectly well that if we attack you, you will respond the same way. But you too will receive the same that you hurl against us. And I think that you also understand this. My conversation with you in Vienna gives me the right to talk to you this way.

This indicates that we are normal people, that we correctly understand and correctly evaluate the situation. Consequently, how can we permit the incorrect actions which you ascribe to us? Only lunatics or suicides, who themselves want to perish and to destroy the whole world before they die, could do this. We, however, want to live and do not at all want to destroy your country. We want something quite different: to compete with your country on a peaceful endeavor. We quarrel with you, we have differences in ideological questions. But our view of the world consists in this, that ideological questions, as well as economic problems, should be solved not by military means, they must be solved on the basis of peaceful competition, i.e., as this is understood in capitalist society, on the basis of competition. We have proceeded and are proceeding from the fact that the peaceful co-existence of the two different social-political systems, now existing in the world, is necessary, that it is necessary to assure a stable peace. That is the sort of principle we hold.

You have now proclaimed piratical measures, which were employed in the Middle Ages, when ships proceeding in international waters were attacked, and you have called this "a quarantine" around Cuba. Our vessels, apparently, will soon enter the zone which your Navy is patrolling. I assure you that these vessels, now bound for Cuba, are carrying the most innocent peaceful cargoes. Do you really think that we only occupy ourselves with the carriage of so-called offensive weapons, atomic and hydrogen bombs? Although perhaps your military people imagine that these (cargoes) are some sort of special type of weapon, I assure you that they are the most ordinary peaceful products.

Consequently, Mr. President, let us show good sense. I assure you that on those ships, which are bound for Cuba, there are no weapons at all. The weapons which were necessary for the defense of Cuba are already there. I do not want to say that there were not any shipments of weapons at all. No, there were such shipments. But now Cuba has already received the necessary means of defense.

I don't know whether you can understand me and believe me. But I should like to have you believe in yourself and to agree that one cannot give way to passions; it is necessary to control them. And in what direction are events now developing? If you stop the vessels, then, as you yourself know, that would be piracy. If we started to do that with regard to your ships, then you would also be as indignant as we and the whole world now are. One cannot give another interpretation to such actions, because one cannot legalize lawlessness. If this were permitted, then there would be no peace, there would also be no peaceful coexistence. We should then be forced to put into effect the necessary measures of a defensive character to protect our interest in accordance with international law. Why should this be done? To what would all this lead?

Let us normalize relations. We have received an appeal from the Acting Secretary General of the UN, U Thant, with his proposals. I have already answered him. His proposals come to this, that our side should not transport armaments of any kind to Cuba during a certain period of time, while negotiations are being conducted—and we are ready to enter such negotiations—and the other side should not undertake any sort of piratical actions against vessels engaged in navigation on the high seas. I consider these proposals reasonable. This would be a way out of the situation which has been created, which would give the peoples the possibility of breathing calmly. You have asked what happened, what evoked the delivery of weapons to Cuba? You have spoken about this to our Minister of Foreign Affairs. I will tell you frankly, Mr. President, what evoked it.

We were very grieved by the fact—I spoke about it in Vienna—that a landing took place, that an attack on Cuba was committed, as a result of which many Cubans perished. You yourself told me then that this had been a mistake. I respected that explanation. . . .

Why have we proceeded to assist Cuba with military and economic aid? The answer is: we have proceeded to do so only for reasons of humanitarianism. . . .

If assurances were given by the President and the Government of the United States that the USA itself would not participate in an attack on Cuba and would restrain others from actions of this sort, if you would recall your fleet, this would immediately change everything. I am not speaking for Fidel Castro, but I think that he and the Government of Cuba, evidently, would declare demobilization and would appeal to the people to get down to peaceful labor. Then, too, the question of armaments would disappear, since, if there is no threat, then armaments are a burden for every people. Then, too, the question of the destruction, not only of the armaments which you call offensive, but of all other armaments as well, would look different.

I spoke in the name of the Soviet Government in the United Nations and introduced a proposal for the disbandment of all armies and for the destruction of all armaments. How then can I now count on those armaments?

Armaments bring only disasters. When one accumulates them, this damages the economy, and if one puts them to use, then they destroy people on both sides. Consequently, only a madman can believe that armaments are the principal means in the life of society. No, they are an enforced loss of human energy, and what is more are for the destruction of man himself. If people do not show wisdom, then in the final analysis they will come to a clash, like blind moles, and then reciprocal extermination will begin.

Let us therefore show statesmanlike wisdom. I propose: we, for our part, will declare that our ships, bound for Cuba, are not carrying any armaments. You would declare that the United States will not invade

Cuba with its forces and will not support any sort of forces which might intend to carry out an invasion of Cuba. Then the necessity for the presence of our military specialists in Cuba would disappear.

Mr. President, I appeal to you to weigh well what the aggressive, piratical actions, which you have declared the USA intends to carry out in international waters, would lead to. You yourself know that any sensible man simply cannot agree with this, cannot recognize your right to such actions. . . .

These thoughts are dictated by a sincere desire to relieve the situation, to remove the threat of war.

Respectfully yours,

/s/ N. Khrushchev

October 26, 1962. *End text*.

Original of letter being air pouched today under transmittal slip to Executive Secretariat.

Kohler

DOCUMENT NO. 16

KHRUSHCHEV'S MESSAGE TO KENNEDY, OCTOBER 27, 1962[16]

By October 27 Khrushchev had received information indicating that an American attack was not as immediate as had been assumed. At the same time, he had received hints that a possible trade of missiles in Cuba for Jupiters in Turkey might be possible. Consequently it might be possible for him to turn a defeat into a victory.

γ   γ   γ

Moscow, October 27, 1962.

DEAR MR. PRESIDENT, I have studied with great satisfaction your reply to Mr. Thant concerning measures that should be taken to avoid contact between our vessels and thereby avoid irreparable and fatal consequences. This reasonable step on your part strengthens my belief that you are showing concern for the preservation of peace, which I note with satisfaction.

I have already said that our people, our Government, and I personally, as Chairman of the Council of Ministers, are concerned solely with having our country develop and occupy a worthy place among all peoples of the world in economic competition, in the development of culture and the arts, and in raising the living standard of the people. This is the most noble and necessary field for competition, and both the victor and the vanquished will derive only benefit from it, because it means peace and an increase in the means by which man lives and finds enjoyment.

In your statement you expressed the opinion that the main aim was not simply to come to an agreement and take measures to prevent contact between our vessels and consequently a deepening of the crisis which could, as a result of such contacts, spark a military conflict, after which all negotiations would be superfluous because other forces and other laws should then come into play—the laws of war. I agree with you that this is only the first step. The main thing that must be done is

[16] Department of State, *Foreign Relations of the United States 1961–1963*. Volume XI *Cuban Missile Crisis and Aftermath* (Washington, D.C., 1966) pp. 257–260.

to normalize and stabilize the state of peace among states and among peoples.

I understand your concern for the security of the United States, Mr. President, because this is the primary duty of a President. But we too are disturbed about these same questions; I bear these same obligations as Chairman of the Council of Ministers of the U.S.S.R. You have been alarmed by the fact that we have aided Cuba with weapons, in order to strengthen its defense capability—precisely defense capability—because whatever weapons it may possess, Cuba cannot be equated with you since the difference in magnitude is so great, particularly in view of modern means of destruction. Our aim has been and is to help Cuba, and no one can dispute the humanity of our motives, which are oriented toward enabling Cuba to live peacefully and develop in the way its people desire.

You wish to ensure the security of your country, and this is understandable. But Cuba, too, wants the same thing; all countries want to maintain their security. But how are we, the Soviet Union, our Government, to assess your actions which are expressed in the fact that you have surrounded the Soviet Union with military bases; surrounded our allies with military bases; placed military bases literally around our country; and stationed your missile armaments there? This is no secret. Responsible American personages openly declare that it is so. Your missiles are located in Britain, are located in Italy, and are aimed against us. Your missiles are located in Turkey.

You are disturbed over Cuba. You say that this disturbs you because it is 90 miles by sea from the coast of the United States of America. But Turkey adjoins us; our sentries patrol back and forth and see each other. Do you consider, then, that you have the right to demand security for your own country and the removal of the weapons you call offensive, but do not accord the same right to us? You have placed destructive missile weapons, which you call offensive, in Turkey, literally next to us. How then can recognition of our equal military capacities be reconciled with such unequal relations between our great states? This is irreconcilable.

It is good, Mr. President, that you have agreed to have our representatives meet and begin talks, apparently through the mediation of U Thant, Acting Secretary General of the United Nations. Consequently, he to some degree has assumed the role of a mediator and we consider that he will be able to cope with this responsible mission, provided, of course, that each party drawn into this controversy displays good will.

I think it would be possible to end the controversy quickly and normalize the situation, and then the people could breathe more easily, considering that statesmen charged with responsibility are of sober mind and have an awareness of their responsibility combined with the ability to solve complex questions and not bring things to a military catastrophe.

I therefore make this proposal: We are willing to remove from Cuba the means which you regard as offensive. We are willing to carry this out and to make this pledge in the United Nations. Your representatives will make a declaration to the effect that the United States, for its part, considering the uneasiness and anxiety of the Soviet State, will remove its analogous means from Turkey. Let us reach agreement as to the period of time needed by you and by us to bring this about. And, after that, persons entrusted by the United Nations Security Council could inspect on the spot the fulfillment of the pledges made. Of course, the permission of the Governments of Cuba and of Turkey is necessary for the entry into those countries of these representatives and for the inspection of the fulfillment of the pledge made by each side. Of course it would be best if these representatives enjoyed the confidence of the Security Council, as well as yours and mine—both the United States and the Soviet Union—and also that of Turkey and Cuba. I do not think it would be difficult to select people who would enjoy the trust and respect of all parties concerned.

We, in making this pledge, in order to give satisfaction and hope of the peoples of Cuba and Turkey and to strengthen their confidence in their security, will make a statement within the framework of the Security Council to the effect that the Soviet Government gives a solemn promise to respect the inviolability of the borders and sovereignty of Turkey, not to interfere in its internal affairs, not to invade Turkey, not to make available our territory as a bridgehead for such an invasion, and that it would also restrain those who contemplate committing aggression against Turkey, either from the territory of the Soviet Union or from the territory of Turkey's other neighboring states.

The United States Government will make a similar statement within the framework of the Security Council regarding Cuba. It will declare that the United States will respect the inviolability of Cuba's borders and its sovereignty, will pledge not to interfere in its internal affairs, not to invade Cuba itself or make its territory available as a bridgehead for such an invasion, and will also restrain those who might contemplate committing aggression against Cuba, either from the territory of the United States or from the territory of Cuba's other neighboring states.

Of course, for this we would have to come to an agreement with you and specify a certain time limit. Let us agree to some period of time, but without unnecessary delay—say within two or three weeks, not longer than a month.

The means situated in Cuba, of which you speak and which disturb you, as you have stated, are in the hands of Soviet officers. Therefore, any accidental use of them to the detriment of the United States is excluded. These means are situated in Cuba at the request of the Cuban Government and are only for defense purposes. Therefore, if there is no invasion of Cuba, or attack on the Soviet Union or any of our other allies, then of course these means are not and will not be a threat to anyone. For they are not for purposes of attack.

If you are agreeable to my proposal, Mr. President, then we would send our representatives to New York, to the United Nations, and would give them comprehensive instructions in order that an agreement may be reached more quickly. If you also select your people and give them the corresponding instructions, then this question can be quickly resolved.

Why would I like to do this? Because the whole world is now apprehensive and expects sensible actions of us. The greatest joy for all peoples would be the announcement of our agreement and of the eradication of the controversy that has arisen. I attach great importance to this agreement in so far as it could serve as a good beginning and could in particular make it easier to reach agreement on banning nuclear weapons tests. The question of the tests could be solved in parallel fashion, without connecting one with the other, because these are different issues. However, it is important that agreement be reached on both these issues so as to present humanity with a fine gift, and also to gladden it with the news that agreement has been reached on the cessation of nuclear tests and that consequently the atmosphere will no longer be poisoned. Our position and yours on this issue are very close together.

All of this could possibly serve as a good impetus toward the finding of mutually acceptable agreements on other controversial issues on which you and I have been exchanging views. These views have so far not been resolved, but they are awaiting urgent solution, which would clear up the international atmosphere. We are prepared for this.

These are my proposals, Mr. President.

Respectfully yours,

N. Khrushchev

DOCUMENT NO. 17

THE EXCOMM MEETING,
OCTOBER 27, 1962[17]

Saturday, October 27, 1962 was the worst day of the Cuban missile crisis for President Kennedy and the ExComm. A message from Khrushchev seemed to contradict his October 26 message, a U-2 plane was shot down, the pilot killed and another plane wandered into Siberian air space—all combined to make it indeed a "Black Saturday."

γ   γ   γ

President Kennedy: [apparently reading from a news ticker] "A special message appeared to call for negotiations, and both nations, Cuba and Turkey, should give their consent to the United Nations to visit their territories. Mr. Khrushchev said that, in the Security Council, the Soviet Union would solemnly pledge not to use its territory as a bridgehead for an attack on Turkey, called for a similar pledge from the United States not to let its territory be used as a bridgehead for an attack on Cuba. A broadcast shortly after said it was out of the question for the U.S. to abandon its Turkish military bases . . . "

Now, we've known this was coming for a week. We can't. It's going to be hung up here now.

Unidentified: We might just request negotiations.

Unidentified: We've done it.

Unidentified: No, we have not.

Rusk: We haven't talked with the Turks. The Turks have talked with us—in NATO.

President Kennedy: Well, have we gone to the Turkish government before this came out this week? I've talked about it now for a week. Have we had any conversations in Turkey, with the Turks?

Rusk: We've asked Finletter and Hare to give us their judgments on it. We've not actually talked with the Turks.

Ball: We did it on a basis where, if we talked to the Turks, I mean, this would be an extremely unsettling business.

[17] Reprinted by permission of the publisher from *The Kennedy Tapes* by Ernest R. May and Philip D. Zelikow, Cambridge, MA: Harvard University Press, Copyright © 1997 by the President and Fellows of Harvard College, pp. 498–501, 510–513, 570–576.

President Kennedy: Well, *this* is unsettling *now*, George, because he's got us in a pretty good spot here. Because most people would regard this as not an unreasonable proposal. I'll just tell you that. In fact, in many ways—

Bundy: But what *most* people, Mr. President?

President Kennedy: I think you're going to find it very difficult to explain why we are going to take hostile military action in Cuba, against these sites, what we've been thinking about. [I'm] saying that he's saying: "If you'll get yours out of Turkey, we'll get ours out of Cuba." I think we've got a very touchy point here.

Bundy: I don't see why we pick that track when he's offered us the other track within the last 24 hours. You think the public one is serious?

President Kennedy: I think you have to assume that this is their new and latest position, and it's a public one.

Rusk: What would you think of releasing the letter of yesterday?

Bundy: I think it has a good deal of virtue.

President Kennedy: Yeah, but I think we have to be now thinking about what our position is going to be on *this* one, because this is the one that's before us, and before the world.

Sorensen: As between the two, I think it's clear that practically everyone here would favor the private proposal.

Rusk: We're not being offered a choice. We *may* not be offered the (a) choice [referring to the private proposal].

President Kennedy: But seriously, there are disadvantages also to the private one, which is this guarantee of Cuba.

But in any case, this is now his official one. And we can release his other one, and it's different, but this is the one that the Soviet government obviously is going on.

Nitze: Isn't it possible that they're going on a dual track, one a public track and the other a private track? The private track is related to the Soviets and Cuba, and the public track is one that's in order to confuse the public scene with additional pressures.

President Kennedy: It's possible.

Thompson: I think, personally, that statement is one that the Soviets take seriously.

Rusk: Well, I think, yes. I think that the NATO-Warsaw Pact arms problem is a separate problem, and that ought to be discussed between NATO and the Warsaw Pact. They've got hundreds of missiles looking down the throat of every NATO country. And [long pause] I think this is—we have to get it into *that context*. The Cuba thing is a Western Hemisphere problem, an intrusion into the Western Hemisphere.

[Unclear group discussion.]

Nitze: I think we ought to stand as much as we can on a separate basis.

Unidentified: Absolutely.

Nitze: Fight the Turkish one with the best arguments we can. I'd handle this thing so that we continue on the real track, which is to try to get the missiles out of Cuba pursuant to the private negotiation.

Bundy: The other way, it seems to me, is, if we accept the notion of a trade at this stage, our position will come apart very fast.

We are in a very difficult position. It isn't as if we'd got the missiles out, Mr. President. It would be different. Or if we had any understanding with the Turks that they ought to come out, it would be different. Neither of these is the case.

President Kennedy: Well, I'd like to know how much we've done about it and how much did we talk about it.

Bundy: We decided *not* to, Mr. President. We decided *not* to play it directly with the Turks.

Rusk: —our own representatives to their—

Ball: If we talked to the Turks, they would bring it up in NATO. This thing will be all over Western Europe, and our position would have been undermined.

Bundy: That's right.

Ball: Because immediately the Soviet Union would know that this thing was being discussed. The Turks feel very strongly about this. We persuaded them that this *was* an essential requirement, and they feel that it's a matter of prestige and a matter of real [unclear].

Bundy: In our own terms it would already be clear that we were trying to sell our allies for our interests. That would be the view in all of NATO. Now, it's irrational and it's crazy, but it's a *terribly* powerful fact.

Thompson: Particularly in the case that this is a message to you and U Thant. It seems to me we ought to get word to Stevenson that, if this is put up up there, he should immediately say we will not discuss the Turkish bases.

Bundy: The problem is Cuba. The Turks are not a threat to the peace. Nobody smells the Turks as—

President Kennedy: I think it would be better, rather than saying that, until we've got time to think about it . . . Than saying: "Well, the fact of the matter is that we received a letter last night from Khrushchev, and it's an entirely different proposal." So, therefore, we first ought to get clarification from the Soviet Union of what they're talking, at least give us . . . As I say, you're going to find a lot of people think this is a rather reasonable position.

Unidentified: That's true.

President Kennedy: Besides, literally, in regard to the guarantee not to intervene in Turkey, we must do the same in Cuba. This means our agreement. It leaves the steering in the hands . . . Well, we know what the problem is here.

Rusk: Well, I think that it's relevant here to be able to say that we supported the declaration of Iran that they would not accept foreign missiles in Iran. The Turkish problem is a NATO-Warsaw Pact problem. And it's an arms problem between these two groups that is something for these two groups to talk about with *each other* as a problem of disarmament with respect to NATO and Warsaw Pact.

Dillon: Well, there's also this thing of upsetting the status quo, and we did not upset it in Iran [unclear].

President Kennedy: He's put this out in a way to cause maximum tension and embarrassment. It's not as if it was a private proposal, which would give us an opportunity to negotiate with the Turks. He has put it out in a way that the Turks are bound to say that they don't agree to this. And therefore—

Dillon: There's another military thing to it. It may be preparations for counteraction against those particular bases once we leave Cuba again. Could be that.

[Unclear discussion.]

President Kennedy: Until we have gotten our position a little clearer, we ought to go with this last night's business, so that that gives us about an hour or two—we don't have Khrushchev. . . .

Robert Kennedy: I'd like to have a consideration of my thought about saying that he—I haven't refined this at all—but that he's offered this arrangement in Cuba—that he will withdraw the bases in Cuba for assurances that we don't intend to invade Cuba. We've always given those assurances. We'd be glad to give them again. That, in his letter to me, he said that he would permit inspection. Obviously that entails inspection not only of Cuba but entails inspection of the United States to ensure that we're not—by United Nations observers—to ensure that we're not getting ready to invade. Now, this is one of the things for U Thant.

The bases in Cuba involve the security of the Western Hemisphere. This is not just a question of the United States. This is a question of all Latin American countries. All have joined together in this effort. Time is running out on us. This must be brought to fruition. The question of the Turkish bases—which is excellent that you brought that up—in that there should be disarmament of the Turkish bases. But that has nothing to do with the security of the Western Hemisphere. It does have to do with the security of Turkey, and we would be happy to assure the Turks that we are making a similar arrangement in Turkey. We will withdraw the bases from Turkey if—and allow inspection of Turkey to make sure that we've done that. And you withdraw your invasion bases of the Soviet Union and permit inspection there.

Bundy: I think it's too complicated, Bobby.

Robert Kennedy: [sharply] Well, I don't think it is.

President Kennedy: It seems to me the first thing we ought to try to do is not let the Turks issue some statement that this is totally unacceptable, so that before we've even had a chance to get our own diplomacy clear . . . .

President Kennedy: Well now, what we have to do first is get, I would think, very quickly to get a chance to think a little more about it.

But what we ought to say is that we have had several publicly and privately different proposals, or differing proposals from the Soviet Union. They are all about complicated matters. They all require some discussion to get their true meaning. We cannot permit ourselves to be impaled on a long negotiating hook while the work goes on on these bases. I therefore suggest that the United Nations immediately, with the cooperation of the Soviet Union, take steps to provide for cessation of the work, and then we can talk about all these matters, which are very complicated.

Bundy: I think it will be very important to say at least that the current threat to peace is not in Turkey; it is in Cuba. There's no pain in saying that, even if you're going to make a trade later on.

I think also that we ought to say that we have an immediate threat. What is going on in Cuba: that is what has got to stop. Then I think we *should* say that the public Soviet, the broadcast, message is at variance with other proposals which have been put forward within the last 12 hours. We could surface those for background.

President Kennedy: That being so, until we find out what is really being suggested and what can really be discussed, we have to get something in words. Maybe we can see if the work's going on.

Bundy: That's right.

President Kennedy: There isn't any doubt. Let's not kid ourselves. They've got a very good proposal, which is the reason they made it public—

Bundy: What's going on, while you were out of the room, Mr. President, we reached an informal consensus that—I don't know whether Tommy agrees—that this last night's message was Khrushchev's. And this one is his own hard nosed people overruling him, this public one. They didn't like what he said to you last night. Nor would I, if I were a Soviet hard-nose.

Thompson: I think the view is, the Kreisky speech, they may have thought this was our underground way of suggesting this, and they felt that—

Unidentified: Who said this?

President Kennedy: The only thing is, Tommy, why wouldn't they say it privately if they were serious? The fact that they gave it to me publicly, I think they know the kind of complexities . . .

Unidentified: Well, they're building up pressure.

Bundy: And it's a way of pinning themselves down.

President Kennedy: Now, let's . . . I would think the first thing we have to do is, as I say, rather than getting to the details, the fact that work is going on is one defensible public position we've got.

They've got a very good product. This one is going to be very tough, I think, for us. It's going to be tough in England, I'm sure, as well as other places on the continent. If we are forced to take action, this will be, in my opinion, not a blank check, but a pretty good check [for the Soviets] to take action in Berlin on the grounds that we are only unreasonable, emotional people. That this is a reasonable trade, and we ought to take advantage of it. Therefore, it makes it much more difficult for us to move [against Cuba] with world support. These are all the things that—why this is a pretty good play of his.

That being so, I think that the only thing we've got him on is the fact that, while they put forward various proposals in short periods of time, all of which are complicated, under that shield this work goes on. Until we can get somewhat of an agreement on the cessation of work, how can we possibly negotiate [with proposals] coming as fast as the waters [run]?. . . .

[Later in the afternoon.]

Robert Kennedy: A U-2 was shot down?

McNamara: Yes. [Unclear name] said it got shot down.

Robert Kennedy: Was the pilot killed?

Taylor: It was shot down near Banes, which is right near a SAM-2 site in eastern Cuba.

Unidentified: A SAM site.

Taylor: . . . saying that the pilot's body is in the plane. Apparently, this was a SAM site that had actually had the Fruitcake radar. It all ties in in a very plausible way.

President Kennedy: Well now, this is much of an escalation by them, isn't it?

McNamara: Yes, exactly. And this—this relates to the timing.

I think we can defer an air attack on Cuba until Wednesday [October 31], or Thursday [November 1] but only if we continue our surveillance, and fire against anything that fires against a surveillance aircraft, and only if we maintain a tight blockade in this interim period. If we're willing to do those two things, I think we can defer the air attack until Wednesday or Thursday and take time to go to NATO.

President Kennedy: How do we explain the effect of this Khrushchev message of last night? And their decision [to shoot down U.S. planes], in view of their previous orders [to fire only if attacked], the change of orders? We've both had flak and a SAM site operation. How do we . . .? I mean, that's a . . .

McNamara: How do we interpret this? I don't know how to interpret it.

Taylor: They [the Soviets] feel they must respond now. The whole world knows where we're flying.

That raises the question of retaliation against the SAM sites. We think we—we have various other reasons to believe that we know the SAM sites [that shot down the U-2]. Two days ago—

President Kennedy: How can we send a U-2 fellow over there tomorrow unless we take out all the SAM sites?

Unidentified: This is exactly the effect.

Unidentified: I don't think we can.

[Unclear group discussion.]

Unidentified: It's on the ground?

Taylor: It's on the ground The wreckage is on the ground and the pilot's dead.

McNamara: It's in the water, isn't it?

Taylor: I didn't get the water part.

Bundy: If we know it, it must be either on friendly land or in the water.

Unidentified: It is on Cuban land at this point.

Taylor: That's what I've got.

McCone: I wonder if this shouldn't cause a most violent protest. Write a letter right to Khrushchev. Here's, here's an action they've taken against—against us, a new order in defiance of public statements he made. I think—

Unidentified: They've fired the first shot.

McCone: If there's any continuation of this, we've got to take those SAM sites out of there.

Unidentified: We should retaliate against the SAM site, and announce that if any other planes are fired on we will come back and take it. . . .

Gilpatric: Earlier today, Mr. President, we said: "Any interference with such surveillance will meet counteraction and surveillance will be continued."

President Kennedy: Do we want to announce we're going to take counteraction, or just take it tomorrow morning?

Unidentified: Take it.

President Kennedy: The U-2 was shot down?

Gilpatric: No, no. This is a general statement that we would enforce surveillance.

President Kennedy: Well now, do we want to just announce that an American plane was shot down—a surveillance plane was shot down in Cuba? It seems to me that's been—

Unidentified: I would announce it after you've taken further action.

Unidentified: I understand, sir, that Havana has announced it. That's how we . . .

President Kennedy: Well, I think that we ought to announce it because it shows off Khrushchev's protestations about Cuba.

Unidentified: Came from over there?

Unidentified: This about the pilot is from Havana.

Unidentified: Oh, that's Havana!

President Kennedy: We haven't confirmed that, have we. There are so goddamn many . . . We could stay here all day.

Well now, let's say if we're sure the U-2 has been shot down, it seems to me we've got to announce it, or it's going to dribble out. Havana's announced it anyway. We ought to announce it.

Unidentified: We don't know that yet.

President Kennedy: Then we ought to not say anything, don't you think? And just take the reprisal without making any announcement?

We don't want to announce that we're going to take a reprisal against that SAM site tomorrow, or would that make our reprisal more difficult?

McNamara: It would certainly make it more difficult.

President Kennedy: I think we ought to announce that action is being taken—action will be taken to protect our various aircraft.

McNamara: Exactly. Then we ought to go in at dawn and take out that SAM site. And we ought to send a surveillance aircraft in tomorrow with the regular flights early in the morning, and we ought to be prepared to take out more SAM sites and knock out the—

President Kennedy: Well, what we want to do, then, is get this announcement written.

Ros, why don't you write this out, plus this thing about what we're going to do. Then we'll get back to what we're going to do about the Turks.

[Overlapping voices.]

McNamara: Well, I think he was shot coming in.

Unidentified: But he came in.

Rusk: There's a map I have showed him the other way around.

Unidentified: Now, he was to go up here.

Well, can we take that SAM site out?

Unidentified: Here's the chart that was just handed us. It shows he was on his way out. Because that's the Banes site.

Robert Kennedy: In addition, there was one other shooting at the low level, wasn't there?

Unidentified: Yes.

Unidentified: Where was that, Bob, do you know?

McNamara: I haven't the detail.

Unidentified: Near [unclear name]?

Unidentified: Possibly.

Taylor: They started the shooting.

President Kennedy: Well now, we're going to get out an announcement about the earlier thing, and we're going to say that . . .

McNamara: We're going to say that it was shot down, and we're going to continue our surveillance protected by U.S. fighter aircraft.

Dillon: Suitable protection.

Unidentified: The assumption is—

McNamara: Well, I'd just say "U.S. fighter aircraft" so you don't leave any doubt about it.

Robert Kennedy: Tomorrow morning, add POL [to the quarantine]?

McNamara: I wouldn't do it tonight, Bobby. I'd just announce this one.

I think tomorrow morning we ought to go in and take out that SAM site, and send our surveillance in with proper protection immediately following it or on top of it, or whatever way the—

Taylor: [3 seconds excised as classified information, possibly because the information came from intercepted Cuban communications.] The plane is on the ground. It is not in the water.

Unidentified: In Cuba?

Robert Kennedy: In Cuba. Well, we don't—we have no—

Unidentified: Well, let's put it out. Otherwise, they will put it out.

Unidentified: We don't know.

President Kennedy: It's overdue anyway, isn't it? So we can assume.

Taylor: Quite. Hours overdue.

President Kennedy: Do we want to say it was shot down? We don't know. Do they say it's been shot down, the Cubans?

Well, why doesn't Ros, and you, General, get a statement which would cover in any case. It may be we don't know it was shot down.

Unidentified: We don't know it.

McNamara: I think—certainly I'd say—it was shot down. Because the probabilities are that it was shot down, and we want an excuse to go in tomorrow and shoot up that SAM site and send in our—

Dillon: If the plane's on the ground there, it was shot down. It didn't just come down and land.

Unidentified: Well, there might have been mechanical failure problems.

President Kennedy: The only point is—the only thing that troubles us—is the other plane was shot at.

McNamara: That's right. Exactly.

President Kennedy: They say—that's why I'd like to find out whether Havana says they did shoot it down.

Unidentified: We don't have anything from Havana yet, do we?

Unidentified: We assume these SAM sites are manned by Soviets.

Unidentified: Yes.

Unidentified: That's the significant part, if it is the SAM site.

Unidentified: You might have Cubans—

Unidentified: No, but they'd be inoperative.

McNamara: You had antiaircraft. This is a change of pattern. Now, why it's a change of pattern, we don't know.

Robert Kennedy: Yeah.

Unidentified: I think the important thing to find out is, if we possibly can, whether it is a SAM site.

McNamara: There's no way to find out. What we know is that that particular SAM is the one that had the Fruitcake radar, which is required for control of the missiles.

Unidentified: Will we know whether it's in operation today?

McNamara: It was in operation, we believe, at the same time that the U-2 was over. We checked it this morning. We checked it.

Alexis Johnson: It's a very different thing. You could have an undisciplined antiaircraft, Cuban antiaircraft outfit, fire. But to have a SAM site, with a Russian crew, fire is not any accident.

Unidentified: Well, if he had been at altitude and had any type of a failure, he could fly to Puerto Rico or Mexico.

Unidentified: He could have had an engine failure of some type that was—

Dillon: But even then he could fly out.

Unidentified: I mean that destroyed him.

Unidentified: But if he blew up they're not going to be recovering his box from the aircraft, not likely.

[Unclear discussion; much clatter; possible sound of song—a cleaning crew?]

President Kennedy: What we got to do is—let's just see if we can get this. Announce the plane that from a base in Cuba was fired upon.

Let's see if . . . George, come up and sit here now. Let's talk a little more about the Turks, how we're going to handle that. NATO and the Turks, that's the one matter we haven't settled today.

Dillon: I am very much concerned that this Castro announcement was late. The reason eludes me.

President Kennedy: I think we ought to . . . Why don't we send an instruction to Hare to have a conversation [with the Turks], but also have the NATO meeting? And to explain to them what's happening over here? Otherwise, we're going to be carrying a hell of a bag.

Dillon? I think you're going to have great pressure internally within the United States, too, to act quickly, with our planes always being shot down while we sit around here.

President Kennedy: Therefore, we've got to move. That's why I think we'd better have a NATO meeting tomorrow. . . .

DOCUMENT NO. 18

A MESSAGE FROM KENNEDY TO KHRUSHCHEV, OCTOBER 27, 1962[18]

Messages from Khrushchev on October 26 and 27 confused the president and the ExComm. Was there a hidden meaning behind the messages? In the first message, Khrushchev proposed to withdraw the missiles from Cuba in return for a pledge by Kennedy not to invade Cuba. In the second message, Khrushchev asked that the president take the Jupiters out of Turkey and promise not to invade Cuba. Khrushchev would remove the missiles from Cuba and pledge not to attack Turkey. Finally, the president and his advisers chose to ignore the second message and answer Khrushchev's first message.

γ γ γ

Washington, October 27, 1962, 8:05 p.m.

1015. Following message from President to Khrushchev should be delivered as soon as possible to highest available Soviet official. Text has been handed Soviet Embassy in Washington and has been released to press:

"Dear Mr. Chairman:
I have read your letter of October 26 with great care and welcomed the statement of your desire to seek a prompt solution to the problem. The first thing that needs to be done, however, is for work to cease on offensive missile bases in Cuba and for all weapons systems in Cuba capable of offensive use to be rendered inoperable, under effective United Nations arrangements.

Assuming this is done promptly, I have given my representatives in New York instructions that will permit them to work out this week and—in cooperation with the Acting Secretary General and your representative—an arrangement for a permanent solution to the Cuban problem along the lines suggested in your letter of October 26. As I read your letter, the key elements of your proposals—which seem generally acceptable as I understand them—are as follows:

[18] Department of State, *Foreign Relations of the United States 1961–1963* Volume XI *Cuban Missile Crisis and the Aftermath* (Washington, D.C., 1996), pp. 268–269.

1. You would agree to remove these weapons systems from Cuba under appropriate United Nations observation and supervision; and undertake, with suitable safeguards, to halt the further introduction of such weapons systems in Cuba.

2. We, on our part, would agree—upon the establishment of adequate arrangements through the United Nations to ensure the carrying out and continuation of these commitments—(a) to remove promptly the quarantine measures now in effect and (b) to give assurances against an invasion of Cuba and I am confident that other nations of the Western Hemisphere would be prepared to do likewise.

If you will give your representative similar instructions, there is no reason why we should not be able to complete these arrangements and announce them to the world within a couple of days. The effect of such a settlement on easing world tensions would enable us to work toward a more general arrangement regarding "other armaments", as proposed in your second letter which you made public. I would like to say again that the United States is very much interested in reducing tensions and halting the arms race; and if your letter signifies that you are prepared to discuss a détente affecting NATO and the Warsaw Pact, we are quite prepared to consider with our allies any useful proposals.

But the first ingredient, let me emphasize, is the cessation of work on missile sites in Cuba and measures to render such weapons inoperable, under effective international guarantees. The continuation of this threat, or a prolonging of this discussion concerning Cuba by linking these problems to the broader questions of European and world security, would surely lead to an intensification of the Cuban crisis and a grave risk to the peace of the world. For this reason I hope we can quickly agree along the lines outlined in this letter and in your letter of October 26.

/s/ John F. Kennedy"

Rusk

DOCUMENT NO. 19

MEMORANDUM FROM ROBERT KENNEDY TO DEAN RUSK, OCTOBER 30, 1962[19]

In order to impress on the Soviet government of the necessity for a speedy decision, President Kennedy sent his brother Robert to meet with Anatoly Dobrynin, the Soviet ambassador, in the evening of October 27. He instructed the attorney general to convey to the ambassador the need for a quick decision because work was continuing on the missile sites in Cuba and a U-2 flying over the island had been shot down and the pilot killed. This is Robert Kennedy's account of this important meeting.

γ   γ   γ

Washington, October 30, 1962.

At the request of Secretary Rusk, I telephoned Ambassador Dobrynin at approximately 7:15 p.m. on Saturday, October 27th. I asked him if he would come to the Justice Department at a quarter of eight.

We met in my office. I told him first that we understood that the work was continuing on the Soviet missile bases in Cuba. Further, I explained to him that in the last two hours we had found that our planes flying over Cuba had been fired upon and that one of our U-2's had been shot down and the pilot killed. I said these men were flying unarmed planes.

I told him that this was an extremely serious turn in events. We would have to make certain decisions within the next 12 or possibly 24 hours. There was a very little time left. If the Cubans were shooting at our planes, then we were going to shoot back. This could not help but bring on further incidents and that he had better understand the full implications of this matter.

He raised the point that the argument the Cubans were making was that we were violating Cuban air space. I replied that if we had not been violating Cuban air space then we would still be believing what he and Khrushchev had said—that there were no long-range missiles in Cuba. In any case I said that this matter was far more serious than the air space over Cuba and involved peoples all over the world.

[19] Department of State, *Foreign Relations of the United States. 1961–1963* Volume XI *Cuban Missile Crisis and Aftermath* (Washington, D.C., 1996) pp. 270–271.

I said that he had better understand the situation and he had better communicate that understanding to Mr. Khrushchev. Mr. Khrushchev and he had misled us. The Soviet Union had secretly established missile bases in Cuba while at the same time proclaiming, privately and publicly, that this would never be done. I said those missile bases had to go and they had to go right away. We had to have a commitment by at least tomorrow that those bases would be removed. This was not an ultimatum, I said, but just a statement of fact. He should understand that if they did not remove those bases then we would remove them. His country might take retaliatory action but he should understand that before this was over, while there might be dead Americans there would also be dead Russians.

He asked me then what offer we were making. I said a letter had just been transmitted to the Soviet Embassy which stated in substance that the missile bases should be dismantled and all offensive weapons should be removed from Cuba. In return, if Cuba and Castro and the Communists ended their subversive activities in other Central and Latin American countries, we would agree to keep peace in the Caribbean and not permit an invasion from American soil.

He then asked me about Khrushchev's other proposal dealing with the removal of the missiles from Turkey. I replied that there could be no quid pro quo—no deal of this kind could be made. This was a matter that had to be considered by NATO and that it was up to NATO to make the decision. I said it was completely impossible for NATO to take such a step under the present threatening position of the Soviet Union.[1]

Per your instructions I repeated that there could be no deal of any kind and that any steps toward easing tensions in other parts of the world largely depended on the Soviet Union and Mr. Khrushchev taking action in Cuba and taking it immediately.

I repeated to him that this matter could not wait and that he had better contact Mr. Khrushchev and have a commitment from him by the next day to withdraw the missile bases under United Nations supervision for otherwise, I said, there would be drastic consequences.

---

[1] The following typed sentence at the end of this paragraph was crossed out: "If some time elapsed—and per your instructions, I mentioned four or five months—I said I was sure that these matters could be resolved satisfactory."

DOCUMENT NO. 20

AMBASSADOR DOBRYNIN'S TELEGRAM TO THE SOVIET FOREIGN MINISTRY, OCTOBER 27, 1962[20]

According to Ambassador Dobrynin's account of his meeting with Robert Kennedy on the night of October 27, the president's brother warned that the situation would only worsen. The president was under pressure to respond with gunfire if United States planes were fired upon again. American generals were itching for a fight. The situation was getting out of control.

γ   γ   γ

Late tonight R. Kennedy invited me to come see him. We talked alone.

The Cuban crisis, R. Kennedy began, continues to quickly worsen. We have just received a report that an unarmed American plane was shot down while carrying out a reconnaissance flight over Cuba. The military is demanding that the President arm such planes and respond to fire with fire. The USA government will have to do this.

I interrupted R. Kennedy and asked him, what right American planes had to fly over Cuba at all, crudely violating its sovereignty and accepted international norms? How would the USA have reacted if foreign planes appeared over its territory?

"We have a resolution of the Organization of American states that gives us the right to such overflights." R. Kennedy quickly replied.

I told him that the Soviet Union, like all peace loving countries, resolutely rejects such a "right" or, to be more exact, this kind of true lawlessness, when people who don't like the social-political situation in a country try to impose their will on it—a small state where the people themselves established and maintained [their system]. "The OAS resolution is a direct violation of the UN Charter," I added, "and you, as the Attorney General of the USA, the highest American legal entity, should certainly know that."

R. Kennedy said that he realized that we had different approaches to these problems and it was not likely that we could convince each other.

---

[20] *Cold War International History Project Bulletin* No. 5 (1995), pp. 79–80.

But now the matter is not in these differences, since time is of the essence. "I want," R. Kennedy stressed, "to lay out the current alarming situation the way the president sees it. He wants N.S. Khrushchev to know this. This is the thrust of the situation now."

"Because of the plane that was shot down, there is now strong pressure on the president to give an order to respond with fire if fired upon when American reconnaissance planes are flying over Cuba. The USA can't stop these flights, because this is the only way we can quickly get information about the state of construction of the missile bases in Cuba, which we believe pose a very serious threat to our national security. But if we start to fire in response—a chain reaction will quickly start that will be very hard to stop. The same thing in regard to the essence of the issue of the missile bases in Cuba. The USA government is determined to get rid of those bases—up to, in the extreme case, of bombing them, since, I repeat, they pose a great threat to the security of the USA. But in response to the bombing of these bases, in the course of which Soviet specialists might suffer, the Soviet government will undoubtedly respond with the same against us, somewhere in Europe. A real war will begin, in which millions of Americans and Russians will die. We want to avoid that any way we can. I'm sure that the government of the USSR has the same wish. However, taking time to find a way out [of the situation] is very risky (here R. Kennedy mentioned as if in passing that there are many unreasonable heads among the generals, and not only among the generals, who are 'itching for a fight'). The situation might get out of control, with irreversible consequences."

"In this regard," R. Kennedy said, "the president considers that a suitable basis for regulating the entire Cuban conflict might be the letter N.S. Khrushchev sent on October 26 and the letter in response from the President, which was sent off today to N.S. Khrushchev through the US Embassy in Moscow. The most important thing for us," R. Kennedy stressed, "is to get as soon as possible the agreement of the Soviet government to halt further work on the construction of the missile bases in Cuba and take measures under international control that would make it impossible to use these weapons. In exchange the government of the USA is ready, in addition to repealing all measures on the "quarantine," to give the assurances that there will not be any invasion of Cuba and that other countries of the Western Hemisphere are ready to give the same assurances—the US government is certain of this."

"And what about Turkey?" I asked R. Kennedy.

"If that is the only obstacle to achieving the regulation I mentioned earlier, then the president doesn't see any unsurmountable difficulties in resolving this issue," replied R. Kennedy. "The greatest difficulty for the president is the public discussion of the issue of Turkey. Formally the deployment of missile bases in Turkey was done by a special decision of the NATO Council. To announce now a unilateral decision by the president of the USA to withdraw missile bases from Turkey—this would damage the entire structure of NATO and the US position as the leader of NATO, where, as the Soviet government knows very well, there are many arguments. In short, if such a decision were announced now it would seriously tear apart NATO."

"However, President Kennedy is ready to come to agree on that question with N.S. Khrushchev, too. I think that in order to withdraw these bases from Turkey," R. Kennedy said, "we need 4–5 months. This is the minimal amount of time necessary for the US government to do this, taking into account the procedures that exist within the NATO framework. On the whole Turkey issue," R. Kennedy added, "if Premier N.S. Khrushchev agrees with what I've said, we can continue to exchange opinions between him and the president, using him, R. Kennedy and the Soviet ambassador. However, the president can't say anything public in this regard about Turkey," R. Kennedy said again. R. Kennedy then warned that his comments about Turkey are extremely confidential: besides him and his brother, only 2–3 people know about it in Washington.

"That's all that he asked me to pass on to N.S. Khrushchev," R. Kennedy said in conclusion. "The president also asked N.S. Khrushchev to give him an answer (through the Soviet ambassador and R. Kennedy) if possible within the next day (Sunday) on these thoughts in order to have a business-like, clear answer in principle. [He asked him] not to get into a wordy discussion, which might drag things out. The current serious situation, unfortunately, is such that there is very little time to resolve this whole issue. Unfortunately, events are developing too quickly. The request for a reply tomorrow," stressed R. Kennedy, "is just that—a request, and not an ultimatum. The president hopes that the head of the Soviet government will understand him correctly."

I noted that it went without saying that the Soviet government would not accept any ultimatums and it was good that the American government realized that. I also reminded him of N.S. Khrushchev's appeal in his last letter to the president to demonstrate state wisdom in resolving this question. Then I told R. Kennedy that the president's thoughts would be brought to the attention of the head of the Soviet government. I also said that I would contact him as soon as there was a reply. In this regard, R. Kennedy gave me a number of a direct telephone line to the White House.

In the course of the conversation, R. Kennedy noted that he knew about the conversation that television commentator Scali had yesterday with an Embassy adviser on possible ways to regulate the Cuban conflict [one-and-a-half lines whited out].

I should say that during our meeting R. Kennedy was very upset: in any case, I've never seen him like this before. True, about twice he tried to return to the topic of "deception," (that he talked about so persistently during our previous meeting), but he did so in passing and without any edge to it. He didn't even try to get into fights on various subjects, as he usually does, and only persistently returned to one topic: time is of the essence and we shouldn't miss the chance.

After meeting with me he immediately went to see the president, with whom, as R. Kennedy said, he spends almost all his time now.

27/X-62   A. DOBRYNIN

DOCUMENT NO. 21

KHRUSHCHEV'S LETTER TO PRESIDENT KENNEDY, OCTOBER 28, 1962[21]

Khrushchev replied quickly, agreeing to withdraw the missiles in return for a pledge by Kennedy that United States forces would not invade Cuba. However, he only had Robert Kennedy's word that the Jupiters would be withdrawn from Turkey. Consequently Khrushchev wanted to work out an agreement with President Kennedy concerning the removal of the Jupiters from Turkey. They would exchange views through Dobrynin and Robert Kennedy. In this message to President Kennedy, Khrushchev sought to formalize the procedure.

γ　　　　　γ　　　　　γ

Moscow, October 28, 1962.

DEAR MR. PRESIDENT, Ambassador Dobrynin has apprised me of his conversation with Robert Kennedy which took place on October 27. In this conversation Robert Kennedy said that it is somewhat difficult for you at the present time to publicly discuss the question of eliminating the US missile bases in Turkey because of the fact that the stationing of those bases in Turkey was formalized through a NATO Council decision.

Readiness to agree on this issue that I raised in my message to you of October 27 was also emphasized. In this context Robert Kennedy said that removal of those bases from Turkey would take 4 to 5 months. Furthermore, a wish was expressed that exchanges of views on this matter between you and I should continue through Robert Kennedy and the Soviet Ambassador, and that these exchanges should be considered confidential.

I feel I must state to you that I do understand the delicacy involved for you in an open consideration of the issue of eliminating the US missile bases in Turkey. I take into account the complexity of this issue and I believe you are right about not wishing to publicly discuss it. I agree that our discussion of this subject be pursued confidentially through

[21] Department of State, *Foreign Relations of the United States. 1961–1963.* Volume VI *Kennedy-Khrushchev Exchanges* (Washington, 1996), pp. 189–190.

Robert Kennedy and the Soviet Ambassador in Washington. You may have noticed that in my message to you on October 28, which was to be published immediately, I did not raise this question—precisely because I was mindful of your wish conveyed through Robert Kennedy. But all the proposals that I presented in that message took into account the fact that you had agreed to resolve, [sic] the matter of your missile bases in Turkey consistent with what I had said in my message of October 27 and what you stated through Robert Kennedy in his meeting with Ambassador Dobrynin on the same day.

I express my great appreciation to you for having instructed your brother R. Kennedy to convey those thoughts.

I hope, Mr. President, that agreement on this matter, too, shall be a no small step advancing the cause of relaxation of international tensions and the tensions between our two powers. And that in turn can provide a good impetus to resolving other issues concerning both the security of Europe and the international situation as a whole.

Mr. President, the crisis that we have gone through may repeat again. This means that we need to address the issues which contain too much explosive material. Not right away, of course. Apparently, it will take some time for the passions to cool down. But we cannot delay the solution to these issues, for continuation of this situation is frought [sic] with many uncertainties and dangers.

Sincerely,

N. Khrushchev

DOCUMENT NO. 22

AMBASSADOR DOBRYNIN'S TELEGRAM TO THE SOVIET FOREIGN MINISTRY, OCTOBER 30, 1962[22]

Robert Kennedy insisted on a meeting with Dobrynin because of Khrushchev's letter of October 28 seeking to work out an understanding with President Kennedy about the removal of Jupiter missiles from Turkey. Khrushchev's letter could be a political time bomb for the Kennedy brothers. The letter had to be returned. Khrushchev would have to accept Robert Kennedy's word concerning his brother's promise.

γ   γ   γ

30 October 1962

Today Robert Kennedy invited me to meet with him. He said that he would like to talk about N.S. Khrushchev's letter to the President yesterday.

The President, Robert Kennedy said, confirms the understanding [*dogovorionnost*] with N.S. Khrushchev on the elimination of the American missile bases in Turkey (Robert Kennedy confirmed that one speaks of an understanding). Corresponding measures will be taken towards fulfilling this understanding within the period of time indicated earlier, in confidential observance of NATO guidelines, but of course without any mention that this is connected to the Cuban events.

We, however, said Robert Kennedy, are not prepared to formulate such an understanding in the form of letters, even the most confidential letters, between the President and the head of the Soviet government when it concerns such a highly delicate issue. Speaking in all candor, I myself, for example, do not want to risk getting involved who knows where and when such letters can surface or be somehow published—not now, but in the future—and any changes in the course of events are possible. The appearance of such a document could cause irreparable harm to my political career in the future. This is why we request that you take this letter back.

It is possible, Robert Kennedy continued, that you do not believe us

---

[22] *Cold War International History Project Bulletin* Nos. 8–9 (1996/1997), p. 304.

and through letters you want to put the understanding in writing. The issue of Soviet missile bases in Cuba has unfortunately introduced a real element of uncertainty and suspicion even into confidential channels of contact. We will however live up to our promise, even if it is given in this oral form. As you know, it was in precisely the same oral form that the President made his promise to N.S. Khrushchev regarding the removal of a certain number of American soldiers from Thailand. That promise was kept. So too will this promise be kept.

As a guarantee, Robert Kennedy added, I can only give you my word. Moreover I can tell you that two other people besides the President know about the existing understanding: they are [Secretary of State Dean] Rusk and [advisor on Soviet affairs Llewellyn] Thompson. If you do not believe me, discuss it with them, and they will tell you the same thing. But it is better not to transfer this understanding into a formal, albeit confidential, exchange of letters (as can be noted, the greatest suspicion in the two Kennedy brothers was elicited by the part of Khrushchev's letter which speaks directly of a link between the Cuban events and the bases in Turkey). We hope that N.S. Khrushchev will understand us correctly. In regard to this Robert Kennedy insistently asked to take the letter back without delay.

I told Robert Kennedy that everything said above I would report to N.S. Khrushchev, emphasizing in doing so that even the President and he, Robert Kennedy, could be sure of the fact that the Soviet government is regarding the understanding that has been reached as strictly secret and not for publication. At the same time, in order to confirm Robert Kennedy's statement about the understanding, I asked him again about whether the President really confirms the understanding with N.S. Khrushchev on the elimination of American missile bases in Turkey. Robert Kennedy said once again that he confirmed it, and again that he hoped that their motivations would be properly understood in Moscow. Taking what they explained into account, I believed it conditionally possible—before receiving any instructions from Moscow—to take this letter [back], since a categorical refusal to do so would, in my opinion, only weaken Robert Kennedy's firm statements on the understanding that has been reached. Moreover, leaving the letter with him, after he had clearly expressed the President's desire not to exchange letters, could scarcely be in the interests of doing business [in the future].

In conclusion Robert Kennedy said that, in his opinion, the events connected with the Cuban issue have been developing quite favorably, and that he hoped that everything would eventually be settled. He added that, on the Turkish issue and other highly confidential issues he was prepared to maintain a direct contact with me as earlier, emphasizing in doing so that the point was the possible oral considerations of the President and the head of the Soviet government N.S. Khrushchev on the exchange of letters on such delicate issues as missile bases in Turkey, or issues which need to be handled more by the State Department than by him personally, taking into account the delicacy of his situation as the President's brother and as Attorney General of the United States. I do not want, Robert Kennedy added, to claim for myself the function of the State Department, but my "solitary diplomacy" may be needed several more times, and we will meeting with each other periodically.

I answered to Robert Kennedy that I was prepared to maintain contact with him on highly important issues in the future, passing over the heads, as he himself suggested, of all intermediaries. Robert Kennedy confirmed this. From what Robert Kennedy said it was clear that the President is trying now to avoid exchanging any documents on issues of a highly delicate nature like Turkey which could leave a trace anywhere, but that he favors the continuation of a confidential exchange of opinions between the heads of the two governments.

We believe it expedient to visit Robert Kennedy once again and to issue a statement, in referring to our mission, that the Soviet government and N.S. Khrushchev personally are prepared to take into account the President's desire for maintaining the secrecy of the oral understanding on the removal of the American missile bases from Turkey. It is also expedient to tell of our willingness, if the President is also prepared for this, to continue the confidential exchange of opinions between the heads of the governments on many important unresolved issues, on whose resolution the lessing of international tension, and of the tension between our two countries in particular, is to a very great degree dependent.

I request instructions.

30.X.62   A. DOBRYNIN

DOCUMENT NO. 23

AMBASSADOR DOBRYNIN'S TELEGRAM TO THE SOVIET FOREIGN MINISTRY, NOVEMBER 12, 1962[23]

Negotiations over the removal of the IL–28 bombers from Cuba were deadlocked. At his brother's direction, Robert Kennedy again met with the Soviet ambassador, Anatoly Dobrynin, in the evening of November 12 at the Soviet embassy. Robert Kennedy brought another gentleman's agreement between the president and Khrushchev over the withdrawal of the IL–28 bombers from Cuba.

γ   γ   γ

Your instruction have been carried out. Robert Kennedy has familiarized himself attentively with the content of N.S. Khrushchev's confidential oral message to the President. When he got to the place that spoke of Nixon's defeat in the elections, he immediately grinned, saying: "Your chairman is a real master of colorful expression that expressed the true essence of the issue. Yes, we are quite satisfied with Nixon's defeat, and in general we are not complaining about the results of the election." It was felt that this portion of the message was received with definite satisfaction.

When Robert Kennedy had familiarized himself with the whole message, he said that for the President, for domestic policy considerations, it was very important to receive the Soviet Union's firm agreement to the removal of the IL–28 planes, especially now that there were essentially no inspections being conducted in Cuba itself. The correspondence between N.S. Khrushchev and President Kennedy of 27 and 28 October implied that an agreement between our countries had been reached. But we understand the difficulties in this area that have now arisen because of Premier Fidel Castro's position, and we are not insisting on this as an unalterable and fundamental condition. But the removal of the IL–28 planes—in an atmosphere of growing criticism within the USA—is a matter of great concern to the President. Let us reach an agreement, continued Robert Kennedy, on the following

[23] *Cold War International History Project Bulletin*, Nos. 8–9 (1996/1997), pp. 331–333.

points: that the Soviet Union will remove its IL-28 planes by a definite
date announced in advance, and that on that same day the USA will
officially lift its quarantine. All this may be announced immediately.

I answered Robert Kennedy that his proposal is entirely unacceptable
for the Soviet side. I then demonstrated the unacceptability of of this
proposal by using the argument contained in N.S. Khrushchev's oral
message that had been passed on to him. In conclusion I expressed my
certainty that conveying his proposal to Moscow would prove fruitless.

Thinking a moment, Robert Kennedy said that he would like to confer with his brother the President, after which he would again contact
me later the same day. I agreed.

After an hour and a half (all this happened in the evening), Robert
Kennedy came to my residence. He said that now, after speaking with
the President, he could formulate the American proposal in the following way:

N.S. Khrushchev and the president would reach an essential agreement that the IL-28 planes would be removed by a definite date. After
such an agreement has been reached, the USA would, as early as the
next day, lift any quarantine even before the removal of the planes had
been completed. The Americans would of course prefer that the date
agreed upon for the removal of the IL-28 planes be publicized. However, if the Soviets have any objections to the public disclosure of that
date, then the President would not insist on it. For him a promise from
N.S. Khrushchev would be entirely sufficient. As far as the date is concerned, it would be good if the planes were removed, let us say, within
30 days. We ask that N.S. Khrushchev be informed of this whole proposal.

Robert Kennedy was told that the President's proposal would of
course be communicated to N.S. Khrushchev. As a personal opinion, however, I noted that it was unlikely that such an imminent date
could be acceptable to us, all the more so since the fundamental USA
obligations—guarantees of non-aggression against Cuba, and other obligations—remain, as before, unfulfilled; moreover, they themselves are
pushing everything later and later. And this is happening in circumstances in which the Soviet government is sincerely fulfilling, and essentially has already fulfilled, its own obligations for the removal of the
missiles. It is now the Americans' turn.

Robert Kennedy said that the time-frame he had referred to—30
days—is not in any way definitive. That time-frame had been "given to

him," but he thought that there was room for negotiation here as long as the period was not too great, and as long as N.S. Khrushchev generally found the President's proposal acceptable. I want now to make note of one more condition, Robert Kennedy continued. After such an agreement has been reached, especially if it is not publicized, it would be important for us that, even if the end of the agreed-upon period for the removal of the IL-28 planes has not yet been reached, at least some planes will have been disassembled by this time, or if they have just been taken out of containers, that a portion of them be returned to their containers. We need all of this, Robert Kennedy remarked, so that we can satisfy our domestic public opinion by reporting that there has been some progress in the removal of the IL-28 planes. This is necessary, since even [West German Chancellor Konrad] Adenauer is starting now to criticize us publicly for trusting the word of the Soviet Union without inspections in Cuban territory—not to mention the Cuban emigres in certain republics [states—ed.] who are making similar accusations. But the President, Robert Kennedy emphasized, has faith in N.S. Khrushchev's word, and is willing to lift the quarantine immediately if the agreement mentioned above can be reached, even though we really do not have any guarantees with regard to inspections in Cuban territory.

I answered Robert Kennedy that it would be much better if Adenauer kept his nose out of everyone else's business, and if the USA government told him so directly (here Robert Kennedy energetically nodded his head in a gesture of agreement). I then said that in the proposal that he had advanced, the issue is once again raised of a full elimination of all the tension that has existed, that is, beyond the immediate lifting of the blockade, the obligations of all the parties should be fixed in appropriate UN documents, and non-aggression against Cuba and a strict observation of its sovereignty should be guaranteed; there would also be UN posts established in the countries of the Caribbean region as guarantees against unexpected actions harming another state.

Robert Kennedy said that he believed that an agreement could be reached on all this points. It is important, from the point of view of American public opinion, to have some inspection conducted in Cuba, even in the form of several UN posts. Castro will scarcely go for this unless a similar procedure is imposed on the other countries of the Caribbean basin. But is possible to resolve this too, Robert Kennedy mentioned, as an alternative to this, the plan put forth by Brazil, but then he immediately said that this aspect of the issue was being studied by

Stevenson, and that he, Robert Kennedy, could not go into details with regard to it. I can however repeat the firm assurances of the President not to invade Cuba. He authorized me once again to say this now. He was grateful to N.S. Khrushchev for the latter's clarification that the IL-28 planes are manned by Soviet rather than Cuban pilots, but nevertheless the issue of the removal of these planes remains a very important one for the President, and he asks that we consider his proposal.

Further discussion came down to a reiteration of the positions of the parties. Robert Kennedy said in conclusion that he was flying now to New York on personal business, and that he would be willing to meet with me at any time.

When he left, he glimpsed a crowd of dancing couples in the embassy's parlor. Realizing that this was a friendly welcome party arranged by the embassy community for the Bolshoi Theater troupe that had just arrived in Washington, he said that he would like to meet with the troupe. Mingling with and greeting almost all the members of the troupe, he delivered a welcome speech in which he said that the President was preparing to attend their premier the following evening. At the end, he kissed Maya Plisetskaya when he found out that he and she had been born in the same year, month, and day, and said they would celebrate their birthdays in a week. None of this needs to be mentioned especially, but all in all the behavior of Robert Kennedy, who is ordinarily quite a reserved and glum man, reflects to some degree the calmer and more normal mood in the White House after the tense days that shook Washington, even though this fact is concealed in various ways by American propaganda.

12.X.62   A. DOBRYNIN

DOCUMENT NO. 24

PRESIDENT KENNEDY'S PRESS
CONFERENCE, NOVEMBER 20, 1962[24]

*Although Khrushchev had agreed to dismantle the missiles, the crisis
dragged on with negotiations deadlocked on the issue of the removal of the
IL-28 bombers. The American naval quarantine was still in effect. After
behind the scenes negotiations, in the afternoon of November 20, 1962,
President Kennedy received Khrushchev's message that the planes would be
removed within thirty days. At a press conference, the president announced
that the bombers would be withdrawn and the naval quarantine lifted.*

γ　　　　　　γ　　　　　　γ

THE PRESIDENT. I have several statements.

[1.] I have today been informed by Chairman Khrushchev that all of
the IL-28 bombers now in Cuba will be withdrawn in 30 days. He also
agrees that these planes can be observed and counted as they leave. Inasmuch as this goes a long way towards reducing the danger which faced
this hemisphere 4 weeks ago, I have this afternoon instructed the Secretary of Defense to lift our naval quarantine.

In view of this action, I want to take this opportunity to bring the
American people up to date on the Cuban crisis and to review the progress made thus far in fulfilling the understandings between Soviet
Chairman Khrushchev and myself as set forth in our letters of October
27 and 28. Chairman Khrushchev, it will be recalled, agreed to remove
from Cuba all weapons systems capable of offensive use, to halt the further introduction of such weapons into Cuba, and to permit appropriate
United Nations observation and supervision to insure the carrying out
and continuation of these commitments. We on our part agreed that
once these adequate arrangements for verification had been established
we would remove our naval quarantine and give assurances against an
invasion of Cuba.

The evidence to date indicates that all known offensive missile sites
in Cuba have been dismantled. The missiles and their associated equipment have been loaded on Soviet ships. And our inspection at sea of

[24] *Public Papers of the Presidents of the United States. John F. Kennedy. January 1 to
December 31, 1962* (Washington, D.C., 1963), pp. 830–831.

these departing ships has confirmed that the number of missiles reported by the Soviet Union as having been brought into Cuba, which closely corresponded to our own information, has now been removed. In addition, the Soviet Government has stated that all nuclear weapons have been withdrawn from Cuba and no offensive weapons will be reintroduced.

Nevertheless, important parts of the understanding of October 27th and 28th remain to be carried out. The Cuban Government has not yet permitted the United Nations to verify whether all offensive weapons have been removed, and no lasting safeguards have yet been established against the future introduction of offensive weapons back into Cuba.

Consequently, if the Western Hemisphere is to continue to be protected against offensive weapons, this Government has no choice but to pursue its own means of checking on military activities in Cuba. The importance of our continued vigilance is underlined by our identification in recent days of a number of Soviet ground combat units in Cuba, although we are informed that these and other Soviet units were associated with the protection of offensive weapons systems, and will also be withdrawn in due course.

I repeat, we would like nothing better than adequate international arrangements for the task of inspection and verification in Cuba, and we are prepared to continue our efforts to achieve such arrangements. Until that is done, difficult problems remain. As for our part, if all offensive weapons systems are removed from Cuba and kept out of the hemisphere in the future, under adequate verification and safeguards, and if Cuba is not used for the export of aggressive Communist purposes, there will be peace in the Caribbean. And as I said in September, "we shall neither initiate nor permit aggression in this hemisphere."

We will not, of course, abandon the political, economic, and other efforts of this hemisphere to halt subversion from Cuba nor our purpose and hope that the Cuban people shall some day be truly free. But these policies are very different from any intent to launch a military invasion of the island.

In short, the record of recent weeks shows real progress and we are hopeful that further progress can be made. The completion of the commitment on both sides and the achievement of a peaceful solution to the Cuban crisis might well open the door to the solution of other outstanding problems.

May I add this final thought in this week of Thanksgiving: there is much for which we can be grateful as we look back to where we stood only 4 weeks ago—the unity of this hemisphere, the support of our allies, and the calm determination of the American people. These qualities may be tested many more times in this decade, but we have increased reason to be confident that those qualities will continue to serve the cause of freedom with distinction in the years to come.

DOCUMENT NO. 25

A POLICY FOR CUBA, JANUARY 22, 1963[25]

The Soviet and the American governments had informed the United Nations secretary general on January 7, 1963 that the Cuban missile crisis no longer needed to occupy the attention of the Security Council. However, on January 22 when President Kennedy reviewed foreign policy with the National Security Council, he singled out Cuba for emphasis.

γ   γ   γ

Washington, January 22, 1963.

Notes on Remarks by President Kennedy before the National Security Council Tuesday, January 22, 1963

I will start by reviewing areas of policy which will be before us in the coming months and indicate the general attitude which I have toward them and to emphasize where we might put our emphasis in the next few months.

The responsibilities of the United States are worldwide and the U.S. is the only country which is recognizing its wide responsibilities. We are part of NATO, SEATO, etc. and support other pacts even though we are not a part of them. Other nations are not doing their share.

Would like to say a word first about Cuba.

The indications are that the importance of timing is of paramount importance in reaching judgments—both by the USSR and the US. Our big problem is to protect our interests and prevent a nuclear war. It was a very close thing whether we would engage in a quarantine or an air strike. In looking back, it was really that it presented us with an immediate crisis and the USSR had to make their judgment and come to a decision to act in twelve hours. In looking back over that four or five day period, we all changed our views somewhat, or at least appreciated the advantages and disadvantages of alternate courses of action. That is what we should do in any other struggle with the Soviet Union—and I believe we will be in one in the future. We should have sufficient time to consider the alternatives. You could see that the Russians

[25] Department of State. *Foreign Relations of the United States 1961–1963*. Volume XI. *The Cuban Missile Crisis and Aftermath* (Washington, D.C., 1996) pp. 668–669.

had a good deal of debate in a 48 hour period. If they had only to act in an hour or two, their actions would have been spasmodic and might have resulted in nuclear war. It is important that we have time to study their reaction. We should continue our policy even though we do not get Europe to go along with us.

The time will probably come when we will have to act again on Cuba. Cuba might be our response in some future situation—the same way the Russians have used Berlin. We may decide that Cuba might be a more satisfactory response than an nuclear response. We must be ready—although this might not come. We should be prepared to move on Cuba if it should be in our national interest. The planning by the US, by the Military, in the direction of our effort should be advanced always keeping Cuba in mind in the coming months and to be ready to move with all possible speed. We can use Cuba to limit their actions just as they have had Berlin to limit our actions.

[Here follows discussion of other subjects.]

BIBLIOGRAPHY

Abel, Elie. *The Missiles of October: The Story of the Cuban Missile Crisis 1962*. Philadelphia: Lippincott, 1966.

Allyn, Bruce J., James G. Blight and David A. Welch. *Back to the Brink: Proceedings of the Moscow Conference on the Cuban Missile Crisis, January 27–28, 1989*. University Press of America: Lanham, 1992.

Ball, George W. *The Past Has Another Pattern: Memoirs* New York: Norton, 1973.

Beschloss, Michael. *The Crisis Years: Kennedy and Khrushchev, 1960–1963*. New York: HarperCollins, 1991.

Blight, James G. and David A. Welch. *On the Brink: Americans and Soviets Reexamine the Cuban Missile Crisis*. 2nd edition. New York: Noonday Press, 1990.

Blight James G., Bruce J. Allyn and David A. Welsh. *Cuba on the Brink: Castro, the Missile Crisis and the Soviet Collapse*. New York: Pantheon, 1993.

Brugioni, Dino A. *Eyeball to Eyeball: The Inside Story of the Cuban Missile Crisis*. New York: Random House, 1991.

Burlatsky, Fedor. *Khrushchev and the First Russian Spring*. London: Weidenfeld and Nicolson.

Chang, Laurence and Peter Kornbluh, editors. *The Cuban Missile Crisis, 1962: A National Security Archives Documents Reader*. New York: New Press, 1992.

Department of State. *Foreign Relations of the United States, 1961–1963*. Volume X *Cuba, January 1961–September 1962*. Washington, DC: United States Government Printing Office, 1996.

Department of State. *Foreign Relations of the United States, 1961–1963*. Volume XI. *Cuban Missile Crisis and Aftermath*. Washington, DC: United States Government Printing Office, 1996.

Department of State. *Foreign Relations of the United States, 1961–1963*. Volume VI. *Kennedy-Khrushchev Exchanges* Washington, DC: United States Government Printing Office, 1996.

Detzer, David. *The Brink: Cuban Missile Crisis, 1962*. New York: Crowell, 1979.

Dobrynin, Anatoly. *In Confidence*. New York: Times Books, 1993.

Fursenko, Aleksandr and Timothy Naftali. *"One Hell of a Gamble." Khrushchev, Castro, and Kennedy, 1958–1964*. New York: Norton, 1997.

Fursenko, Aleksandr and Timothy Naftali. "The Pitsunda Decision: Khrushchev and Nuclear Weapons," *Cold War International History Project Bulletin*. No. 10 (March 1998), pp. 223–227.

Gaddis, John Lewis. *We Now Know: Re-thinking Cold War History*. Oxford: Clarendon Press, 1997.

Garthoff, Raymond. *Reflections on the Cuban Missile Crisis*. Rev. edition. Washington, DC: Brookings Institution, 1989.

Gribkov, Anatoli I. and William Y. Smith. *Operation ANADYR: U.S. and Soviet Generals Recount the Cuban Missile Crisis*. Chicago: Edition Q, 1994.

Hagerman, George M. "The Lively Voyage of a Navy Reefer." *All Hands* (March, 1963), pp. 18–21.

Hersh, Seymour M. *The Dark Side of Camelot*. Boston: Little Brown, 1997.

Hershberg, James G. "More Evidence on the Cuban Missile Crisis: More Documents from the Russian Archives," *Cold War International History Project Bulletin*. Nos. 8–9(Winter 1996/1997), pp. 270–278.

Hershberg, James G. "More on Bobby and the Cuban Missile Crisis," *Cold War International History Project Bulletin*. Nos. 8–9 (Winter 1996–1997), pp. 274, 344–347.

Hershberg, Jim. "Anatomy of a Controversey: Anatoli Dobrynin's Meeting with Robert F. Kennedy, Saturday, 27 October 1962," *Cold War International History Project Bulletin*. No.5 (Spring, 1995), pp. 75–80.

Higgins, Trumbull. *The Perfect Failure: Kennedy, Eisenhower, and the CIA at the Bay of Pigs*. New York: Norton, 1989.

Kagan, Donald. *On the Origins of War and the Preservation of Peace*. New York: Doubleday, 1995.

Kennedy, Robert F. *Thirteen Days: A Memoir of the Cuban Missile Crisis*. New York: Norton, 1969.

Kramer, Mark. " 'Lessons' of the Cuban Missile Crisis for Warsaw Pact Nuclear Operations," *Cold War International History Project Bulletin*. Nos. 8–9 (Winter 1996/1997), pp. 348–354.

Khrushchev, Nikita S. *Khrushchev Remembers*. Edited and translated by Strobe Talbott. Boston: Little Brown, 1970.

Khrushchev, Nikita S. *Khrushchev Remembers: The Glasnost Tapes*. Translated and edited by Jerrold L. Schechter with Yacheslav V. Luchkov. Boston: Little Brown, 1990.

Lebow, Richard Ned and Janice Gross Stein. *We All Lost the Cold War*. Princeton, NJ: Princeton University Press, 1993.

McAuliffe, Mary S., editor. *The Secret Cuban Missile Crisis Documents/Central Intelligence Agency*. New York: Brassey's (US), 1994.

May, Ernest R. and Philip D. Zelikow. *The Kennedy Tapes: Inside the White House during the Cuban Missile Crisis*. Cambridge: Harvard University Press, 1977.

"The Mikoyan-Castro Talks, 4–5 November 1962: The Cuban Version." *Cold War International History Project Bulletin*. Nos.8–9 (Winter 1996/1997), pp. 320, 339–343.

Nash, Philip. *The Other Missiles of October: Eisenhower, Kennedy and the Jupiters, 1957–1963*. Chapel Hill: University of North Carolina Press, 1997.

Nathan, James, ed. *The Cuban Missile Crisis Revisited*. New York: St. Martin's Press, 1992.

Quirk, Robert E. *Fidel Castro*. New York: Norton, 1993.

Reeves, Richard. *President Kennedy: Profile of Power*. New York: Simon and Schuster, 1993.

"Russian Documents on the Cuban Missile Crisis," *Cold War International History Project Bulletin*. Nos.8–9 (Winter 1996/1997), pp. 278–338.

"Russian Foreign Ministry Documents on the Cuban Missile Crisis," *Cold War International History Project Bulletin*. No. 5 (Spring 1995), pp. 58, 63–77.

Sagan, Scott D. *The Limits of Safety: Organizations, Accidents, and Nuclear Weapons*. Princeton, NJ: Princeton University Press, 1993.

Schlesinger, Arthur M. Jr. *A Thousand Days: John F. Kennedy in the White House*. Boston: Houghton Mifflin, 1965.

Schlesinger, Arthur M. Jr. *Robert Kennedy and His Times*. New York: Ballantine, 1979.

Sorenson, Theodore. *Kennedy*. New York: Harper and Row, 1962.

Szulc, Tad. *Fidel: A Critical Portrait*. New York: William Morrow. 1993.

U.S. National Archives and Records Service. *Public Papers of the Presidents of the United States: John F. Kennedy, 1961–1963*. Washington, DC: United States Government Printing Office, 1962–1964.

Utz, Curtis A. *Cordon of Steel: The U.S. Navy and the Cuban Missile Crisis*. No. 1 The *U.S. Navy in the Modern World Series*. Washington, DC: Naval Historical Center.

White, Mark J. *The Cuban Missile Crisis*. London: Macmillan, 1996.

White, Mark J. *Missiles in Cuba: Kennedy, Khrushchev, Castro and the 1962 Crisis*. Chicago: Ivan R. Dee, 1997.

Wydon, Peter. *The Bay of Pigs: The Untold Story*. New York: Simon and Schuster, 1979.

Zubiok, Vladislav and Constantine Pleshkov. *Inside the Kremlin's Cold War: From Stalin to Khrushchev*. Cambridge, MA: Harvard University Press, 1996.

INDEX